ONE
WORLD
ORDER

SOCIALIST DICTATORSHIP

DR. JOHN COLEMAN

For permissions, or serializations, condensations, adaptations, or for our catalog of other publications, write the Publisher at the address below.

Library of Congress Cataloging-in-Publication Data

Coleman, Dr. John, 1935-
One World Order: Socialist Dictatorship
p.   cm.
Includes biographical references and index.
1. Socialism — United States. 2. Conspiracies — United States.
I. Title
HX86.C695   1998
320.973--dc21   98-43399
                                                                      CIP

ISBN 0-9640104-9-6 (alk. paper)

Published by
BRIDGER HOUSE PUBLISHERS, INC
P.O. Box 2208, Carson City, NV 89702, 1-800-729-4131

Cover design by The Right Type
Printed in the United States of America
10 9 8 7 6 5 4 3 2 1

"The enemy in Washington is more to be feared than the enemy in Moscow." This is a sentiment I have expressed over and over again. Communism did not destroy tariff protection erected by President George Washington. Communism did not force the United States to adopt graduated income tax. Communism did not create the Federal Reserve Board. Communism did not get the United States into WWI and WWII. Communism did not force the United Nations on America. Communism did not take the Panama Canal away from the American people. Communism did not create the Global 2000 Report mass genocide plan. It is SOCIALISM that has brought these evils upon the United States!

Communism did not give the world AIDS! Communism did not give America disastrous levels of unemployment. Communism did not mount unrelenting attacks on the Constitution of the United States.

Communism did not force America to adopt "foreign aid," that cursed tax on the American people which is involuntary servitude.

Communism did not force an end to school prayers. Communism did not promote the falsehood of "separation of church and state." Communism did not give America a Supreme Court packed with justices bound and determined to undermine the Constitution of the United States. Communism did not send our soldiers to fight an illegal war in the Gulf to protect the interests of the British crown.

Yet, for all these years, while our attention was focused on the evils of Communism in Moscow, the Socialists in Washington were busy stealing America! "One World Order: Socialistic Dictatorship" tells how this was, and is, being accomplished.

TABLE OF CONTENTS

INTRODUCTION I

1   How Fabian Socialism Began And Subsequent History 1

2   What Socialism Is — Why It Leads to Slavery 23

3   Socialist Controlled Education — The Road to Slavery............69

4   The Female of the Species...89

5   Subverting The Constitution Via the Legislative Route...........109

6   Brightest Stars in the American Socialist Firmament 115

7   Socialist Penetration and Permeation of Religion...................149

8   Planned Destruction of the United States Through Free Trade.................165

9   A Nation Undone 187

Epilogue..205

Sources and Notes...211

Index 219

INTRODUCTION

"We will build the New World Order piece by piece right under their noses" (the American people). "The house of the New World Order will have to be built from the bottom up rather than from the top down. An end run around sovereignty, eroding it piece by piece, will accomplish much more than the old fashioned frontal attack." Richard Gardner, leading American Socialist, Foreign Affairs, the journal of the Council on Foreign Relations (CFR), April 1974.

In this, my third book ("The Committee of 300" and "Diplomacy By Deception,") I tell how Gardner's statement gives notice of the Fabian Socialist agenda for the United States. The ideas, thoughts and people who have worked diligently to establish Socialism, the principal, fatal political disease of modern nations is explained in clear detail.

There is an account of the various Socialists goals set by the British Fabian Society, whose motto is, "Make Haste Slowly." When asked to explain Communism, Lenin replied, "Communism is Socialism in a hurry." Socialism has no where to progress but to Communism, is something I have often said. The book explains why so many of the ills that plague our society today have their origin in careful Socialist planning and execution.

Socialism is inherently evil because it forces people to accept deliberately engineered changes they have neither requested nor want. The power of Socialism is disguised in soothing terms and hides behind a mask of humanitarianism. It is also found in far reaching, fundamental changes in religion, which the Socialists have long used as a potent vehicle for gaining acceptance, after which they spread their influence inside churches to the detriment of all religions.

The goal of Socialism is the liquidation of the free enterprise system, which is true capitalism. Scientific Socialism goes under several disguises, and its promoters call themselves Liberals or Moderates. They wear no badge and are not recognizable, as they would be if they called themselves Communists.

There are more than 300,000 Socialists inside the United States Government, and careful estimates have it that in 1994, 87 percent of the members of Congress are Socialists. Executive orders are an unconstitutional Socialist ruse to use the legislative route to make the Constitution of the United States of no effect, where direct methods are not possible to bring about desired Socialist changes blocked by the Constitution.

Socialism is revolution without openly violent methods but never the less does the utmost violence to the psyche of the nation. It is a movement governed by stealth. Its slow advance on the United States from its home base in England was almost imperceptible up to the 1950s. The Fabian Socialist movement remains distinct from so called Socialist Party groups and its forward crawl was thus almost imperceptible to the majority of Americans. "When you wound a Communist, a Socialist bleeds" is a saying that dates back to the early days of Fabian Socialism.

Socialism ardently welcomes proliferation of central government power which they strive to secure for themselves, always pretending it to be for the common good. The United States and Britain are full to the brim with false prophets pushing the New World Order. These Socialist missionaries preach peace and humanitarianism and common good. Fully aware that they could not overcome the resistance of the American people to Communism by direct means, the insidious Fabian Socialists knew they had to move silently and slowly, and avoid alerting the people to their real objectives. Thus was 'scientific Socialism' adopted as the way to overcoming the United States and making of it the leading Socialist country in the world.

How far Fabian Socialism has succeeded, and where we stand today is told in this book. Presidents Wilson, Roosevelt, Eisenhower, Carter, Kennedy and Johnson were eager, willing servants of Fabian Socialism. Their mantle was passed to President Clinton. Democracy and Socialism go hand-in-hand. All United States presidents since Wilson have repeatedly stated that the United States is a Democracy, when in fact, it is a Confederated Republic. Fabian Socialism directs the destiny of the world in a way which is disguised to render it unrecognizable. Socialism is the author of graduated income tax, the destroyer of nationalism, the author of so-called "free trade."

This book is no dull account of the philosophies of Socialism, but a dynamic, dramatic telling of how it became the foremost menace to free men everywhere, but more especially, in the United States, which has still to confront it, head-on. The bland, smooth surface of Socialism hides its true intent: A Federal World Government under Socialist control, in which We, the People, will be their slaves in a New World Order of the New Dark Age.

1

HOW FABIAN SOCIALISM BEGAN AND SUBSEQUENT HISTORY

"Like all Socialists, I believe that the Socialist Society evolves in time into a Communist Society." — John Strachey, Labor Party Cabinet Minister.

"In American newspaper jargon, John Strachey would be described as 'Marxist No. 1' and the title would be deserved." "Left News," March 1938.

Fabian Socialism began with the Fabian Society, which in their words, "consists of Socialists who allied themselves with the Communist Manifesto of 1848," written by Karl Marx, a Prussian born Jew who lived the better part of his life in Highgate, London. In the "Basis of the Fabian Society" we learn the following:

"It therefore aims at the reorganization of society by the emancipation of land and industrial capital from individual ownership and vesting them in the community for the general benefit. In this way only can natural and acquired advantages of the country be shared by the whole people..."

This was the principal that Fabian Socialism exported to the United States, one which they have tirelessly forced upon the American people to the great detriment of the nation.

Marx died in solitary "digs" in October of 1883, without ever realizing the vision he shared with Moses Mendelssohn (Mendelssohn is generally recognized as the father of European Communism), and was buried in the small, walled Highgate Cemetery in North London. That the Communist Manifesto gave life to Socialism, was admitted by Professor Harold Laski, the man most closely identified with the movement from its inception, and up to the time of his death in 1950.

But Socialism actually, was born with the founding of the Ethical Society of Culture, formerly the Fellowship of New Life, in New York. Although the political economy of John Stuart Mill as expressed in Henry George's Socialist book, "Progress and Poverty" the spiritual side of Socialism should not be ignored. Webb and his wife Beatrice ran the Fabian Society from its beginning. Most of the members of the Fellowship of New Life which preceded the Ethical Society of Culture, were Freemasons affiliated with Madame Blavatsky's occult Theosophy to which Annie Besant also subscribed.

Not that Laski was in any sense a "spiritual man," being more like Marx than Ramsay McDonald, who went on to become prime minister of England. Laski was a most powerful influence on scores of British political, economic and church leaders, and is credited with having compellingly influenced Presidents Franklin Delano Roosevelt and John F. Kennedy. Victor Gollancz, the Socialist publisher, said on many occasions that Socialism is necessary for world domination: "Socialism centralizes power and makes individuals completely subject to those who control that power," the publisher said.

Having withdrawn from the Fellowship of the New Life, Fabian Socialism tried several paths already trodden by Communists, Bakounists, Babuovists (anarchists) and Karl Marx, always vehemently denying any connection with these movements. Consisting mainly of intellectuals, civil servants, journalists and publishers like the great Victor Gollancz, Fabian Socialism had no interest in getting involved with street fighting anarchist revolutionaries. The founder members of Fabian Socialism perfected the technique first used by Adam Weishaupt — that of penetrating the Catholic Church and then "boring away from inside until just an empty husk was left." It was called, "penetration and permeation." Apparently neither Weishaupt nor Gollancz thought Christians would be smart enough to see what was happening.

Gollancz was reported as saying: "Christians are not exactly bright, so it will be easy for Socialism to lead them down the garden path through their ideals of brotherly love and social justice." Fabian Socialism targeted political, economic and educational organizations, in addition to the Christian Church. Later Gollancz's Left Wing Books gave special discounts to Christians who were interested in Socialist ideas. On the selection committee of the Left Book Club were Gollancz himself, Professor Harold Laski, and John Strachey, a Labour Party member of Parliament. Gollancz, who also owned The Christian Book Club, was a strong believer in Bolshevik Russia as an ally of Socialism. At the urging of Beatrice Webb, he published one of the Fabian Society's best sellers, "Our Soviet Ally."

Fabian Socialism set out from the very beginning of its history to penetrate and permeate the British Labor and Liberal Parties, and, as it turned out, also the Democrat Party in the United States. It was relentless in its zeal and energy to create "feminist" Socialism, at which it was to become highly successful. Socialism succeeded in gaining the ascendency of school boards, town councils and labor unions under the guise of bettering the lot of the working man. Fabian Socialism's determination to capture education mirrors what Madame Zinoviev had long counseled in Bolshevik Russia.

In 1950, Gollancz published, "Corruption in a Profit Economy" a widely read work by Mark Starr. Starr was a product of Fabian Socialism, and although considered a bit rough around the edges (he began life as a coal miner,) he was not rejected by the Ivy League Socialists of Harvard and Yale, to which the Fabian Society had gained access in its orderly progression up the ladder from its humble beginnings in London. Starr emigrated to the United States in 1928, after earning his Socialist credentials at the National Council of Labour Colleges.

Tutored by the formidable Margaret Cole, the founder of the Fabian Research Center, Starr was THE link between the Fabian Society in London and the burgeoning Socialist movements in America. Starr served at the Brockwood Labor College from 1925-1928, at an early age subjected to a Socialist education second to none. The Socialist Garland Fund gave Starr a grant of $74,227, a considerable sum of money in those days. He later became educational director of the International Ladies Garment Workers Union (ILGWU) from 1935 to 1962. His work on labor politics and labor education was outstanding in the cause of Socialism. As far as Starr was concerned, education meant teaching that private profit was wrong and should be abolished.

In 1941, Starr was appointed vice president of the American Federation of Teachers, an avante-garde Socialist teachers body of the day. After taking American citizenship, Starr was named by President Harry Truman to the United States Advisory Commission, authorized by Public Act 402, "to advise the State Department and the Congress on the operation of information centers and libraries maintained by the United States Government in foreign countries, as well as on the exchange of students and technical experts." This was indeed a "coup" for Socialism in the United States!

Fabian Socialism attracted many of the upper elite of society in Britain and the United States. It is said of American Socialists that they "aped their English betters, admiring their command of the language, their quick turn of phrase and their genteel respectability, perhaps personified by Professor Graham Wallas, Sir Stafford Cripps, Hartley Shawcross and Richard Crossman."

Professor Graham Wallas lectured at the New School for Social Research in New York City, a Socialist "think tank" founded by the "New Republic" magazine, that catered for leftwing professors, of which the United States had more than its share. Wallas was one of the earlier intellectuals to join the then nondescript Fabian Society, which, back in 1879, faced a very uncertain future and was not considered to be a threat to Government or Church. Wallas' early interest in education is mirrored by one of his earliest jobs — that of County School Management Committee of the School Board. As we shall see in other chapters, the Fabian Socialists hierarchy considered control of education the kingpin in their strategy to capture the world.

That ideal was further reflected by Wallas' teaching appointment at the London School of Economics, founded by Sydney Webb, and then still a fledgling Socialist institution of learning. Wallas had only four students in his class.

Wallas believed that the way to Socialize a country was through applied psychology. The way to Socialize America, Wallas contended, was to take the mass of the population by the hand like children (he did not have a very high regard for the standard of education in the United States) and like children, lead them one step at a time down the road to Socialism, to which I would add, and ultimate slavery. Wallas is an important name in this account of Socialism, as he wrote a book which was adopted, word-for-word by President Lyndon Johnson, as Democrat Party official policy.

The sinister creeping progress of Socialism that began to blanket England, might have been avoided, but for WWI. The flower of Christian British youth who would have resisted the onward march of this alien concept, lay dead in the fields of Flanders, their lives uselessly thrown away on a nebulous ideal of "patriotism." Numbed by the horrific loss of their sons, the older generation did not care about what Socialism was doing to their country, believing that "there will always be an England."

Social psychology was a weapon used deftly used to deflect attacks on American Fabianist organizations. Americans for Democratic Action (ADA), said it was not part of the Fabian Society, and its mouthpiece, "The Nation" sought vehemently to deny attempts to tie the two in with each other.

In 1902, Wallas was teaching outright Socialism at the Philadelphia University summer sessions. He had been invited to the United States by wealthy American Socialists who attended Oxford summer schools in 1899 and 1902, the period when the summer school indoctrination classes were at the height of their popularity with rich Americans who had nothing better to do. The year 1910 found Wallas as the mentor of American Socialist leaders like Walter Lippmann, delivering the Lowell Lectures at Harvard. Graham Wallas was recognized as being among the Big Four Socialist intellectuals in Britain, and as such, he was sought out by the American Socialist Ray Stannard Baker, the emissary Colonel Edward Mandel House sent to the Paris Peace Conference to represent him, and find out what the delegates were doing.

Between 1905 and 1910, Graham Wallas wrote "The Great Society" which was to become the blueprint for President Johnson's program of the same name, and which embodied social psychology principles. Wallas made it very plain, that the object of social psychology was to control human conduct, thus preparing the masses for the coming Socialist State that would ultimately lead them into slavery — although he was careful not to spell it out that far. Wallas became a conduit into the United States for Fabian Socialists ideas, much of them going into Roosevelt's "New Deal," written by Socialist Stuart Chase, Kennedy's "New Frontier" written by Socialist Henry Wallace and Johnson's "Great Society" written by Graham Wallas. From these facts alone, the tremendous impact of Fabian Socialism upon the American political scene can be gauged.

Like Professor Laski, Wallas had the same good disposition and kindly nature which was to make such a big impact on political and religious leaders in the United States. Both men were to be the Fabian Society's most successful missionaries to universities and colleges all across the United States, not to mention their impact on the leaders of the aggressive "feminist" movement which was just getting started.

Thus, from the beginning of Fabian Socialism in America, this dangerously radical movement was falsely clothed in a mantle of benigness that was able to deceive "the very elect," to paraphrase the Bible. It was a cover for revolution on both sides of the Atlantic while remaining aloof from the violence generally associated with the word, "revolution." History will one day record that the Fabian Socialist revolution far exceeded in scope and breadth the violent Bolshevik Revolution. While the Bolshevik Revolution ended more that fifty years ago, the Fabian Socialist revolution is still gathering momentum and growing ever stronger. This unobtrusive movement has literally "moved mountains," and vastly changed the course of history, and nowhere more so than in the United States.

The two guiding lights who remained in control of Fabian Socialism to the end of their days were George Bernard Shaw and Sydney Webb. Later, they were joined by men like Graham Wallas, John Maynard Keynes and Harold Laski, whose dream of a Socialist conquest of Great Britain and the United States they knew could only be realized by the progressive weakening of the financial system of each country, until they collapsed into a total welfare state. We see this now in effect having overtaken Britain which has become a bankrupted, welfare state.

Fabian Socialism's second course of action was against the constitutional separation of powers mandated by the United States Constitution. Professor Laski and his colleagues felt that if Fabian Socialism could remove this obstacle, they would have the key to dismantling the entire Constitution of the United States. Thus, it was imperative that Socialism train and deploy special change agents who would be in a position to undermine this, the most important provision in the Constitution. The Fabian Society set about doing just that, and the success of their mission can be seen in the shocking manner in which Congress blithely surrenders its powers to the executive branch in a manner which can only be described not only as reckless, but 100 percent unconstitutional.

A good example would be Line Item Veto powers given to the President Clinton in defiance of the Constitution. Another good example was the surrender of powers in trade negotiations which properly belong in the House of Representatives. As we shall see in the chapters dealing with NAFTA and GATT, this is precisely what Congress has done, thereby wittingly or unwittingly — it matters not — playing right into the hands of the Socialist enemies of this Nation.

Sydney Webb and George Bernard Shaw are the men who set the Fabian Socialist course: penetration and permeation, rather than anarchy and violent revolution. Both were determined to ensure that the public be led to believe that Socialism didn't necessarily mean LEFT, and certainly not Marxism. Both journeyed to Bolshevik Russia at the height of the terror, ignoring, rather than commenting on the butchery that was public knowledge. Of the two, Webb was the more impressed with the Bolsheviks and wrote a work, "Soviet Socialism — A New Civilization?" It came out later, after a Soviet foreign office official defected, that Webb apparently did not actually write the book, which was the work of the Soviet Foreign Office.

Shaw and Webb became known as the "demons of Socialism waiting to be exorcised," before Socialism could unfold its wings and as Shaw put it, "rescue Communism from the barricades." Although Shaw pretended not to care about FORM, he nevertheless expressed the belief that Fabian Socialism would become a "constitutional movement." Even with the "greats" of Socialism pouring into the movement, Toynbee, Keynes, Haldane, Lindsay, H.G. Wells and Huxley, Shaw and Webb kept their grip on the London Fabian Society and steered it in the direction they had chosen so many years before.

The nearly always penniless Shaw had his indigence relieved through marriage to Charlotte Payne Townshend, a lady of considerable means, which was, as some would have it, is the reason why the irascible Shaw married her. This is born out by the fact that before the marriage vows were exchanged, Shaw insisted that he be taken care of in the form of a large prenuptial settlement.

Shaw was no longer given to soap box orations nor basement meetings, but aspired to mix socially with Socialism's upper crust. Men like Lord Grey and Lord Asquith became his good friends, and while Shaw still took one or two trips to Moscow, he cooled toward Communism. Although an avowed atheist, this did not stop Shaw from cultivating those whom he felt could be used to further his career, such as Lord Asquith in particular. Shaw did not take orders from anybody, let alone the "newcomers" like Hugh Gaitskell, future prime minister of England, and a protege of the Rockefeller family. Shaw definitely considered himself as "old guard" along with Sydney and Beatrice Webb. These tough, hardened professional Socialists weathered many a storm over policy and never flinched in the face of often considerable outside opposition and "family feuds."

Fabian Socialism began life in 1883 as a debating society, "Nueva Vita" (New Life) with meetings in a small room at 17 Osnaburgh Street, London. It was not unlike the start of the German Nationalist Socialist movement which Hitler later took over. One of the aims of "Nueva Vita" was to bring together in an amalgam, the teachings of Hegel and St. Thomas Aquinas.

But the word "Socialism" was not new, having been around since 1835, long before "Nueva Vita" began its infant steps in 1883, the very evening that Marx went to his death. The leader of the group — numbering four people — was Edward Pease, and their aim was to use education as a vehicle for Socialist propaganda, which was to have such a profound effect on education and politics on both sides of the Atlantic. This would seem to have been a tall order for a group of men who did not have the required public school education, a necessity for would-be leaders in Victorian England, and yet, an examination of the Fabian Society shows that is exactly what they accomplished.

In rather grandiose style, the young men named their group after Quintas Fabian, a Roman general of note, whose tactics were said to be based upon waiting patiently for the enemy to make a mistake and then striking hard. The Irishman, George Bernard Shaw joined the Fabian Society in May of 1884. Shaw came from the Hampstead Historical Club, a Marxist reading circle. It is odd how both Shaw and Marx came to Socialism within a short distance of each other — Hampstead Heath is not that far from Highgate. And both frequented the British Museum. (I happen to know this area well, having lived in the area of Hampstead and Highgate and spent many years of study at the British Museum.) So in a sense, my perception of what Fabian Socialism was about, may have been clearer because of these circumstances.

Never admitting to knowing Marx, although he courted his daughter Eleanor, Shaw is suspected of having been Marx's "front runner" to bring Socialism home to audiences he, Shaw, addressed more often that not, four times a week, anywhere he could find them. A study that I made in the British Museum leads me to believe that Communism invented Socialism as a vehicle for its radical ideas that would not otherwise have gone down well in England or the United States, the two countries most prized for conquest by Communism.

There is little doubt in my mind that Shaw was Marx in "disguise" as Socialism was Communism "in disguise." My theory gains added weight when we learn that Shaw attended the Socialist International in London in 1864, as a Fabian delegate. As we know, Marx was the creator of the Socialist Internationals at which his flawed theories were preached ad-infinitum alongside outright Communist propaganda. Karl Marx never tried to hide the unholy alliance between the Communist International and his own Socialist International, but Shaw and the Webbs, and later, Harold Laski, vehemently denied any connection with Marxism or Communism.

Endless hours were spent by the Fabians splitting hairs whether it was "Social Democracy" or "Democratic Socialism" which was to be the battle cry. In the end it was "Democratic Socialism" that was to be used in the United States with such stunning success, Shaw's idea that Socialist intellectuals (in which category he included himself) would lead the charge at election time, while labor would provide the money. This was successfully co-opted by ADA, who flooded Congressional committees with "experts" shuttled to and from Harvard, to confound and confuse Senators and Representatives, unschooled and inexperienced in the ways of Socialist treachery and treason.

Socialism IS NOT ABOUT EQUALITY AND FREEDOM. Nor is it about helping the middle class and working people. On the contrary, it is about enslavement of the people by gradual, subtle means, a fact that Shaw once admitted to in an unguarded moment. Graham Wallas' book "Great Society" and Lyndon Banes Johnson's "Great Society" were the same thing, and on the surface, looked as if the people would be the beneficiaries of government largess, but in truth, it was merely an enslavement trap baited with Socialist honey. AS LONG AS SOCIALISM IS ALIVE, COMMUNISM CANNOT BE DEAD, AND THAT IS WHERE SOCIALISM IS LEADING THIS NATION — INTO THE STEEL TRAP OF COMMUNISM.

We need to remind ourselves what the great President Andrew Jackson said about the hidden enemy in our midst: "Sooner or later your enemy will show himself, and you will know what to do....you will be confronted by many unseen enemies of your hard-fought liberty. But they will show themselves in time — time enough to destroy them." Let us hope that the American people, blinded by false Socialists policies of four presidents, will have the scales removed from their eyes before it is too late.

A second Marxist in disguise was Sydney Webb, so disdainfully dismissed by Sir Bertrand Russell in later years as a "clerk in the Colonial Office." Webb was angry in his denials that he had ever met Marx, but as it was with Shaw, there is circumstantial evidence that Webb did indeed meet with Marx quite regularly. Unlike Shaw who married late, Webb married Beatrice Potter quite early on, a wealthy, formidable women who was to advance his career more than he ever cared to admit.

Beatrice was the daughter of a Canadian railroad magnate, who had fallen in love with Joseph Chamberlain, but rejected by him due to class difference. In those days, having money didn't mean automatic admission to the best circles. One had to come from the "right" background, which usually meant a public school education (A "public school" in England is the same as a private school in America). From their very first meeting Shaw and the Webbs were on the same wavelength, and became an excellent team act.

The Socialist revolution proposed by the Fabian Society was to cast a long, dark shadow across England and later the United States. Its aims differed little from those set out in the Communist manifesto of 1848: "It therefore aims at the reorganization of society by the emancipation of land and Industrial capital from individual and Class ownership and vesting them in the community for general benefit. It accordingly works for the extinction of private property in land... It seeks to achieve these ends by general dissemination of knowledge as to the relations between the individual and Society in its economic, ethical and political aspects."

There was no denouncement of religion, no long-haired anarchists running around with bombs. Nothing like that. Fascists, were also welcome, witness the fact that Sir Oswald Mosely and his wife, nee Cynthia Curzon, were both firmly committed Socialists before they were called to Fascism. Shaw, the "old guard" Socialist had high praise of Hitler in the years leading up to WWII. Instead of showing its true colors, Fabianism put on genteel airs and graces that belied its dangerous revolutionary intent: the unwritten constitution of England and the written Constitution of the United States were to be subverted and replaced by a system of State-run Socialism, through a process that was known as "gradualism" and "penetration and permeation."

There are some similarities here between Hitler and the Fabianists: in the beginning, nobody took the slightest notice of them. But unlike Hitler, for Shaw and Webb, the vision was one where the world would evolve into a New World Order in which everyone would be happy and contented, this having been brought about without resort to violence and anarchy.

The Fabians began to spread their wings and by 1891 were ready to publish their first "Fabian News." It was during this period that Beatrice Webb began teaching radical feminism and developed the Fabian Research program, later used with great success by Justice Louis Brandeis and known as the "Brandeis Brief." This consisted of volume after volume of "research" material, enough to swamp opponents, covered with the thinnest of legal briefs. Not much encouragement was given to nondescript unimportant new members: Webb and Shaw felt their movement was one for the elite — they were not interested in mass movements of people without money and influence.

For this reason they turned their attention to Oxford and Cambridge Universities, where the sons of the elite were educated and who were later to take the Fabian message (suitably disguised as "reforms") into the heart and soul of the Parliament. The Fabian Society's goal was to get Socialists installed in positions of power, where their influence could be counted on to bring about "reforms."

This program, somewhat modified, was practiced in the United States also, and produced Roosevelt, Kennedy, Johnson and Clinton — Socialists all. Such agents of change were trained in the Fabian way of combining sociology with politics to open doors. Mere numbers was never its style. One of their elite, Arthur Henderson, who was Britain's Foreign Minister in 1929, was the guiding, leading light in getting diplomatic recognition for the monstrous Bolshevik regime, with the United States following suit a few years later.

The first Fabian Society cell in Oxford opened in 1895, and by 1912 there were three more, with students forming more than 20 percent of the membership. This was perhaps the most profound period for the Fabian Society's growth; students being inducted into Socialism, many of whom went on to be world leaders.

The little movement that nobody paid any attention to in 1891, had arrived. One of the most dangerous radical, revolutionary movements of the 20th century had taken root in England, and was already starting to spread to the United States. Laski, Galbraith, Attlee, Beaverbrook, Sir Bertrand Russell, H.G. Wells, Wallass, Chase and Wallace; these were some of the Fabian Socialists who were to have a profound effect in shaping the course the United States was to take.

This was particularly true of Professor Laski. Few in the government of the thirty years that Laski spent in America, ever became aware of the depth of his penetration into education and the very government itself. This was a man who put the tenets of Socialism into daily practice. Laski lectured in many of the States and at the Universities of Oregon, California, Colorado, Columbia University, Yale, Harvard and Roosevelt University, in Chicago. During all of this time, he constantly urged the adoption of a Federal program of "social insurance" which he omitted to say, would lead to the Socialist goal of a TOTAL welfare state.

In later years, Laski, Wallas, Keynes, and many of the Fabian Society political leaders and economists would go to the Tavistock Institute of Human Relations to learn the methods of John Rawlings Reese, which became known as "inner conditioning" and "long range penetration." It was to this school that Henry Kissinger was also sent.

Gradually, as was their custom, Fabianists began to penetrate both the Labor and Liberal Parties, from where they exerted great influence in the socializing of the Englishman, formerly sturdily independent and not known to accept government aid. While the Webbs claimed credit for the "penetration" technique, the claim was rudely upset in 1952 by Colonel I.M. Bogolepov, who said that the entire plan was written for the Webbs in the Soviet Foreign Office, as had much of the material in the many books the Webbs claimed to have written. Bogolepov went on to say that much of the material in Webb's books he had personally written. "They changed it just a bit here and there, otherwise it was a copied verbatim," the colonel said.

As is so often the case when leftist or socialist heroes are debunked, the press covers up and praises the exposed one with masses of irrelevant verbiage until the charge is all but forgotten. We see this almost daily in the press with regard to the moral character and political ineptitude of President Clinton. "He is theirs, and no matter what is said of him, they will not let the mud stick," an intelligence colleague of mine said. And wash Clinton they do. In analyzing reports of Clinton's questionable morality and political mistakes, one cannot help but be impressed by the Fabian Socialist damage control: "wash" the target and smother the attacker in verbiage that has little relevancy to the issues.

In studying the history of the Fabian Society in the British Museum in London, I was struck by the awesome progress of the tiny band of unknowns who went on to bring some of the most important politicians, writers, teachers, economists, scientists, philosophers, religious leaders and publishers into the Fabian Society's orbit, while the world seemed never to notice its existence. Why the profound changes that were coming into being were not cause for alarm can be explained. Every single move made by Fabianists was cloaked in the mantle of "reforms" and the Fabian technique of equating "reforms" with "beneficial," "just," or "good" was the key to their success.

The same things held good for American Socialists. Every major move made by the Socialist Fifth Column in Washington is disguised as "reforms," that are going to benefit the people. The trick is as old as the hills, yet voters fall for it every time. Roosevelt's "New Deal" was lifted straight out of a Fabian Socialist book of the same title written by Stuart Chase, yet, seemingly, it was accepted as a genuine "reform" of the system. Even Woodrow Wilson's recognition of the treasonous Kerensky government, was clothed in language crafted to intentionally deceive the American people that "reforms" going on in Russia were for the benefit of the common people. Johnson's "Great Society" was another "American" program lifted straight out of a book written by Graham Wallas, called "The Great Society."

With the London School of (Socialist) Economics established, although nowhere near as pretentious in the beginning as the title sounded, Fabian Socialists became increasingly influential in shaping monetary policies on both sides of the Atlantic. The facility was vastly upgraded when the Rockefeller foundation gave it a substantial grant. The method of funding Socialist institutions through grants by the wealthy elite, and its day-to-day programs for the poor, is believed to be the idea of Shaw, which he activated after he attended a lecture at the London School of Economics.

Basically, making the poor pay for "local" programs came down to starting trade unions among the working class, and then using member's dues to facilitate and fund Socialist programs. It is rather like the Freemasons, who are prone to let us know that they contribute generous amounts of money to charities. But the money usually comes from the public, not from Mason coffers. In the United States the Shriners are famous for donating money to hospitals, but the money comes from the public by street parades the Shriners hold. None of their OWN money goes to hospitals.

The "Four Pillars of the House of Socialism," written by Sydney Webb shortly after WW I, became the blueprint for future Socialist action, not only in Britain, but also in the United States. The plan called for the destruction of the system of production of goods and services based on competition, unlimited taxation, massive state welfare, no private property rights and a One World Government. These objectives did not differ all that much from the principles laid down by Karl Marx in the Communist Manifesto of 1848. The differences lay in method of application, style, rather than in substance.

In detail, state-financed welfare was to be the first principle. The right of women to vote was included (the birth of women's rights movements), all land to be nationalized, with no private property rights. All industries "serving the people" (rail, power, light, phone, etc.) to be nationalized, "private profit" to be eliminated from the insurance industry, confiscation of wealth via taxation to be stepped up and finally, the concept of a One World Government was spelled out: International economic controls, international courts providing international legislation governing social affairs.

A cursory examination of the Communist Manifesto of 1848 reveals where the "research" for the "Four Pillars" was done. While "Four Pillars" dealt quite exclusively with socializing Britain, many of its ideas were put into practice by Wilson, Roosevelt, Johnson, Carter, and now, Clinton. "Labour and the New Social Order" had made the big time in the United States, where its thoroughly revolutionary aims went unrecognized, even as Hitler was being held up as the greatest threat to the world. Whether we like it or not, the policies and programs instituted by Wilson, Roosevelt, Kennedy, Johnson, Carter and Reagan all bore the stamp, "Made in England By the Fabian Society." This is truer with Clinton than with any of the former presidents.

Ramsay McDonald, sent to the United States to "spy out the land" went on to become Britain's first Fabian Society Socialist prime minister. McDonald set the pattern for future prime ministers to surround themselves with Fabian Socialist advisors, a tradition carried on by Margaret Thatcher and John Major. Across the Atlantic, Fabian Socialists surrounded President Wilson and presented a program to socialize the United States. It was an altogether spectacular achievement for those few men under the leadership of Pease, who set out to change the world at the turn of the century, and did so by making full use of "presidential advisors."

One of the rising stars in the Fabian Society's inner circle was Sir Stafford Cripps, a nephew of Beatrice Webb. Sir Stafford played a major role in advising American Socialists on how to get the United States to join in WWII. In 1929, Cripps had been a guiding light for the upper-crust entre into Fabianism, this, in spite of the fact that Fabianism and Communism had become blurred along the edges, and several leading conservatives of the day warned that there was little to choose between Fabian Socialism and Communism, other than the lack of membership cards for Fabian Socialists.

The year 1929 also saw the rise of another star who was destined to shake the economic and financial policies of many nations, including his own England, but perhaps more importantly, those of the United States. John Maynard Keynes had become a virtual Fabian Society icon thanks to men like Gollancz, with his giant left publishing house and Left Book Club, and Harold Joseph Laski. (1893-1950)

Rare Fabian Society papers I saw in the British Museum were of the opinion that without the blessing of Laski, Keynes would not have amounted to much. Laski was once described in these papers as "everybody's idea of a Socialist."

Even the great H.G. Wells bowed the knee to Laski, calling him, "the greatest Socialist intellectual in the English-speaking world."

Laski came from Jewish parents in moderate circumstances and it is said the rise of Hitler was what turned him to a militant for Jewish rights in Palestine. Clashes with Earnest Bevin, Socialist prime minister of Britain were frequent and furious. On May Day, 1945, Laski, as chairman of the British Labor Party, made a speech in which he reiterated that he did not believe in the Jewish religion, because he was a Marxist. But now, Laski said, he believed the rebirth of the Jewish nation in Palestine was vitally necessary. This was confirmed by Ben Gurion himself.

Laski's opinion was conveyed to President Truman and Rabbi Stephen Wise on April 20,1945. Truman had inherited Roosevelt's hardline stand in favor of Jewish aspirations, as dictated by Laski, and when trouble began brewing over the question of Jewish settlers being allowed into Palestine, Truman sent a copy of what many believed was a Fabian-Socialist report on the status of refugee camps in Europe, urging then Foreign Secretary Bevin to let 100,000 Jews emigrate from these camps and settle in Palestine.

Truman's message caused Bevin to take deep umbrage with both Laski and Truman. Bevin's image of Jews was neither pro nor anti. His views were decidedly tempered by those of Clement Attlee, then Prime Minister of England. As Bevin saw it, the Jews were not a nation, while on the other hand, the Arabs were. "The Jews don't need a state of their own," Bevin said. He told Laski that he would not pay the slightest attention to Truman's suggestion, putting it down to, "pressure from the New York Jewish vote." Bevin's refusal to see it (Laski's and Truman's way) resulted in endless squabbling.

Bevin adhered to his policy based on his belief that "the Arabs were essentially indigenous to the region and pro-British, while a Zionist state meant an intrusion of an alien, disruptive element, which would weaken the region and open the doors to Communism." Even when Weitzman went to meet with him, Bevin refused to offer more than a monthly quota of fifteen hundred Jews who could go to Palestine. From this had to be deducted the number of illegal Jewish immigrants who entered Palestine each of the months. This was one of the very few occasions that Fabian Socialism and Laski suffered a severe defeat.

Ayn Rand is said to have used Laski as her model for her 1943 novel, "The Fountainhead," and Saul Bellow wrote, "I shall never forget Mosby's observations on Harold Laski: on packing the Supreme Court, on the Russian Purge trials, and on Hitler. "Laski's influence is still felt in the United States, forty-four years after his death. His association with Roosevelt, Truman, Kennedy, Johnson, Oliver Wendell Holmes Jr, Louis Brandeis, Felix Frankfurter, Edward R. Murrow, Max Lerner, Averill Harriman, and David Rockefeller was to profoundly change the course and direction on which the Founding Fathers had set this nation.

Laski taught as a Professor of Political Science at the London School of Economics and was chairman of the British Labor Party when Aneuran Bevan was Prime Minister. Laski was like George Bernard Shaw; he would not hesitate to walk up and introduce himself to anyone he wanted to meet. He cultivated friendship with the most important people in the furtherance of Socialist causes. His personality was described by close associate Richard Crossman as, "warm and gregarious, a man who made it to the top on his own, a public intellectual." It is said of Laski that he was generous and kind and that people liked to be with him, all the while the indefatigable Socialist crusader.

A notable milestone of progress for Fabian Socialism came in the 1940s with the Beveridge Report on a series of essays simply entitled, "Social Security." The year 1942 was chosen precisely for psychological reasons. Britain was facing its darkest days of WWII. Now was the time for Socialism to offer hope. Laski offered the scheme to John G. Winant, United States ambassador to the Court of St. James. Mrs Eugene Meyer of the Washington Post described the attention of Roosevelt. In Britain, Fabian Society notables like Lord Pakenham made hundreds of high-profile speeches in favor of the miracle of abolishing want and deprivation. The British public was ecstatic.

But five years later found the British government "borrowing" heavily from the United States to make social security work. John Strachey, so idolized by the Fabian Socialists, discovered that no matter how much he regulated the amount of social security, increasing it when needed, it was still not enough to generate purchasing power, so Strachey, the No.1 Marxist and Minister of Food Supply, had to ration supplies. The Socialists had almost bankrupted the country, in one year, 1947, spending $2.75 billion on their Socialist programs, the money "borrowed" from the United States! The "loans" were the work of Laski, and Harry Dexter White of the United States Treasury, and a Soviet informant.

It is truly amazing that the American people stood silent in the face of the kind of financing of Socialist pipe dreams that they were expected to carry. The only reason which comes to mind as to why the American people did not protest is, quite simply, that the truth was hidden from them. The Federal Reserve "lent" Britain $3 billion dollars in the 1920s so that the "dole" (welfare) system could continue, while at home, war veteran's pensions were cut by $4,000,000 a year as a partial contribution. Could such a thing ever happen again? Informed opinion is that not only can it happen again, but that the reaction from the American people would be the same; for the most part, one of total indifference.

But even with the unstinting, albeit unofficial help of Harry Dexter White, Socialism could not on its own fund its grandiose schemes and when the Congress finally discovered the full extent of White's financial help for Socialist Britain, Sir Stafford Cripps had to come right out with it and tell the British people that henceforth, social security would have to be funded through taxing their incomes. In the period 1947-1949, taxes mounted, food became scarce, incomes dwindled, and although one Fabian brain trust after another worked tirelessly to come up with a solution that would make Socialism work — other than borrowing money from the United States — they always came back to the same thing: deficit spending or scrap Fabian Socialist programs as unworkable.

Britain was reduced from a profitable renderer of goods and services and brokerage agents for other nations, to a beggar nation. In short, Socialist programs were responsible for the destruction of its centuries old, thriving economy. Britain began to resemble a banana republic. Grabbing at straws, the Labour Party (its leadership Fabian Socialists almost to a man) thought it could make things work by more nationalizing and more rationing, but the electorate did not give the Fabian Society the chance, turning Labour out of office in general elections in 1950.

The Fabian Society's legacy? An empty treasury, gold reserves gone, production down to an all time low, it sought to distance itself from the discredited Labor Party on the grounds that "the Fabian Society is not a political party."

Speaking in the House of Commons, a notable Socialist, Albert Edwards said: "I have spent years discoursing on the defects of the capitalist system. I do not withdraw those criticisms. But we have seen the two systems side by side. And the man who would still argue for Socialism as the means of ridding our country of the defects of capitalism is blind indeed. Socialism just does not work."

Yet, in spite of the total and abject failure of Socialism in practice as opposed to theory, there were still those in the United States who were determined to thrust failed Socialist policies down the throats of the American people. Roosevelt, Truman, Kennedy, Johnson, Nixon, Bush and Carter seemed determined to ignore the Great Socialist Debacle on the other side of the Atlantic, and, urged on by their Socialist advisors, plunged ahead with American versions of the same old failed Fabian Socialist theories and policies.

Still tied to Britain through a common language and a common heritage, the Socialists were able to enmesh the United States in their dream of a One World Government through the so-called Atlantic Alliance or Atlantic Union. Ignoring the wisdom of President George Washington's Farewell Address, successive American governments went ahead with what was essentially a Fabian Socialist scheme for a world government in which Americans for Democratic Action (ADA) played no small part. Also much to the fore in this strictly Socialist enterprise was the Royal Institute for International Affairs (RIIA) headquartered at Chatham House, St. James Square, London, the "mother" of the American Council of Foreign Relations (CFR).

The "Socialist Hands Across The Sea" drive was bolstered by the presence of Owen Lattimore, at Leeds University. Lattimore, a Johns Hopkins professor, is best remembered for his treasonous conduct while in charge of the Institute for Pacific Relations (IPR), which is blamed for the instigation of United States trade policies toward Japan. That spurred the attack on Pearl Harbor and got the United States into WWII, at a time when the German Army had thoroughly trounced the so-called "allies" who were staring defeat in the face in Europe.

The rise of Harold Wilson as the future prime minister of England could be laid at the door of the Kennedy administration, which having dispatched Harold MacMillan "with one Skybolt" as one commentator put it, the Kennedy administration exuded kindness and know how toward the "Oxford Socialist in grey flannels," as Wilson was described. Wilson went to America to find a way of sloganeering himself into office, and he found it among the Madison Avenue advertising agents. Strange, that Socialism had to turn to capitalism to find out how things are done!

Yet, no sooner was Wilson installed as prime minister than he told the House of Commons that his policies would be socialism as usual: nationalizing of industries, "social justice" and of course tax REFORM, a bigger bite out of the incomes of corporations, payroll levies and the whole Socialist nine yards. An excited Wilson told his Fabian Socialist colleagues that they could be sure of success, because "we have an American government in sympathy."

What Wilson really meant was that the American government appeared more willing than ever to pay the bills for extravagant Socialist spending by his Labour government. Again, we emphasize in contribute toward "world socialism."

Prime Minister Wilson, making good use of his American connections, borrowed four billion dollars from the International Monetary Fund, (the largest funder of which was, and remains, the United States.) Once again it was demonstrated that Socialist programs could not support their own weight, and like the dinosaur, would collapse if not propped up. The IMF was established by Lord Keynes, who described it as "essentially a Socialist conception."

But some voices were being raised in the United States against the alarming Socialist penetration of government that had begun with Wilson, accelerated with Roosevelt, and grown larger and bolder and more outspoken in the Kennedy administration. One of those was Senator Joseph McCarthy from Wisconsin. A true patriot, McCarthy was determined to root out the Socialists and Communist agents of change with which the United States State Department had become infested, a battle that McCarthy began in 1948 with the Truman administration, and continued with the Eisenhower administration.

The Fabian Society became thoroughly alarmed. How was it to defend its penetration of the United States government and its institutions against public exposure? For help, Fabians turned to Americans for Democratic Action, who set about mounting a massive campaign of vilification against the senator from Wisconsin. Without this force to reckon with, there is no doubt that McCarthy would have achieved his goal of exposing just how far the American government and its institutions had been taken over by Fabian Socialism, which McCarthy mistakenly identified as "Communism."

The ADA spent hundreds of thousands of dollars in efforts to curb McCarthy, even going so far as to distribute thousands of copies of the Senator's personal finances, in violation of Senate rules, which were disclosed to the Senate Subcommittee. The Socialist publication "New Statesman" suddenly became concerned with the Constitution and the Bill of Rights — suggesting that the McCarthy hearings were imperiling these "sacred rights." The ADA — sponsored resolution condemning McCarthy was proof positive that then, as now, the Democrat Party was in the hands of international Socialists of the Fabian Society variety. ADA was not at all shy about claiming credit for having "stopped McCarthy."

With the downfall of Senator McCarthy, the Fabian Society breathed a collective sigh of relief: this was about as close to exposure it had come. The one man who could have foiled the ADA attack failed to show up at the Senate hearing. Senator John F. Kennedy, a professed admirer of the senator from Wisconsin was reputedly confined to a hospital bed when the vote came up. It has not been explained why he failed to pair his vote. Kennedy actually owed his rise to power to McCarthy, who refused to campaign for Henry Cabot Lodge, when Lodge was running against Kennedy in Massachusetts.

That fact, not well known, bodes ill for the independence of the United States and the Republic for which its stands. In the future, unless Socialism is radically checked, and then uprooted, the Pledge of Allegiance might well go something like this:

"I pledge allegiance to the flag of United States and to the Socialist Government for which its stands..."

Let us not think this far-fetched. We should recall the small band of unimportant young men who started their movement in London, a movement that spread its dangerous poison across the entire world, were also considered "farfetched" in their day. The Fabian Society was now reinvigorated. With the McCarthy threat disposed of, and a new, young, president in the White House, one educated by Harold Laski at the London School of Economics and influenced by John Kenneth Galbraith, the Socialists looked set fair to make a quantum leap into the very sinew and muscle of the United States Government. After all, wasn't Kennedy's "New Frontier" actually a book written by the great Socialist Henry Wallace?

Wallace had not flinched in putting Socialism's goals firmly in view:

"Socially disciplined men will work cooperatively to increase the wealth of the human race and apply their inventive skills to changing society itself. They will modify (reform) governmental and political machinery as well as the momentary and price system, to achieve far wider possibility of social justice and social charity (welfare) in the world...men may rightfully feel that they are serving a function as high as any minister of the Gospel. They will not be

Communists, Socialists or Fascist, but plain men trying to gain by democratic methods the professed objectives of Communists, Socialists or Fascists..."

That the Kennedy administration originally embarked on a program that looked even more radical than that of the Roosevelt era, is not disputed. Even the fact that the ADA selected his cabinet and advisers almost to a man is well known. In Britain, the Fabian Socialists wore broad smiles: their time, it seemed had arrived. But their happiness began to be tempered with reservation as news from the United States had it that Kennedy was not living up to their Socialist expectations.

The ADA's mouthpiece, "New Republic" said in an editorial published June 1, 1963: "In general the Kennedy performance is less impressive than the Kennedy style." Laski's vision of "a new Jerusalem" in the English-speaking world and the building of a new, Socialist society, seemed to have been put on hold — at least for a while. Laski had known how to manage Labour Party leaders Attlee, Dalton, McDonald, the Kennedy brothers, the question was, would his successors be able to handle the "American side" as well as he had done?

The rise of Fabianism in the United States could be traced back to the Fellowship of New Life and later, to the Boston Bellamy Club, which came into being after the visit of Sydney Webb and R.R. Pease, historian of the Fabian Society — one of the original four Fabians, to visit the United States in 1883. The Bellamy Club was brought into being by General Arthur F. Devereux and Captain Charles E. Bowers, backed by newspapermen Cyrus Field, Willard and Frances E. Willard. The club did not have its intention the advance of Socialism. Devereux's main concern was the huge influx of untrained immigrants into the United States, which he said, was not ready to receive them.

General Devereux felt that the situation should be nipped in the bud before it got completely out of hand. (He could not have foreseen the horrendous, deliberately contrived immigration situation that developed in the United States in 1990—thanks to Socialist policies.) As Devereux and his friends were getting ready to found the Boston Bellamy Club, Webb arrived from England in September of 1888 and was put in touch with the club's founders. Sensing an opportunity, Webb and Pease were able to include in the club's principles the nationalization of private industry, with the name to be changed to the Boston Nationalist Club. The opening meeting was attended by Webb and Edward Bellamy. On December 15, 1888, the seed of Fabian Socialism in the United States that was to sprout and grow into a huge tree, was planted.

Advancing into the arts, in 1910, Shaw's plays were being put on by the Theater Guild in New York City by Professor Kenneth MacGowan of the Harvard Socialist Club, using methods learned from the Moscow Arts Theater. The League of Industrial Democracy, Americans for Democratic Action was still far in the future, but the foundations for their organizations had already been laid.

Shaw and H.G. Wells were puffed by literary agents all over America, particularly in college towns, and socialist magazines, "The New Republic" and "The Nation" and "The Socialism Of Our Times," edited by Norman Thomas and Henry Laidler, were taking off.

A frequent contributor to the "New Republic," Laski taught at Harvard all through WWI. His unkind critics say thus he was to avoid any possibility of having to serve in some capacity or another in the British war effort. It was from the "New Republic" that Woodrow Wilson received support, not only for getting the United States into that conflagration, but right throughout its disastrous course. If ever there was a "Socialist War," this was it. "New Republic" did not have the same concerns for the terrible slaughter going on in Russia under the guise of Bolshevising Russia.

Laski was an enthusiastic admirer of Felix Frankfurter and some of his letters in praise of Frankfurter revealed the extent of the penetration of Fabian Socialism into the United States justice system. While on one of his many visits to the United States, Laski urged the ADA and other American Socialists to take active measures in getting higher taxation laws passed: newer, higher taxes on unearned high incomes was the way to get taxation equitably distributed, Laski said. He also kept in constant touch with his friend Judge Felix Frankfurter, urging him to press for "reforms" of the United States Constitution, particularly the constitutional separation of powers between the executive, legislative and judicial branches.

Laski was constantly at the side of Frankfurter and constantly attacking the United States Constitution, derisively referring to it as, "Capitalism's strongest safeguard, a class document." Laski called Roosevelt, "the sole bulwark against the Fascist form of Capitalism." That Laski was not charged with sedition for trying to overthrow the United States Constitution was a big mistake. A frequent visitor to the Roosevelt White House, he was also very secretive about it, such visits never mentioned in the press.

Meetings were always arranged through Felix Frankfurter. During one visit, Laski is alleged by his biographer to have told Roosevelt, "Either Capitalism or Democracy must prevail" and urged the president to "save democracy." By "democracy" Laski obviously meant SOCIALISM, the Socialists having long ago adopted "democracy" as the standard bearer of Socialism. During WWII, Laski frequently urged Roosevelt to make the world safe by laying a foundation for postwar Socialism. The Socialist education Roosevelt received from Laski is said to have almost equaled that received by John F. Kennedy while Laski's pupil at the London School of Economics.

There were some who were aware of what was going on. Congressman Tinkham introduced into the Congressional Record, House, January 14, 1941, a letter written by Amos Pinchot. The Pinchot letter stated: "Many young Socialists declare that what is generally called the Roosevelt Program is in reality the Laski program, imposed on New Deal thinkers and finally on the President, by the London Professor of Economics and his friends." The only thing wrong with that bold statement is that Laski was a professor of political science, not economics. Otherwise, the observation was right on target!

Laski carried on lengthy correspondence with Frankfurter, urging him to be vigilant and push the "political psychology" of Fabian Socialism. There can be no doubt whatsoever that Laski's advice to Frankfurter served as the basis for sweeping changes made by the Supreme Court, changes that completely altered the course and the character of the United States. If ever it could be said that the "New Deal" had a father, that father was not Roosevelt, but the Fabian Society's Professor Harold Laski.

Even to this day, so few Americans are aware of the vast influence Fabian Society Professor Laski had on Roosevelt. Six months after Pearl Harbor got the United States into WWII as planned, Eleanor Roosevelt invited Laski to be the keynote speaker at the International Students Congress that was set to take place in September of 1942, the one that Churchill refused to let Laski attend.

Congressman Woodruff of Michigan put it very succinctly, when he denounced Laski as having "a key to the back door of the White House." Had patriots been able to access the private letters between Laski, Frankfurter and Roosevelt, they might have aroused enough righteous indignation to get Laski expelled from the country, a fate he richly deserved.

Graham Wallas was another leading Socialist whose influence over Frankfurter and Justice Oliver Wendell Holmes is said to have turned American jurisprudence upside down. It is said that through William Wisemen, head of MI6 North American Desk, Laski got Frankfurter appointed to one of the very first purely Socialist-oriented panels: The Mediation Commission On Industrial Unrest.

In Britain, Fabianism penetrated every comer, every nook and cranny of the civil and military scene. No facet of society was immune to its penetration, which is the path it was to follow in its invasion of the United States. Truly, Socialism is a more deadly enemy than was ever faced by George Washington and his troops during the American War of Independence. This ongoing war never ceases, day or night, the battle for the hearts, minds, and the souls of the American nation goes forward.

One of the bulwarks against Socialism penetration is the Christian religion. Clemment Atlee, a leading Fabianist who went on to become prime minister of England put the successes of the Fabian Socialists down to its penetration of labor. But Irish Catholic labor was never penetrated by Webb, Shaw, or any of the other leading lights of the Fabian Society. There is much hope in this for us today as we seek to find ways of halting Socialism's relentless march across the North

American continent, a march that will end in the camps of Communist slavery, for indeed, Socialism is the road to slavery.

The slippery, slimy, treasonous methods adopted to spread Socialism is no place better demonstrated that in the prominent Socialists who were never recognized as such. These leading lights appeared in positions of great power, while never openly admitting their Socialist aspirations. A few names will help to illustrate the point: In Britain:

The Rt. Hon L. S. Amery. Lectured at Livingston Hall, an important education center.

Professor A.D. Lindsay, lecturer at Kingston Hall, an important education center.

Annie Besant, leader of the Theosophist movement.

Oswald Mosley, M.P., and Fascist leader in England.

Malcolm Muggeridge, author, scholar, lecturer.

Bertrand Russell, elder statesmen, the Committee of 300, Kingsway Hall lecturer.

Wickham Steed, perhaps one of the most famous of all British Broadcasting Corporation (BBC) commentators whose opinions influenced millions of the BBC's listeners.

Arnold Toynbee, Kingsway Hall lecturer.

J.B. Priestly, author.

Rebecca West, Kingsway Hall lecturer.

Anthony Wedgewood Benn, Kingsway Hall lecturer.

Sydney Silverman, lecturer and parliamentarian.

On the American side, the following personalities kept their Socialist beliefs well hidden:

Archibald Cox, Watergate special prosecutor.

Arthur Goldberg, Secretary of Labor, United Nations Rep. etc.

Henry Steel Commager, writer and publisher.

John Gunther, writer, reporter for LIFE magazine.

George F. Kenan, specialist on Bolshevik Russia.

Joseph and Stewart Alsop, writers, newspaper columnist opinion-makers.

Dr. Margaret Meade, anthropologist, author.

Martin Luther King, Southern Christian Leadership Conference civil rights leader.

Averill Harriman, Industrialist, roving representative, prominent Democrat.

Birch Bayh, United States Senator.

Henry Fowler, under Secretary, United States Treasury.

G. Mennen Williams, industrialist, Department of State.

Adlai Stevens, Politician.

Paul Volcker, Federal Reserve Board.

Chester Bowles.
Harry S. Truman, President of the United States.
Lowell Weicker, United States Senator.
Hubert Humphrey, United States Senator.
Walter Mondale, United States Senator.
Bill Clinton, President, United States.
William Sloane Coffin, Church leader.

There are hundreds more names, some prominent, others not so prominent, but the foregoing are enough to make the point. The careers of these people fit very neatly the type of enemy described by President Andrew Jackson.

One person who contributed a great deal to the spread of Socialism in Britain and the United States was the famous Malcolm Muggeridge. The son of H.T. Muggeridge, Malcom enjoyed a distinguished career writing for "Punch," with good connections in Moscow. The fact that he was a nephew of the great lady, Beatrice Webb, did not hurt. Muggeridge wrote for the "New Statesman" and the "Fabian News" and was much sought-after as a speaker at the Society's weekend schools. Malcolm Muggeridge became one of the main draw-cards for Socialism in the United States, and was often featured very prominently on television interviews.

2

WHAT SOCIALISM IS:
WHY IT LEADS TO SLAVERY

"Where the ends they seek are concerned, Socialism and Communism are virtually interchangeable terms. Indeed, Lenin's party continued to call itself, 'Social Democrat' until the Seventh Party Congress of March, 1918, when it substituted the term, 'Bolshevik' as a protest against the non-revolutionary attitude of the Socialist parties of the West."...Ezra Taft Benson — A Race Against Time, Dec. 10, 1963.

"Through restructuring, we want to give Socialism a second wind. To achieve this, the Communist Party of the Soviet Union returns to the origins and principles or the Bolshevik Revolution, to the Leninist ideas about the construction of a new society." Mikhail Gorbachev, in a speech at the Kremlin in July 1989.

These highly revealing comments, and other which we shall quote as we proceed, put Socialism in its proper perspective. Most modern day Americans have only a vague idea of what Socialism is about, viewing it as a semi-benign movement whose goals are a general improvement of the living standards of the ordinary people. Nothing could be further from the truth. Socialism has one place to go, and that is Communism. We have been besieged by the media, led to believe that Communism is dead, but some thinking will convince us otherwise.

The Fabian Socialists closely followed the Communist Manifesto of 1848, but in a more genteel, less abrasive manner. Their aims however, were the same: A world revolution which would end in a One World Government — New World Order in which capitalism would be replaced by Socialism in a welfare state, in which every individual would be beholden to a dictatorial Socialist hierarchy for everything in life.

There would be no private property, no constitutional government, only authoritarian rule. Every individual would be beholden to the Socialist state for his sustenance. Outwardly, this would in theory be of great benefit to the ordinary people, but an examination of the Socialist experiments in England, reveals the system as a complete, unworkable failure. As we show elsewhere, Great Britain of 1994 has totally collapsed because of the Socialists and their welfare state.

The Fabian Socialists set out to achieve their goals in England and the United States by placing intellectuals in key positions from where they were able to exert undue influence in changing the direction of both countries. In the United States, the two prime agents in this regard undoubtedly were Professor Harold Laski and John Kenneth Galbraith. In the background, one of the "old guard" of British Fabianism, Graham Wallas, was director of propaganda. Together, they wrote the "Basis of The Fabian Society of Socialists."

"The Fabian Society therefore aims at the reorganization of society by the emancipation of land and Industrial Capital from individual and class ownership, and vesting of them in the community for the general benefit...The Society accordingly works for the extinction of private property in land...The Society further works for the transfer to the Community of such Industrial capital as can be conveniently handled by Society. For the attainment of these ends the Fabian Society looks to the spread of Socialist opinions, and the social and political changes consequent thereon...It seeks to achieve these ends by the general dissemination of knowledge as to the relation between the individual and the Society in its economic, ethical and political aspects."

In 1938, the aims and objects of the Society were somewhat altered:

"The Fabian Society of Socialists."

"It is therefore the aims at the establishment of a society in which the economic power of individuals and classes shall be abolished through the collective ownership and democratic control of the economic resources of the community. It seeks to secure these ends by the methods of political democracy. The Fabian Society shall be affiliated with the Labour Party. Its activities shall be in furtherance of Socialism, and the education of the public along Socialist lines by the holding of meetings, lectures, discussion groups, conferences and summer schools; the promotion of research into political, economic and social problems and periodicals; and by any other appropriate means."

One is at once struck by the number of times "community" appears, alongside the playing down of individual rights. In this, it appears that Fabian Socialism set its face against Christianity from the earliest gatherings of the original few in London. The determination to nationalize industrial projects that served the public was very evident and bore a striking resemblance to what the Communist Manifesto of 1848 said on the subject. It was also evident that the purpose of Fabian Socialism was to establish a National Cooperative Common wealth Society, in which everyone would have the same rights to the economic wealth of the nation.

The Boston Bellamy Club, which opened in 1888, succeeded the Fellowship of New Life with its Theosophical learnings and became the first Fabian Socialist enterprise in the United States. The Basis was somewhat different:

"The principal of the Brotherhood of Humanity is one of eternal truths that govern the world's progress on lines which distinguish human from brute nature. No truth can prevail unless practically applied. Therefore those who seek the welfare of man must endeavor to suppress the system founded on brute principles of competition and put in its place another based on the nobler principles of association..."

"We advocate no sudden or ill-considered change; we make no war upon individuals who have accumulated immense fortunes simply by carrying out to a logical end the false principles upon which business is now based. The combinations, trusts, and syndicates of which people at present complain, demonstrate the practicability of our basic principle of association. We merely seek to push the principle a little further and have industries operated in the interests of the nation—the people organized, the organic unity of the whole people."

The prose was the work of Sydney Webb, and Edward Pease, Fabian Society historian, who traveled to the United States in the 1880s to set in motion American Fabian Socialism. The mildness of the tone and the choice of words belies its iron-hard inner core of revolutionary aims. The use of the word "reforms" was intended to disarm critics as were Fabian publications like "The Fabian News" which advocated "reforms" that would prove particularly injurious to the United States Constitution. It paved the way for the ongoing revolution that is changing the United States from a Confederated Republic into a Socialist Welfare State. (It was George Washington who described the United States as a Confederated Republic).

In the "American Fabian" of 1895, (unlike the disguised Socialists who infest the United States House and Senate and the Judiciary and who act as advisers to the President) the Fabian Socialist aims for America were rather plainly stated:

"We call our paper, 'The American Fabian' for two reasons; we call it 'Fabian' because we desire to make it stand for the kind of educational Socialist work which is so ably done by the English Fabian Society...We call our paper, 'The American Fabian' because our policies must in a measure differ from those of the English Fabians. England and America are alike in some things; in some things they are utterly unlike. England's constitution readily admits to constant though gradual modification. Our American Constitution does not readily admit to such change. England can thus move into Socialism almost imperceptibly. Our Constitution being largely individualist *must be changed to admit Socialism and each change necessitates a political crisis."*

Thus from the very beginning it was clear that the main challenge to introducing Socialism to the United States was the Constitution and that from that day onwards, it became the target of Socialist attacks on the institutions that make up the Confederated Republic of the United States of America. As we shall see, to this end, callous, hardened Socialists like Walt Whitman Rostow were employed to undermine the very foundation of the nation. As trained observers were quick to recognize, Fabian Socialism was not just a nice, friendly debating society run by professors and educated ladies, who talked with polished accents and projected an air of sweet reason ableness.

Fabian Socialism developed the art of dissembling and lying without seeming to lie. Many were deceived in England, and later, in the United States, where we are still being deceived on a grand scale. But there were occasions when Socialist leaders could not contain themselves, such as the occasion of the 1936 Eastern Spring Conference of Professional Schools for Teachers. Roger Baldwin explained the double meaning of words so often used by Fabian Socialists: "progressive" meant "'the forces working for the democraticizing of industry by extending public ownership and control," while "democracy" meant "strong trade unions, government regulation of business, ownership by the people of industries that serve the public."

Senator Lehman was another Socialist who was unable to contain his eagerness to introduce Fabian Socialism into the United States. Speaking on the occasion of the American Fabian League Anniversary Symposium on "Freedom and the Welfare State," Lehman had this to say:

"A hundred and seventy years ago the welfare state concept was translated into the basic law of this land by the founders of the republic...The founding Fathers were the ones who really originated the welfare state." Lehman, like so many of his Socialist colleagues in the Senate, had not the foggiest notion of the Constitution, so it was not surprising that he got it mixed up with the Preamble to the Constitution, *which was never made a part of the Constitution simply because our Founding Fathers rejected the concept of a welfare state.*

The Preamble to the Constitution: "to create a more perfect union and to promote the general welfare..." Sen. Lehman seemed to be engaging in wishful thinking for this clause is not part of the United States Constitution. He also appeared to be engaging in the favorite Socialist technique of twisting words and their meaning.

There is a General Welfare Clause in the United States Constitution and it is found in Article 1, Section 8 of the delegated powers of Congress. But in this setting it means the general welfare of ALL citizens, that is to say, their state of well being which is a far cry from the Socialist meaning of a general handout, the dole, i.e. individual welfare provided by the state.

Probably the first time the American Socialists tried to implement their plan to attack industrial capital, came with a crafty scheme proposed by Rexford Guy Tugwell. The scheme involved appointing consumers to the twenty-seven industry boards that were to be set up under what was called "The National Recovery Act." Tugwell was really trying to do away with the profit motive; stripped of its seemingly benevolent intention of reducing prices to consumers, the real intention was to slice the profits of the entrepreneurs and increase the wages of the workers accordingly, but the scheme was declared unconstitutional by a unanimous decision of the Supreme Court. In 1935, the Court was not yet packed with "Liberal" (i.e. Socialist) judges.

Roosevelt was quick to change that "imbalance." It is safe to say that the Supreme Court in the 1920s-1930s really saved the United States from being taken over by the Fabian Socialists who had come pouring into every level of government, banking, industry, and the Congress, in an effort to literally overwhelm the country.

Socialists, in their endeavor to get past the Constitution with so called "laws" like the unconstitutional Brady bill, do not know that the United States Constitution is "the perfect equipoise, equilibrium or balance of the common law." The way in which the Constitution was drafted was that all of its provisions meet in the center to neutralize each other, which why bills the Socialist try to slip through on the premise that they can divide the Constitution, are null and void. The Constitution has to be read as a whole, it cannot be isolated and parted to fit the weird aspirations of men like President Clinton. This is what Ramsey McDonald came up against, and it is what totally frustrated Professor Laski.

The Fabian Society of London and its American counterpart were not known for letting obstacles stand in their way. To get around constitutional safeguards, the American Fabian League came up with the idea that any of their proposals that ran counter to the constitution should be subjected to a referendum. Obviously, with their considerable resources, and with almost the entire jackal press in their pockets, the Fabians felt sure that they could swing public opinion their way. Just look at what they did in standing behind George Bush's *totally illegal* Gulf War.

Being aware of the true nature of Socialism and its aims, makes it easier to understand why the Bolshevik Revolution was bought and paid for by City of London and Wall Street bankers, backed by government action which seemed always to help the Bolsheviks. The Bolshevik Revolution which was so beloved by Gorbachev, was not an indigenous revolution of the Russian people. Rather, it was a foreign ideology, forced upon the Russian nation at the cost of millions of lives. Bolshevism was neither wanted nor requested by the Russian people; they had no say and no defense against this monstrous political, social and religious force that overcame their land.

It is just so with Socialism, which forces human beings to accept deliberately engineered changes of a most far-reaching nature which they don't want and which are carried out against their wills. Take the so-called Panama Canal treaty as an example. The only difference between Bolshevism and Socialism is that in the former, brute force and terror tactics are used, while the Socialist does his work slowly and stealthily, the intended victim never knowing who the enemy is nor what the end result will be.

In "World Revolution" we find the true aims of the Communists and their Socialist twin:

"The goal of world revolution is not the destruction of civilization in a material sense: the revolution desired by the leaders is moral and spiritual revolution, and anarchy of ideas by which all standards set up through the nineteen centuries shall be reversed, all honored traditions trampled underfoot, and above all, the Christian ideal finally obliterated." A study of Franklin Roosevelt's book, "On Our Way," yields substantially the same conclusions.

Emma Goldman, one of the Socialist's bright stars, engineered the murder of President McKinley. This was the "direct" method favored by Communism, but in the last two decades we have seen the type of Socialist anarchy that uses calumny, slander, traducery, maligning and denigration of individual members of the House, Senate and the Presidency, who have attempted to reveal the dreadful Senator Joseph McCarthy, Senator Huey Long, Vice President Agnew — the list is much longer but these names should suffice to make the point.

Fabian Socialist "nobility" is far from being true. They want to gain control of education and the publishing business for the sole purposes of altering the minds of the people by falsely changing the premises upon which opinions are made, individually, and en-mass. A small group of Fabian Socialists set out to accomplish this by moving silently and stealthily, thereby not alerting the audience they wished to capture, as to their real purpose. It can be said with a certain degree of accuracy, that today, in 1994, this small group has come a long way in that they virtually control the destiny of the English-speaking world.

The Bolshevik Revolution would never have got off the ground were it not for the full backing and financial resources of leading Socialists in Britain and the United States. The rise of Bolshevism, and how it was financed by Lord Alfred Milner and the Wall Street banks, controlled on a day-to-day basis by Milner's emissaries, Bruce Lockhart and Sydney Reilly of British intelligence MI6, is detailed in "Diplomacy By Deception."

In the United States the Socialist purveyors hang other signs outside their political shop windows. No one ever calls himself or herself a Socialist, at least not in public. They wear no badge, registering themselves, "Liberals," "Progressives" and "Moderates." Power hungry moves are disguised in terms of "peace" and "humanitarianism." In this regard, the American Socialists are no less devious than their British controllers. They adopted the British Fabian Socialist attitude toward nationalism, declaring it to be irrelevant and not essential to achieving what they call, "Social equality," i.e. Socialism. American Socialists joined with their British cousins in declaring that the best way to break down nationalism and advance the cause of Socialism is via a graduated income tax program.

Fabian Socialists can be identified by the company they keep and the programs they support. This rule of thumb is very helpful in singling out its secretive men and women. In the United States they work at a slower pace than their British counterparts, never showing the direction in which they are traveling. One of their number, Arthur J. Schlesinger Jr., who won a Pulitzer prize for his Socialist leadership, wrote, "There seems no inherent obstacle to the GRADUAL (emphasis added) implementing of Socialism in the United States through a series of 'New Deals' which is a process of backing into Socialism." (Partisan Review 1947)

We should be aware that traditional liberties we take for granted are gravely threatened by Socialism, which brings far-reaching, damaging, changes on the installment plan. All the while, thanks to their control of the book industry, publishing in general and the press, we are going through a non-stop process of being conditioned through "psychopolitics" to accept these Socialist-mandated changes as inevitable. The deadly, destructive Socialist programs forced upon the United States, beginning in the Wilson presidency, have always appeared to be beneficial and helpful, while in reality, destructive and divisive.

Socialism can be fairly described as a dangerous conspiracy cloaked in a mantle of reforms. Almost without exception, their programs have been, and are always described as "reforms." The Socialists "reformed" education, and they are "reforming" health care. They "reformed" the banking system, which "reform" gave us the Federal Reserve Banks. They "reformed" trade laws and broke down protective tariffs that had provided most of the revenue needed to run the country, right up until 1913.

In education, the Fabian Socialists seek to create a "mediocre majority" that has the semblance, but not the substance, of being educated.

The Fabian Socialists fought a secret war to gain control of education, which began in the 1920s and triumphed in 1980 with the passage of the Department of Education signed into law by President Carter. This great victory for Socialism guaranteed that henceforth only mediocre students would leave high school. That was the sum and substance of Socialist "reform" of education. There is a misconception abroad that we are smarter today than our forbears. Yet, if we look at the school curriculum in 1857, we find this is an absolutely false idea. The subjects in which high school students had to be proficient enough to graduate included:
"Thompson's Arithmetic"
"Robinson's Algebra"
"Davie's Algebra"
"Davie's Geometry"
"Comstock's Philosophy"
"Willard's History"
"Cutter's Physiology"
"Brown's Grammar"
"Mitchell's Geography"
"Sander's Series"

Looking at the curriculum of colleges in the late 1880s leaves one astounded by the complexity and number of subjects taught. In those days students studied history and knew all about Napoleon and Alexander the Great. There was no such thing as sheer guesswork, i.e., "multiple choice" questions. Students could answer the questions in their exam papers or they could not. If they did not know them, they were failed and had to stay back to do further study.

There were no elective methods to get by what you did not know. Today, there is one elective after another, which leaves students uneducated and unprepared for the outside world. Mediocrity is the result, and that is the desired goal of Fabian Socialism educational "reforms," to produce a nation with a mediocre educational level.

The great Socialist mischief that laid education in the United States low came with the U.S. Supreme Court case, "Brown vs. School Board, Topeka, Kansas." In this case the Socialists arranged matters so that educational standards were set just above the lowest common denominator, slightly above the more backward elements in the class room. This was the level at which *all children were henceforth to be taught.* Obviously, the upper range of intelligent students were held at the mediocre levels.

So far has education regressed in the United States, that even those whom we think we elect to serve us in Congress, do not understand the language of the Constitution of the United States and our Senators, in particular, grow more incompetent in the Constitution with each passing year.

Returning to the Bolshevik Revolution. The deception was the Socialist leaders in England gave the false impression that it was a "Socialist" revolution meant to improve the lot of the Russian people and put paid to the tyranny of the Romanovs. In fact, the Romanovs were the most benign of all monarchs in Europe, with a genuine love and caring for their people. Deception is the hall mark of Socialism. Its motto. "Make Haste Slowly" is deceptive, because Socialism has not gone slowly and it is not a friend of the working people. Socialism is Communism proceeding more cautiously, but the goals are the same, although the means differ in some instances. The common goal of Communism and Socialism is to liquidate the true capitalist free enterprise system and replace it with a strong central government which has control of every aspect of production and distribution of goods and services. Anyone who stands in their way is immediately labeled "reactionary," "rightwing extremist" a "McCarthy reactionary," "fascist," "religious extremists" and so on. When you hear these words spoken, then you know the speaker is a Socialist.

Communism and Socialism have as their common objective an ushering in of a federal, One World Government, or as it has become more popularly known, the "New World Order." Learn what their leaders had to say:

"I am convinced that Socialism is correct. I am an adherent of Socialism...We are not going to change Soviet power, of course, or abandon its fundamental principles, but we acknowledge the need for changes that will strengthen Socialism" — Mikhail Gorbachev.

"The ultimate aim of the Council on Foreign Relations (CFR) is to create a One World Socialist system and make the United States an official part of it." — Senator Dan Smoot, "The Unseen Hand."

"The American people will never knowingly, accept Socialism, but under the name of Liberalism, they will adopt every fragment of the Socialist program, until one day America will be a Socialist nation without knowing how it happened...The United States is making greater strides toward adopting Socialism under Eisenhower than under President Franklin D. Roosevelt. — Norman Thomas. "Two Worlds."

To understand the full plan and purpose of Florence Kelley's "legislative action" of American Socialists, one must first carefully read the Declaration of Principles of the Fabian Socialists and international Socialism:

"It's purpose is to secure a majority in Congress and in every State legislature, to win the principal executive and judicial offices, to become the dominant party, and when in power, to transfer the industries to ownership by the people, beginning with those of public character, such as banking, insurance etc."

In the United States, the vast majority of Socialists are found in the Democrat Party, with a smattering of "progressives" in the Republican Party. In this sense, Fabian Socialism is a political party, albeit by adoption, as it was in England with the takeover of the Labour Party. It will be recalled that Kelley was the driving force behind the highly destructive false psycho judicial "Brandeis Briefs" which changed the way rulings are arrived at by the Supreme Court. Kelley was a close friend of Socialist lesbian Eleanor Roosevelt. (The "Brandeis Briefs" method totally sabotaged our legal system and is another example of unwanted, undesirable Socialist-originated changes being forced on the people of the United States.)

In pages 9962-9977, Congressional Record, Senate, May 31, 1924, we find the Socialists and Communists aims spelled out even more plainly:

"In short, American Communists themselves admit that it is impossible to promote revolution in this country unless the rights of the States are destroyed, and a centralized bureaucracy, under an entrenched cast of bureaucrats similar to those in Europe, for Communists (and Socialists) the basic conditions for revolution." While this is slanted toward the Communist goals, let us not forget that it is also the Socialist's goal, differing only by method and in degree.

To which I would add that under Presidents Johnson, Carter, Bush and Clinton, the Socialist agenda for the United States has gone into high gear. Clinton will be a single-term president, but will do more to strongly promote Socialist plans, and do more actual damage than either Roosevelt, Eisenhower or Johnson.

It is plainly evident to those who seek the truth that Communism is not dead. It is only taking a temporary respite and is presently waiting in the wings while Socialism catches up. What we have today is what Karl Marx called "Scientific Socialism." It was also called "psychopolitics" by Professor Harold Laski. President Kennedy adopted "scientific Socialism—his "New Frontier" program taken directly from the British Fabian Society blueprint, "New Frontiers," by Henry Wallace (New York, Reynal and Hitchcock 1934).

"Psychopolitics" was summed up by Charles Morgan in his book, "Liberties of the Mind:"

"...we are all being conditioned to accept limitations of freedom...I fear that unconsciously, even if we are ready to accept this new infection...There is no immunity in the great mass of our people and no consciousness of danger...One can think of many ways in which the population as a whole is being conditioned or prepared for this mental change, this loss of individuality and identity." A clearer explanation of Socialism boring away from within would be hard to find.

The Socialists have been practicing psychopolitics upon the people of England and the United States since the appearance of the Communist Manifesto of 1848. That is why we find in 1994, our senators arguing over the merits of one "national health plan" over another, instead of *rejecting outright* the whole idea as a *Socialist* subterfuge. It was Lenin who said that a national health plan is the arch of Socialism. Likewise, we had the Senate debating the merits of the so called Brady bill, instead of rejecting it out of hand as a *Socialist* subterfuge to get around the Constitution of the United States. An entire book could be written on this subject alone.

The Kennedy administration contained 36 Fabian Socialists. Two were cabinet members, three were White House aides, two were undersecretaries and one was an assistant secretary of state. The remainder were in policy making positions of vital importance. That is why so many Kennedy-era policy decisions ran contrary to the best interests of the United States and its people and seemed oddly at variance with what Kennedy said he stood for.

Since the death of Kennedy, Socialism has taken deep root in the United States, always watered and nurtured by those who are called "Liberals," "Moderates" and nursed with great bouts of "tolerance." Colonel Mandel House, and Sir William Wiseman, director of the North American desk for British intelligence M16 "ran" President Wilson, who became the first openly Socialist American President to sit in the Oval Office.

Fabian Socialism dominated six United States presidents, starting with Woodrow Wilson. The Socialists goals never varied, particularly in what they described as "the difficulties to be overcome," and these were, and in some instances still are:

1. Religion, especially the Christian religion.

2. National pride of nation states.

3. Patriotism.

4. The United States Constitution and States constitutions.

5. Opposition to a graduated income tax.

7. Breaking down trade barriers. These goals are described in their blueprint, "American Fabian Techniques," based on obscurantism.

The Fabian Socialist movement was only interested in recruiting the elite of British society, men like Clement Atlee, Sir Stafford Cripps, Herbert Morrison, Emmanuel Shinwell, Ernest Bevin, Lord Grey, Lord Asquith and Ramsey MacDonald, who went on to work their will on England from Parliament. While these names may be foreign to American readers, these men played a vital role in directing the course the United States was to take, and as such, are worthy of mention.

An interesting sidelight on the Fabian Society is that its committee determined that no more than 5 percent of the population were worthy of becoming good Socialist leaders. Some British Fabian Socialists played vital roles in changing the course and direction of the United States and we shall return to this aspect. Fabian Socialist MacDonald, who went on to become prime minister of England, was dispatched to the United States in 1893, to spy out the land. On his return on January 14, 1898, MacDonald told his committee members, "The great bar to Socialist progress in the United States is its written Constitution, Federal and State, which give ultimate power to a law court."

MacDonald further stated that it would be necessary to work diligently to carry out the directive of Edward Bellamy, an American Fabian Socialist. Most of us will know him as the author of the book, "Uncle Tom's Cabin" which was drafted by his mentor, Colonel Thomas Wentworth, a noted Abolitionist and as ardent a Fabian Socialist as one could find.

Bellamy was an true believer and follower of the British Fabian Society and one of its first American Fabian chapter members. Writing in the "American Fabian" in February, 1895, three years before MacDonald delivered his fact-finding report of his tour of the United States, Bellamy stated, "...our Constitution being largely individualistic must be changed to admit Socialism, and each change necessitates a political crisis. This means the raising of great issues."

Didn't Wilson raise "great issues" and didn't Roosevelt, Truman, Eisenhower, Kennedy, Johnson and Bush do the same thing and isn't it remarkable that Clinton is constantly "raising great issues?" This is the methodology of Socialism: raise "great issues" like the so called "healthcare reform" and behind the clouds of dust raised by the issue, do the dirty, underhand work of undermining the Constitution of the United States.

Herein lies the root explanation of the political actions taken by Presidents Wilson, Roosevelt, Truman, Eisenhower, Kennedy, Johnson, Bush and Clinton.

MacDonald's proposals followed very precisely the model laid down by Bellamy. MacDonald stressed that the need to alter the Constitution of the United States should be preeminent in the thinking of Fabian Socialist. We stress once again that Fabian Socialism differed somewhat from European Socialism, more especially in that it claimed to have no party affiliations. This would be true, if we ignored the fact that by "penetration and permeation" it took over the British Labour and Liberal Parties and has now taken over the Democrat Party of the United States.

MacDonald reported that the underlying principles of the United States Constitution rested on the rights guaranteed by the Fifth Amendment, especially the right to own property as a corollary to Isaac Newtons' Natural Law. Therefore, said MacDonald, changing the Constitution was to be done in an obliquely, highly secretive way and over a period of many years. He also pointed to the block to Socialist tactics of penetration and permeation posed by the separation of powers between the three departments of government.

MacDonald's words were an echo of what Bellamy had proposed in February of 1895. At least Bellamy was better educated in the constitution than are the vast majority of judges and politicians in this day and age. He readily admitted that the Constitution of the United States was not flexible. This shows up the ignorance of Judge Ruth Ginsberg, lately appointed to the Supreme Court by Socialist President Clinton, who told a Senate Judiciary Sub-Committee hearing that the Constitution is "flexible," whereas it is immutable.

The great vision of Fabian Socialism of the 1890s was to "revise" the United States Constitution, that is, "reform" it. Although it appeared on the surface that such a task was beyond its abilities, Fabian ability to work silently and secretly was unfortunately under estimated and overlooked. It reminds me of the popular Frank Sinatra song about some ambitious ants and a rubber tree. The ants had no chance of taking the tree away in one operation, but they nevertheless accomplished the impossible, carrying it away, leaf by leaf, until the rubber tree was demolished. I believe this is a good analogy of how Fabian Socialism has been working since 1895 (a task which still is ongoing) to carry off the United States Constitution piece by piece.

Bellamy and MacDonald might be described as "visionaries," but they were Fabian Socialist visionaries with definite ideas about how to succeed. The methods described by "The American Socialist" called for establishing a Socialist elite in the United States, and then schooling the elite cadre on how to take advantage of every local, state and national crisis for the covert ends of Socialism and to gain support for such ideas through a well-organized penetration of the press. The crystallizing of American Fabian Socialism began in earnest in 1905.

"The American Socialist" also called for forming a cadre of Fabian Socialist professors who in later years would act as advisors for a series of presidents, thereby steering them in the direction of the grand design to socialize the United States. These far-left-of-Marx and Lenin professors were drawn mainly from the ranks of Harvard University Law School. "Educational work" was undertaken by the elite Harvard Socialist Club, which when overlaid on the British Fabian Society — one of the few times they were bold enough to show their Socialist colors — revealed a close match.

Charter members of the Harvard Socialist Club included Walter Lippmann, one of those selected by MacDonald and Bellamy to establish a Socialist elite cadre in the United States. Lippmann spent years penetrating the business world. The role played by Lippmann in turning this country toward Fabian Socialism will be explored at another time. As we shall see, Socialists in the inner circles of power were an enemy more to be feared than Communism, although the Americans public was never allowed to see it this way. As I have so often said in the past, "the enemy in Washington is more to be feared than the enemy in Moscow."

The average American, when he did hear anything about Socialism under its own label, was repelled. In the 1890s, the American Fabian Society was a fledgling organization much in need of guidance, especially in the technique of going slowly and obscuring its goals. Thus, when Socialism was mentioned at all, it conjured up visions of weird sexual practices — which today, Socialists are striving to make culturally acceptable — and how to make the dole (welfare) affordable for everybody. Thus, it was not taken seriously, except by a handful of scholars who saw it as a greater danger than Bolshevism, at least to America.

And when Engels, the deceptive practices role model of Socialists and Marxists visited the United States in 1886, a mistake was made by promoting his vitriolic, book, "Origin of the Family" which later became the Bible for the abortionists, the homosexuals and the so called "women's lib" movement of Molly Yard, Patricia Schroeder, Eleanor Smeal. There is some proof that the purpose of the visit by Engels was to lay the foundation of the new, American Fabian Socialist Club.

Similarly, when Eleanor Marx — Karl Marx's daughter who was known to be the mistress of George Bernard Shaw — toured the United States with another lover, this time the live-in Edward Aveling, public reaction was highly unfavorable. The public uproar about "free love" caught European Socialists by surprise, having no idea just how entrenched Christian values were in American society at that time. They had miscalculated in espousing "free love" (the basis of abortion, i.e. free love without responsibility) and their attacks on the values of the family brought nothing but angry responses.

This taught the American Socialists a big lesson: More haste was a losing philosophy. It had to be "make haste slowly." But the Socialists never gave up, never lost sight of their goals, and as a result, today, the evils of Socialism dominate America on every hand, gaining strength, culturally, religiously and social acceptance as they never did when Engels and Eleanor Marx and Edward Aveling were touting their wares. Readers are probably aware that Aveling was the official translator from German to English of "Das Kapital," the best known of the works written by Marx.

In order to deflect criticism away from Socialism, the British Fabian Society decided to form a group in the United States that became known as the American Economic Association which convened on September 9, 1885. Only the elite cadre of American Socialists in the making were invited to attend. (It was following this meeting that the British Fabian Socialists decided that Mac Donald would have to visit the United States to ascertain what problems were in the way of Socialism, and how to overcome them.)

The American Economic Association drew all the leading Socialist and would-be Socialist leaders of the day to Saratoga, New York on September 9, 1885. Many of the "distinguished guests" as they were described in the New York newspapers, were leading Socialist professors, among them, Woodrow Wilson who was to become the first *openly Socialist* president of the United States.

Others in attendance were Professors Ely, H. R. Adams, John R. Commons and E. James, Dr. E. R. Seligman of Columbia, Dr. Albert Shaw and E.W. Bemis, who went on to become the leading disciples of Socialism in America. None were known outside of their limited academic circles, and Socialism was not given any thought as a serious threat to the American way of life. This was a mistake that was to be made many times in the future, one which is being repeated today. From this small beginning has grown the oak tree of Socialism in the United States, whose spreading branches now threaten the Confederate Republic of the United States. Wilson, then at Bryn Mawr College, went on to teach Socialism at the Philadelphia University Extension in 1902, disguised as Political Science.

There he was immersed with other leading Socialist in promoting Socialist ideas in teaching. Included in the list of Socialist professors were British Fabian Society members, Sydney Webb, R.W. Alden and Edward R. Pease; Ely and Adams, two of his American associates we have already mentioned. Other prominent American Socialists who fed Wilson on a diet of their Socialist ideas were Morris Hilquitt and Upton Sinclair. Their contacts with British Fabian Socialists extended to meetings held at Oxford between 1805 and 1901.

Dr. Seligman of Columbia University sponsored the meetings and is credited with the foresight of having the presidency go to Wilson. The similarity between the rise of Wilson and Clinton is quite remarkable: Both were strongly Socialist by persuasion, both were surrounded by a large number of Socialist intellectuals, and both had Socialist ideals indelibly imprinted on them though contact with Oxford University.

Wilson was greatly influenced by such a Fabian Socialist publications as,

"The New Freedom." Moreover, he was the first United States President to accept university professors as advisors — a radical departure from past traditions and an outright Socialist strategy— methodology of forcing unwanted unacceptable changes upon the American people. The rationale was that nobody would suspect academics of infamous purposes.

Very early on, Wilson was backed by British Fabian Socialist Dr. Albert Shaw who got Wilson elected by splitting the vote, running Theodore Roosevelt on an independent ticket, the so-called Bull Moose Party. As Dr. Seymour said at the time, "Roosevelt's defection put Wilson in the White House." The subterfuge included House "denouncing" Roosevelt as "a wild radical," and it worked. Wilson became the President of the United States and his friend Albert Shaw was appointed to the Labor Committee as a reward when Wilson entered the White House.

Although carefully concealed from the public, the British Fabian Socialist selected Wilson, based on his propensity for Socialist issues, and on the strong recommendation of House, whose brother in-law Dr. Sydney Mezes, was a long-time affiliate of the British Fabian Society and president of the City College of New York. Mezes played a prominent role in pre and post WWI Socialist planning.

Added to this was that a large percentage of members of the Fabian Society were Marxists, one of the most notable in the London Fabian Society was Professor Harold Laski, who went on to play a profoundly disruptive role in socializing of the United States, right up to the time of his death in 1952. It is not disputed that Bernard Baruch, who went on to be Wilson's absolute controller during his years in the White House, was also a Marxist.

The entire agenda for Woodrow Wilson's presidency was set by Socialist advisors, both here and in Britain. One of the first of Wilson's Socialist efforts was to federalize powers that were prohibited to the federal government, being reserved to the several States. These included the police powers of health, education, labor and police protection guaranteed to the States by the 10th Amendment to the United States Constitution.

In later years Professor Harold Laski was to put great pressure on President Roosevelt to break down and destroy through executive action the separation of powers between the legislative, executive and judicial branches of government. This was the key to the back door of breaking down and making the Constitution of "no effect." One of the main items on the Wilson agenda was the destruction of Customs tariffs, which, up to 1913 had provided the United States with enough income to pay the bills of the nation and still have a surplus. The hidden agenda was to destroy this source of income and replace it with the Marxist-inspired graduated income tax. Apart from what else it would achieve, the Marxist graduated income tax was designed to forever burden the middle class. It will be recalled that one of the principle obstacles that Ramsey MacDonald said had to be overcome was resistance to graduated income tax. Thanks to President Wilson, the British Fabian Society was able to impose this onerous burden on the American people, thus realizing one of their cherished ambitions.

It is necessary to say this, and to say it loud and clear: *Communism, although the originator, did not bring graduated income tax to the United States. This was solely the work of the British Fabian Society.* For the past 76 years the American people have been dunned into believing that Communism is the biggest danger to a free world. We hope that in the pages of this book will be found enough evidence to point out that the danger from Socialism, transcends anything thus far seen from Communism. Socialism has wrought a thousand more times havoc within the United States than Communism ever did.

Twice found to be unconstitutional by the United States Supreme Court, graduated income tax was proposed to Wilson by the British Fabian Society and its passage, urged by the American Fabian Socialists, was finally realized by 1916, just in time to pay for WWI. While the American people had their attention focused on events in Europe, the Sixteenth Amendment was slipped through Congress, aided and abetted by a whole flock of Socialist legislators.

The Sixteenth Amendment not ever having been ratified by all of the States, remains outside the pale and ken of the Constitution, but that has not stopped its Socialist backers from having their way. Wilson attempted to equate democracy with the Democratic Party, while in fact, there could be no such party. The correct title should be the Democrat Party. We cannot have a "Democratic Party" in a Confederate Republic or a Constitutional Republic.

Wilson's book "The New Freedom" (actually written by Socialist William B. Hayle) denounced capitalism. "It is contrary the common man" Wilson said. At a time when the United States was enjoying prosperity and industrial progress such as never seen before, Wilson called the economy "stagnant" and proposed a revolution to get things moving again. Strange reasoning indeed — that is if we overlook the fact that Wilson was preaching unadulterated Socialism:

"We stand in the presence of a revolution — not bloody revolution, America is not given to spilling blood — but a silent revolution, whereby America will insist upon recovering in practice those ideals which she has always professed, upon securing a government devoted to the general and not special interests." The most important thing that was omitted in the speech was that this was to be a SOCIALIST REVOLUTION, one of stealth and boundless in its deceit, based upon British Fabian Socialist ideals and principles.

Wilson then made a prophetic prediction — at least, seemingly prophetic, except that upon close examination, he was merely spelling out the Socialist agenda for the United States:

"...We are upon the threshold of a time when the systematic life of the country will be sustained, or at least supplemented, at every point by government activity. And we now have to determine what kind of a governmental activity it shall be; whether, in the first place, it shall be directed from government itself, or whether it shall be indirect, through instrumentalities which have already constituted themselves and which stand ready to supersede government."

The people of America remained largely ignorant of the fact that a sinister force was at play, totally foreign to themselves and the Constitution, which had somehow insinuated itself into power by placing a chief executive in the White House, a leader totally beholden to a ruthless and power-hungry group as could be found anywhere in the world — including Bolshevik Russia — that power being the Fabian Socialists in Britain and the United States.

This trend has continued until today, and as we are seeing, now has President Clinton as its eager, and anxious to please chief executive. The "high hopes" of the ants seeking to carry off the rubber tree plant is slowly, and inexorably, being realized. A great nation, the United States of America, seems totally unaware of the criminality behind Socialism and ignorant of its purposes, and is therefore ill prepared to call a halt to the criminal depredations taking place before its very eyes.

How was it possible for Wilson to have deceived the American people on such a monstrous matter as graduated income tax, something foreign to the Constitution, and which the country had been able to do without up to 1913? For answers we need to look again at Socialist ability to implement their program by stealth, by deceit and by outright falsehood while couching it in language that seemed to indicate the poisonous dish it was preparing was for the good of the people.

The first hurdle Wilson had to overcome was disbanding trade tariffs that had protected America's trade and made it a prosperous nation, with living standards the envy of the world, On July 4, 1789, President George Washington told the First Congress of the United States, "A free people should promote such manufactories as tend to render them independent on others for essential, particularly military supplies."

These wise words set in motion a system of tariff barriers that imposed Customs duties on countries wishing to sell their goods in the United States market, the antithesis of so-called "free trade" which was nothing more than a subterfuge devised by Adam Smith to allow Britain to dump its goods on the market with no reciprocity for American goods on the English market. The impression was somehow cultivated — possibly through control of the press — that the United States had developed the living standard of its people on the basis of "free trade," whereas, in reality, the opposite was true.

We saw this deception come to the fore during the Perot-Gore Debate, when Gore, falsely and with malice aforethought against the people of the United States, denounced tariff barrier protectionism as the cause of the 1929 Wall Street

Crash. Perot was not versed in the Smoot — Hawley Act to defend it against the lies of the Vice President.

"Free trade" was spelled out as a Marxist doctrine in a speech made by Marx in 1848. This was not a new thing, but one first proposed by Adam Smith to undermine the economy of the young American nation. A wise Washington realized that protection of America's fledgling industries was needed. This wise protection policy was carried on by Lincoln, Garfield and McKinley. For 125 years, Americans benefited greatly from this wise policy, until the Wilson Socialist wrecker's ball was used to change the face of the United States:

Even as late as up to WWII, only two percent of the economy of the United States depended on foreign trade, yet, to hear it now, the United States will perish if it does not do away with the last vestiges of our wise tariff barriers. What Wilson did was treason and the Congress committed sedition by going along with his devastating attack on the living standards of the American people.

For the most part the Wilson administration badly mauled the Constitution. No soon had the Fabian Socialists got Wilson elected, than he called for a Joint Session of the Congress. By 1900, a mostly Republican government had maintained existing trade barriers and erected fresh tariff barriers to protect the American farmer, industry, and producers of raw materials. The agitation against protective tariff barriers had its origin in London among members of the Fabian Society Socialist, who were in control of the Royal Institute for International Affairs (RIIA). Ideas for breaching the tariff barriers were fed to Wilson via the seditious Mandel House, directly from London.

The anti-tariff propaganda that spewed forth from London in a never ending stream, and which had begun in earnest in 1897, and the following is an example:

"The American manufacturer reached the highest level of inefficiency in 1907, following a noticeable decline which began in 1897, in several important fields, American manufacturers cannot hold their own against foreign competitors in the domestic market. This fact should be brought to the attention of the American people on the basis that because of tariffs, they are paying a higher price for goods than would be the case if tariff barriers which impede trade were removed. The phrase, 'the mother of all trusts' might be a useful way to describe protectionism, especially if linked to the rising cost of living which can be attributed to protectionist policies." Note: The Fabian Society's Research Department began churning out papers they called "tracts" as if they were allied with Christian missionary efforts. These thousands of "tracts" were later assembled into books and position papers. The above quotation is taken from a tract published in 1914.

What this lying propaganda did not say was that there was no link between the rising cost of living between 1897 and 1902, since tariff rates had no effect on domestic prices. But this did not stop a concerted attack by the major newspapers, owned by foreign investors (particularly the New York Times) from blasting tariff protection as a cause in the rise in the cost of living. This was echoed by the "London Economist" and other magazines owned by City of London bankers.

Sedition was not confined to Democrats. Many so-called "progressive Republicans" ("progressive" and "moderate" have always meant Socialist) joined in the attack on protective tariffs. How did the Socialists succeed in getting the Congress to go along with their plans to wreck our trade, the envy of the world? They did it by combining sociology with politics, which technique pushes Socialists to high positions, from where they can exert the utmost undue influence on national issues of vital importance.

As an example, take the matter of diplomatic recognition for the barbarous Bolshevik government. Thanks to the good offices of Arthur Henderson, in 1929 British recognized the Bolshevik butchers as the legitimate government of Russia. They then turned their attention to the United States, and thanks to Socialists installed in high places, got the United States to do likewise. These actions by the leaders of the English — speaking world, gave the Bolsheviks prestige and respect to which they were obviously not entitled, and opened doors to diplomatic contacts, trade and economic matters that would otherwise have remained firmly shut for decades — perhaps for all time.

Fabian Socialists, both in the United States and Britain appeared in such a benign light and their highly-cultured background and great personal charm made it very hard to believe those who were warning that these affable, social elite were a subversive group desirous of stripping the right to own property and threatening to carry off the United States Constitution, piece by piece. It just didn't seem possible to think of this elite group as revolutionaries and anarchists — which in essence is exactly what they were.

A prime example of this was Colonel Edward Mandel House, who was not only properly conventional in every sense of the word, but conservative in manner and speech — at least while in earshot of the public, but one who moved in circles that were far from what one would imagine a group of anarchists to look like.

It was this group of "affable anarchists" who elected Woodrow Wilson. As House saw it, United States citizens were little better than dolts, who could be deceived by appearances. So certain that the voters would not see the nomination of Wilson as a candidate "Made In England," House sailed for Europe on the day that Wilson was nominated at the Democrat convention in Baltimore in 1912. "I feel no need to watch the proceedings" House told Walter Hines, who had introduced him to Wilson the year before. On his arrival in England, House told a gathering of Fabian Socialists of the RIIA, "I was confident that the American people would accept Wilson without question." And so it was.

Wilson went on to become the president, his main task being to undermine the Constitution as mandated by Ramsey McDonald, without the American people ever becoming aware of it, in true Fabian Socialist style. House had often expressed his hatred of the Constitution in private discussions with his secret backers on Wall Street. He called the United States Constitution, "a creation of 18th century minds, not only outmoded, but grotesque," adding, "it ought to be scrapped at once." We shall return to the man Wilson called his greatest friend.

As House put it, "Wilson was elected to carry out a Socialist agenda without alarming the people." How this was to be done was laid out in a fictionalized version of the blueprint of Fabian Socialist long range goals. "Philip Dru, Administrator" was a remarkable confession of Socialist planning and strategies to be used against the American people, very revealing in how Socialists expected the presidency of the United States to be subverted and undermined.

Published by Fabian Socialist B.W. Huebsch, the book should have set alarm bells ringing across America, but unhappily, failed to make clear to the American people what House stood for. It set the agenda for the Wilson presidency as clearly as if it had been presented to the Congress by House himself. "Philip Dru" (actually House) proposed that he become the ruler of America by a series of Executive Orders. Among the tasks "Dru" set himself was establishing a panel of economists to work on the destruction of tariff law which would eventually, "lead to the abolition of the theory of protection as government policy." The panel would also work out a system of graduated income tax and institute new banking laws. Note the sly use of the word "theory." Protective tariffs were no mere theory: Customs duties had earned the United States a living standard that was the envy of the world. Trade protection was *an established doctrine set in place by George Washington, which had proved its worth for 125 years, and was not mere theory.*

How could "Dru" call tariff protection a "theory?" Obviously, it was an attempt to denigrate and belittle the concept and open the way for the Socialist ideal of "free trade" which would begin the decline of the living standards of the American people. It a was also where Wilson got his income tax idea from, which once in place, would further erode the middle class living-standard.

Wilson violated his oath to uphold the United States Constitution on at least 50 separate occasions. In Wilson, the Committee of 300 had found the ideal man to begin the Socializing of America, just as in later years, they found another ideal candidate for their anarchistic purposes in Bill Clinton. A second parallel between Wilson and Clinton is to be found in the type of advisers with whom they surrounded themselves.

In the Wilson inner circle were prominent anarchists-Socialists and Communists Louis D. Brandeis, Felix Frankfurter, Walter Lippmann, Bernard Baruch, Sydney Hillman, Florence Kelley and of course, Edward Mandel House. House, a close friend of Roosevelt's mother, lived two blocks away from N.Y. State Governor Franklin D. Roosevelt and met frequently to give him advice on how to pay for his coming Socialist programs.

The first attack on the Constitution was Ramsey McDonald's declaration that the Constitution had to be altered. The second attack was carried out by House, whose father had made millions of dollars during the Civil War by doing the bidding of the Rothschilds and the Warburgs. After his meeting with Wilson in 1911 through the good offices of Walter Hines, House was certain that he had found the right man to carry out the job of altering the United States Constitution as mandated by McDonald on January 14, 1898.

House began to cultivate Wilson, who was flattered by the attention of a man who seemed to know everybody in Washington. There is a distinct parallel between House and Mrs. Pamela Harriman, who saw in Clinton the ideal man to carry out a wide variety of Socialist reforms without alarming the people. Mrs. Harriman also knew everybody in Washington.

House knew that Wilson would need tutoring by an ardent Socialist, so he arranged for Wilson to meet Harvard law professor Louis D. Brandeis. The meeting was to prove ominous for the future well being of the nation, as Brandeis was committed to making the Constitution of no effect using the legislative route. Brandeis was already writing his predilections into law by "interpreting" the Constitution in such a manner as to make it of no effect based on sociological premises and not Constitutional law.

The third Fabian Socialist attack on the United States Constitution came with the founding of the American Civil Liberties Union (ACLU) in January, 1920 by Fabian Socialist Philip Lovett. Huebsch, the publisher of "Philip Dru, Administrator" was a founder member of this Socialist body whose main purpose in life was to alter the United States Constitution by what Florence Kelley called "the legislative route."

Although it is denied, investigations showed that there were four known Communists on the ACLU board. In the 1920s, Kelley and her associates worked hard to destroy the United States Constitution through a series of false fronts such as the National League of Women's Voters, and we shall return to that later. This was the beginning of the "defeminising" of women by the Socialists.

Many of the most important Socialist (and Communist) leaders in the United States were closely associated with the ACLU, while some even sat on its national committee. One of these was Robert Moss Lovett, a director and a close friend of Norman Thomas and Paul Blanchard who were allied with "Protestants and Other Americans United for the Separation of Church and State."

Thomas was a former clergyman turned Communist. Lovett's charming manner and pleasant demeanor belied the fact that under his affable manner lurked a dangerous anarchist-radical of the worst stripe. In an intemperate fit, Lovett once blew up and revealed his true character: "I hate the United States, I would be willing to see the whole world blow up, if it would destroy the United States." Lovett personified the highly dangerous side of the Fabian Socialist.

In researching statements made by Communists against the United States, I was never able to find one so venomous in intent as that made by Lovett of the ACLU. It might be worthwhile to give a short history of the ACLU at this point in the book:

The ACLU grew out of the 1914-1918 Civil Liberties Bureau, which was against militarism. One of its first directors was Roger Baldwin who had spent time in prison for evading the draft. In a very revealing advisory letter to members, affiliates and friends of the ACLU, Baldwin used traditional Fabian Socialist deceptive tactics to conceal the real intent and purpose of the ACLU:

"Do steer away from making it look like a Socialist enterprise. We want also to look like patriots in everything we do. We want to get a good lot of flags, talk a great deal about the Constitution and what our forefathers wanted to make of the country and show that we are really the folks that really stand for the spirit of our institutions." If ever the later emblem of the British Fabian Society fit, this was it — the wolf in sheep's clothing par excellence.

In 1923 Baldwin forgot his own advice, revealing his true colors:

"I believe in revolution — not necessarily the forcible seizure of power in armed conflict, but the process of a growth of class movements determined to expropriate the capitalist class and take control of all social property. Being a pacifist — because I believe non-violent means best calculated in the long run to achieve enduring results, I am opposed to revolutionary violence. But I would rather see violent revolution than none at all, though I would not personally support it because I consider other means far better. Even the terrible cost of bloody revolution is a cheaper price to pay to humanity than the continued exploitation and wreck off human life under the settled violence of the present system."

In 1936 Baldwin explained some of the terminology used by Fabian Socialists:

"By progressive, I mean forces working for the democraticizing of industry by extending public ownership and control, which alone will abolish the power of the comparatively few who own the wealth...Real democracy means strong trade unions, government regulation of business, ownership by the people of industries that serve the public."

Just how far the Socialists have come down the road to enslaving the United States can be seen by visiting any factory. On the walls of the office will be seen a bewildering array of "permits" empowering one thing or another. OSHA, EPA and "Equal Opportunity" inspectors have the "right" to come in unannounced at any time, interrupt and even stop operations, while they carry out an inspection to see whether the conditions laid out in their "permits" have been violated.

The deceptive language used by Baldwin did not mean what the average American took them to mean. Baldwin was practicing Fabian Socialist techniques on an elite "rearguard" group who would lead American gently by the hand down the road to slavery. This is Socialism at its very worst. No one could have explained the aims and methods of Socialism better than the chairman of the ACLU, which today, has not altered its stance and methods one single iota. Although its membership never exceeded 5,000 between the 1920-1930s, the ACLU nevertheless succeeded in infiltrating and permeating every aspect of American life, which it then proceeded to turn upside down.

The foremost task of the ACLU in the 1920s was to legally block the large number of arrests and deportation of Communists, anarchists. In the early 1920s the Socialists were starting their drive to subvert the United States Constitution through underhand means, using foreign-born aliens to preach — and carry out — acts of sedition. Harvard Socialist Professor Felix Frankfurter acted as the legal guide for the ACLU, whose Roger Baldwin, described anarchists, Communists, seditionists as "victims of the law, members of labor and welfare movements who are being insidiously attacked by unscrupulous men working under the cloak of patriotism."

Frankfurter — assisted by Harold Laski from behind the scenes — helped President Wilson set up a Mediation Committee, which Committee prompted by Frankfurter, kept on using the Constitution to qualify the seditionists, anarchist, avowed enemies of the United States for protection under the United States Constitution. It was a sordid tactic which has worked remarkably well: Since 1920, the MISUSE of the United States Constitution to grant "rights" and protection to every Dick, Tom and Harry trying to undermine the Confederated Republic has burgeoned to a dreadfully alarming degree.

Others who threw their weight behind "persecuted immigrants" and "victims of the law" in which category was recorded every leftist, arsonist, Socialist agitator, murderer and seditionist, were Professor Arthur M. Schlesinger Sr. and Harvard Law Professor Francis B. Sayre, Wilson's son-in-law. It was the beginning of a huge campaign to trammel underfoot the real purpose and intent of the United States Constitution, and it was crowned with success beyond the wildest dreams of the sappers of Socialism in this country.

This was a period when the United States was trying to rid the country of a flood of Communists who came here to commit acts of sedition in an attempt to Communize and Socialize the country. Socialist Upton Sinclair wrote reams in defense of hard-core seditionists and Harvard Law School sent some of its best Socialists into the fray, including its dean, Roscoe Pound. The news media, including magazines like "The Nation" and the "New Republic" did their level best to cloud the straightforward legal issues by constantly referring to "the Red scare."

In 1919, the Overman committee on Bolshevism of the United States Senate, after exhaustive enquires, came to the conclusion that Fabian Socialism was a grave threat to the citizens of the United States, especially to women and children.

The ACLU has been in the vanguard of "defeminising" women under the guise of "women's rights. "The ACLU has successfully protected the prime movers of Socialism, by rushing to their defense whenever they fear the real leaders and purposes of Socialism might be exposed. That is the primary purpose of the ACLU: Deflect the attacks on the Socialist intellectual leadership, the "reformers" with "good intentions" and the Harvard Law professors in the rear.

From 1920, the modus operandi of the ACLU has remained the same, and can better be described by itself:

"Against those indiscriminate federal, state and local measures which though aimed at Communism, (note the exclusion of Socialism) threaten the civil liberties of all Americans; to make an effective civil rights program the law of the land; against both governmental and private pressure group censorship of movies, books, plays, newspapers, magazines, radio and to promote fair procedures in court trials, congressional and administrative hearings."

The ACLU left no doubt that it intended to rewrite the Constitution "by the legislative route." *Nor can there be any doubt that this important Socialist apparatus has changed the face of America* In an interview with Fareed Zakaria of "Foreign Affairs," Lee Kuan Yew, former prime minister of Singapore, was asked: "What in your view has gone wrong with the American system?"

"It is not my business to tell people what is wrong with their system. It is my business to tell people not to foist their system in discriminately on societies in which it will not work," Yew replied. Zakaria then asked, "Do you not view the United States as a model for other countries?" to which Lee responded:

"...But as a total system, I find parts of it (the United States) totally unacceptable. . .vagrancy, unbecoming behavior in public, the expansion of the right of the individual to behave as he pleases has come at the expense of orderly society. In the East the main objective is to have a an orderly society so that everybody can have maximum enjoyment of his freedom. *This freedom only exists in an ordered state and not in a natural state of contention and anarchy."*

"...The idea of inviolability of the individual (in the United States) has been turned into dogma. And yet nobody minds when the army goes and captures the president of another state and brings him to Florida and puts him in jail. (This was in reference to the bandit-action of former President George Bush kidnaping General Noriega of Panama).

Zakaria then asked: "Would it be fair to say that you admired America more than 25 years ago? What, in your view, went wrong?" Lee answered: "Yes, things have changed. I would hazard a guess that it has a lot to do with the erosion of the moral underpinnings of society and the diminution of personal responsibility. The liberal, intellectual tradition that developed after WWII claimed that human beings had arrived at this perfect state where everybody would be better off if they were allowed to do their own thing and flourish. It has not worked out and I doubt if it will. Certain basics about human nature do not change. Man needs a certain moral sense of right and wrong. There is such a thing called evil and it is not the result of being a victim of society..."

There can be no doubt about the crucial role played by the ACLU in stretching existing "rights" and inventing rights that do not exist in the Constitution to the extent that the United States today is in a virtual state of anarchy. Take as an example the "Gay Pride" parade staged in San Francisco on Father's Day Sunday, June 19, 1994.

The choice of day and date was no accident, but a deliberate, studied insult Christianity, the tradition of marriage and family. The parade consisted of lesbians roaring around on motorbikes, naked, and semi naked, (so-called "Dykes on Bikes") men in obscene drag costumes and hordes of other men with their genitals fully exposed and lopping about as they ran hither and thither. This was an altogether disgusting display of vulgarity on city streets that would never have been tolerated before, and should not now be tolerated.

But let anybody bring up the disgusting "parade" and perhaps suggest suitable action to curb such ugly, utterly baneful displays in the future, then they will be sure to find the ACLU charging in to protect the "civil rights" of the most unmoralized, amoral sector of the population. The deplorable "parade" was praised by the San Francisco Chronicle, which also carried a rave review of a movie about two lesbians "falling in love." The paper described this disgusting piece of amorality as "suitable for straights." Thus far have we, as a society, sunk to the bottom of the Socialist cesspool. Fabian Socialists have always been great admirers of Karl Marx. They do not readily admit to this "hero worship" lest the sheep that they so despise should become alarmed. During my five year stint of intensive study at the British Museum in London, I examined Marx's economic writings in some depth. I could do this because Karl Marx had spent 30 years studying in the same British Museum, and some of my mentors knew which books he liked and read the most, told me what they were.

What I discovered about his writings was how little of it was original thought. This is common to most of the great Socialist "thinkers." All of Marx's theories about economics, stripped of dense verbiage surrounding them, can be boiled down to seven or eight basic mathematics equations that I could do when I was in the eighth grade.

All that Marx's theories add up to is the precept that capitalists who finance business ventures end up stealing large sums of money from the workers. This completely ignores the real premise that having taken all the risks in starting up the venture, the investor is entitled to his profit. That, in essence, is the sum and substance of Marx's and his verbiage-ridden theories.

Ranking second only to the ACLU was the League of Industrial Democracy (LID). Founded in 1905, which came out of the Inter-collegiate Socialist Society, the League was to play an important role in distorting education, industry and labor. LID was supported by Eleanor Roosevelt all of her life, as did Florence Kelley and Frances Perkins. Eleanor Roosevelt promoted "social democracy" inside and outside of the organization along with Frances Perkins, her husband's New York State Commissioner of Labor and a great friend of Socialist Justice Harlan Stevens.

Morris Hillquit served as LID treasurer from 1908 to 1915. Lovett, the ACLU leader for so long, was always closely affiliated with the League for Industrialized Democracy, once calling that period of his Socialist career as, "the happiest days of my life." Morris Hillquit had very early on in his socialist career advocated "industrial socialism."

Hillquit and Eugene V. Debbs always followed the London Fabian Society model of not having programs and platforms, but rather in using educational institutes as a captive audience and so inspire students with Socialist ideas and philosophies that they would later be able to infiltrate existing political parties. Courses in Socialism were discreetly introduced, at least in the early 1900s, but by the 1970s, in true Fabian Socialist orthodoxy, the process had been considerably speeded up in many institutes of learning

It is said that the League of Industrial Democracy revitalized American Socialism, which in 1900 was flagging. At that point, several prominent members of the elite in American society, visited the Fabian Socialists in England. Among them were religious leaders, teachers and politicians: Paul Douglas who went on to be Senator Douglas, Arthur M. Schlesinger whose son rose to prominence in the Kennedy and Johnson administrations, Melvyn Douglas the actor and his wife, Helen Douglas, and Walter Raushenbusch, a former minister at the Second Baptist Church of New York. Raushenbusch was a devoted disciple of Giuseppe Mazzini, John Ruskin, Edward Bellamy and Marx. Mazzini was a world leader of Masonry. Ruskin was a self-styled "Old School Communist" who taught at Oxford. Bellamy was the leading Socialist in America at that time.

Raushenbusch gave up preaching Christianity for preaching Socialist politics, which he tried to indoctrinate in as many fellow Baptists as he could reach. LID was on the list of United States military intelligence as a subversive organization, but along with many similar Socialist and Communist organizations, Woodrow Wilson ordered the military to destroy the lists it was holding, which was a loss that could not ever be made again good. The fact that Wilson had no powers under the Constitution that allowed him to give such an order, was tossed aside as inconsequential by the Socialists in his administration at Harvard and on Wall Street.

But it was neither German agents in WWI nor Russian agents in the Cold War era, but British Fabian Socialists who penetrated and permeated every aspect of government, its institutions and the presidency itself. Education was recognized as the way that Socialism could be advanced, so a great effort was made to capture the "student market." When the Lusk Committee was investigating New York's Rand School, reference was made to this: "We have already called attention to the Fabian Society as a very interesting group of intellectuals who engage in a very brilliant campaign of propaganda."

Apparently the Lusk Committee was somewhat taken in by the false air of candor that permeated LID publications and no violent revolutionary types were allowed to sully its membership lists. The Lusk Committee, distracted and looking for Communists — just as the United States has been doing ad infinitum — completely missed the highly subversive and dangerous LID. It never ceases to amaze observers just how skillfully the Socialists were able to deflect attention away from themselves by repeatedly referring to "the Red scare" and denigrating all efforts to ensure internal security as based on a non-existent "Communist threat." We are still largely being fooled in the same way in 1994 as was the Lusk Committee in 1920.

After WWI, LID teamed up with several prominent Socialist organizations in the United States, among them the ACLU, Federated Press and the Garland Fund which was cited by military intelligence as being kindly disposed toward funding Communists and some decidedly Socialist organizations. Robert Moss Lovett of the ACLU was a director in all of the aforementioned bodies including "Protestants and other Americans United for the Separation of Church and State."

LID members were encouraged to disavow Socialism in public and disavow their parent, the Fabian Society, founded by Sydney and Beatrice Webb. This was standard Socialist practice: deny, deny, deny. When one the Fabian Society's most honored member was asked if he was a Socialist, John Kenneth Galbraith replied "of course not." During WWII, when it was obvious that Roosevelt would do anything to get the United States committed to the war against Germany, LID felt it expedient to changes its stance and in 1943 published a statement that said LID had as its goal increasing an understanding of democracy through education, and not making war.

What LID did not say was the "democracy" it had in mind was what Karl Marx called "scientific Socialist democracy." That the United States was a republic and not a democracy, was merely waved aside. Thus by subterfuge, by stealth and by cunning, LID became the leading Socialist body in the United States, dedicated to the downfall of the Republic. The history of LID shows that it played a key role in bringing Socialist "reforms" to the front burner in both the Wilson and Roosevelt administrations.

When Roosevelt was Governor of New York, he appointed Frances Perkins to be his Industrial Commissioner. (We give the remarkable achievements of Perkins in the chapters on women Socialists.) Perkins called on LID economist Paul H. Douglas to draft an unemployment relief program which was adopted by

Governor Roosevelt. One of her collaborators was Dr. Isadore Lubin, a dedicated Socialist, who along with Perkins, pushed for preferential treatment for the Soviet Union, advice that Roosevelt was quick to accept.

Perkins and Lubin began the long process based on British Fabian Socialist strategy of transforming the United States from a Capitalist into a Socialist state, via a welfare state. Included in this plan was the "national health insurance plan" lifted straight out of the Soviet Union. It is worthy of note that "health care reform," nationwide old age pensions and unemployment insurance, were all part of the plan to alter the structure of the United States, in which "social security" was no small part.

In 1994 we have another female Socialist, Hillary Clinton, latching onto the term, "health care reform" as though it were her own invention, when in fact it was the term used by Presotonia Martin Mann, one of the most devoted female Socialists on the American scene, who in turn had borrowed it from the British Fabian Socialist leader Sydney Webb. The phrase was a masterpiece of applied psychology on a level with another piece of applied psychology intended to deceive, the "Social Security Act," invented in England and brought to this country by Father Ryan. The Fabian Socialist blueprint was then adapted for American conditions by Prestonia Martin as we find in her book, "Prohibiting Poverty," championed by Eleanor Roosevelt.

LID never claimed any credit for its behind the scenes in the endeavors of Perkins and Martin, as indeed it never claimed that Felix Frankfurter was one of its very own. The extensive damage to the United States done by LID is remarkable, given the relative smallness of the group. This is precisely the way Fabian Socialism works — blend into the background, infiltrate all of government and important decision-making bodies, and then promote (always from the background) a rising political star to initiate Socialist designed programs.

This is the way Socialism worked in the 1920s, and still works in this way in the United States, which is how the Socialists and their Marxist/Communist allies, came perilously close to taking over the United States in the 1920s and early 1930s. Near perfect examples of Socialism working through rising politicians were Wilson, Roosevelt, Johnson, Bush and now, President Clinton and his wife, Hillary Clinton. Clinton was selected by the British Fabian Society, but the job of "puffing" him was given in secret to Socialist Pamela Harriman.

One term President Clinton has the task of rushing Socialist programs of far reaching and devastating consequences into law. His successes by mid 1994 include, the largest income tax increase in the world, One World Government trade agreements, and possibly "national health reform." Three times before, British Fabian Socialism has changed the face of America by using leadership groups and "advisors" to the president, and via the courts, to achieve Socialist objectives. It was left to LID to supply the personnel Perkins and Roosevelt needed to implement the "New Deal." Of more than a passing interest is that the "New Deal" was a carbon copy of a British Fabian Socialist book. *The fourth drive to Socialize America has come with the Clinton presidency.*

One of the "greats" of LID was Walter Reuther. But in typical Socialist fashion, Reuther chose to deny that he was a Socialist. In a "Face the Nation" interview in 1953, Reuther was pointedly asked about his Socialist background. He trotted out the standard Socialist excuse, "...that I was when I was very young and very foolish, and I got out very quickly, for which I am very thankful." But the truth was far from that. Reuther had in fact served on a committee of the LID of which he had been a member since the early 1940s. In 1949 he was an honored guest at a Fabian Socialist dinner party in London.

LID members played a leading role in pushing Socialist programs through the Senate, and their effect on schools knew no boundaries. Theodore "Ted" Sorenson, who went on to be a key player in the Kennedy administration, was a lifelong Socialist who got his appointment through LID's Senator Paul Douglas. Other United States Senators who had qualified in Socialism with LID, were Senators Lehman, Humphrey, Neuberger and Morse (from "conservative Oregon.") To the list can be added Senators Jacob Javitts, and Philip Hart. Although they vigorously denied it to a man, in 1950, former Attorney General Francis Biddle (a former chairman of Americans For Democratic Action (ADA) — successor to LID named them as known members of LID and its successor, the ADA.

An examination of Javitt's Senate voting record shows that he supported LID and ADA in 82 out of 87 Socialist measures on which he voted. Of Eastern European parents who settled on the lower East Side of New York in the garment district, Javitts joined LID in his early adult years, and became one of LID's highly prized speakers, while staunchly denying any connection with Socialism in his personal beliefs and connections with Socialist groups like LID. Never the less, Javitts was the keynote speaker at the 1952 LID-sponsored seminar under the title, "Needed, *A Moral Awakening In America.*" "Non Socialist," Walter Reuther, also attended the function which studiously avoided discussing corruption in labor while vigorously attacking employer-corporations and businesses in general.

Congressional Record Senate, October 1962, carried a long list of Socialists prominent in government, health, education, women's rights movement, religion, trade unions. The list contained the names of more than 100 professors and educators from some of the nations' most prestigious colleges and universities. The list named of more than 300 members and former members of LID who had spread out and infiltrated every branch of government, law, teaching, foreign policy advisors, churches and so-called women's rights organizations. When LID underwent a name change to Americans For Democratic Action (ADA), many former LID members could be found in the ADA membership list.

The Inter-Collegiate Socialist Society (ISS), which preceded LID, opened doors to universities and gave opportunities to spread Socialist programs among impressionable students. It was the hidden Socialist agenda that was to change the face of education in the United States.

None of this was apparent at the birth of this Fabian Socialist enterprise. The first ISS meeting was held at Peck's Restaurant in New York, on September 12, 1905. Those in attendance included Colonel Thomas Wentworth, Clarence Darrow, Morris Hillquit and two young Socialist authors Upton Sinclair and Jack London. The two authors were enthusiastic Socialists who went across the country preaching the Fabian Socialist gospel at universities and Socialist clubs.

Another notable of a somewhat rougher hew who attended the Peck's Restaurant dinner party was William Z. Foster, who went on to play a leading role in the Communist Party of the USA. Foster's love of Karl Marx had been amply demonstrated for a number of years. Not revealed until 25 years later was the true purpose of the dinner party: It was in fact the first meeting of the American Fabian Society.

Hillquit will best be remembered as the driving force behind the American Socialist Party formed in 1902. Two years later, the Socialist Party gained 400,000 votes in the election — mostly from garment trade workers who had flocked to the United States from Russia in the early 1890s, bringing with them an assorted gaggle of revolutionists and anarchists. Yet, in spite of its ugly revolutionary face, the Socialist Party of America attracted an astonishing number of the elite from the top-drawers of New York society. But the Fabian Socialists in Britain advised caution — making haste so hastily would bring disaster and so it was that the "party" was quietly disbanded.

As the London Fabian Society secretary Edward R. Pease put it: "European countries with their great capitals have developed national brains. America, like the lower organisms, has ganglia for various purposes in various parts of its gigantic frame." Pease was from the elite in the Fabian Society who could not abide America, having never forgiven the Colonists for having inflicted so severe a defeat on the armies of King George III. In spite of this studied insult, a number of prominent Americans went to London and signed on with the Fabian Socialists.

The long-range objectives of the British Fabian Society relative to the United States had still to be defined and developed. A president who would be wide-open to Socialist ideas had yet to be found and appointed, so that the well concealed Socialist techniques of gaining power via the surreptitious route could be implemented. As Ramsey McDonald had said, the United States would be very difficult to Socialize — but not impossible.

The main stumbling block was of course, the Constitution. Coupled with that was the huge size of the country and the six different racial groups with widely diversified religious beliefs. Education and good paying jobs, it was deemed, were two other hurdles that had to be surmounted. As Webb put it, "motherhood and apple pie" stood in the way of the ambitious promoters of Socialism. London ordered the Socialist Party to disband and fade away to regroup under another name at a time better suited for its methods to guarantee success.

Forming a political party was not on the Socialist agenda. The ISS model of "leagues" and "societies" was to be followed. It was by subterfuge that they hoped to eventually co-opt existing political parties, but never again would they try to form a party of their own. So in 1921,the League of Industrial Democracy, (LID)and ISS was founded and it became the British Fabian Society's Socialist headquarters in the United States.

One of the subtlest ways devised by American Socialists to hide their intentions and their tracks was to appoint Socialist professors as presidential policy makers. The technique began with Wilson and has continued ever since. The professor policy makers seldom announced their agenda, instead wrote position papers which they signed. The position-papers had a strictly limited circulation, which kept the general public right out of the picture.

Outside of the circle of professors were other notables who played a major role in the Wilson presidency. Of these, Walter Lippmann, stood head and shoulders above the rest. The British trained Fabian Socialists was ranked their No. 1 apostle in the United States, who, together with Mandel House, had fashioned the "14 points," the first attempt by an American president to shape a "new world order." It is generally recognized that Wilson's war speech delivered to the Congress of the United States on April 6, 1917, rang down the curtain on old order, forcing the United States to take the first steps down the long Socialist to slavery.

Wilson laid the foundation of lies on which American Socialism was to be built. Americans are the most lied to people on earth. Since Wilson came on the political scene, and of course, even before that, the whole Socialist structure consisted of lies upon lies upon lies. One of the biggest lies is that we belong to the United Nations. Others lies say abortion is legal, that school busing and so-called "gun control" is legal; GATT, NAFTA, the Gulf War, Waco, FEMA, "King" George Bushs' raid on Panama and kidnaping of its head of state and Mandela's rule of South Africa, are but the tip of an enormous iceberg of layer upon layer of Socialist lies.

Perhaps one of the more singular of its big lies is that Socialism strives to better the lot of the common people and, unlike capitalism, Socialists are not interested in personal wealth. Socialists are always preaching about the evils of capitalism. But a quick look at some of the leading Socialists quickly reveals that the leadership is drawn from the most elite elements of our society, people using Socialist causes to feather their own nests.

Nothing was too base and no cesspool too deep to plumb for Franklin D.

Roosevelt and his family in the pursuit of money. The Delanos (Roosevelt married Sara Delano) made a fortune out of the opium trade. One of Roosevelt's closest "advisors," Bernard Baruch, and his partner had monopoly on the copper industry that enabled Baruch to make millions upon millions of dollars out of WWI, while the "common man" was dying by the millions in the mud and blood of the trenches in France.

Roosevelt was on the board of the International Bankers Association up to the time that he became Governor of New York. During his tenure as a banker, he secured loans for European nations amounting to billions of dollars at a time when the American worker was struggling to pay off mortgages, and later during the depressions years, find a job. Roosevelt was a consummate Socialist liar, up there with the best of them. He didn't tell the American people that the money would go to bankers whose factories would churn out goods to sell on the American markets, thanks to the abolition of tariff barriers by his predecessor, Wilson. It is estimated that 12 million men lost their jobs thanks to the Wilson — Roosevelt assault on our trade barriers designed to protect American jobs.

One glaring example out of thousands of Roosevelt big lies is found on pages 9832-9840, Congressional Record, Senate, May 25,1935: "...and owing to his announcement to the convention that he was for the Democratic platform 100 percent, it was hardly feasible that the people would understand if he immediately, with his subservient Congress, reduce the tariffs (Customs duties on imported agricultural products and ancillary manufactured goods) with 12 million men out of work. So he and his big banker friends and big business (meaning Committee of 300 companies) immediately conceived the idea of starting the N.R.A — the so called National Recovery Act, better known today as the 'National Ruin Act'."

"It was reported that Bernard Baruch and his friends established 1800 factories in foreign countries and the Republican tariffs were a little too high for them to make our market with cheap foreign labor to satisfy their big money ideas. So why not, under the guise of a war on depression foist upon the people the National Racketeer Association and place Barney Baruch's partner, Brigadier 'Crackup' Johnson in charge of seeing that prices were raised to the levels of 1928 while at the same time setting the prices of agriculture between 1911 and 1914."

"The farmers would not notice the disparity and if they did — since under the circumstances he could control the newspapers, the radio, the movies and every avenue of information of people with taxpayer's money, fill their ears with propaganda he desired..." Roosevelt the American Socialist leader and his international banker friends aided by sedition committed by the Federal Reserve played with the lives of the people of the nation and willfully brought on the 1922 recession, the 1929 Wall Street crash, WWII and beyond. Roosevelt desired greater powers as president than his power-mad predecessor Wilson had enjoyed.

Although the American people did not know it — and millions still do not know it — Wilson engineered the United States into WWI and his unelected advisor, Mandel House, set the stage for WWII. Roosevelt made quite sure that the process of international banks lending billions to European powers to start wars was continued. According to documents made available to me in the British Museum, Lord Beaverbrook, the great British Fabian Socialist, practically used the White House as his Washington office, showing Roosevelt how to pour billions and billions of dollars into Germany to finance Hitler's rise to power.

Wilson showed no scruples in placing openly-avowed Socialists in key positions in his administration, from where they were able to do the maximum to advance the cause of Socialism in the United States. Fred C. Howe, one of the Wilson Socialist appointees was made Commissioner of Immigration at New York. His favorite pastime was to release seditionist and anarchists being held at the port of New York pending deportation.

Another "ex-officio" House appointment was Walter Lippmann as secretary of a "brain storm" group put together to make up plausible war aims and reasons why the United States should get into WWI. It was Lippmann who invented the slogan, "peace without victory," which became the basis of the Korean and Vietnam Wars. The appointment of scandal monger Ray Stannard Baker as confidential correspondent to Wilson at the Treaty of Versailles talks, was another of those "crucial appointments."

It was said that Baker was chiefly responsible for making Wilson so dependent on the British Fabian Society that he was unable to make any decisions of his own at the Paris Peace Conference, without first consulting Sydney Webb, founder of the Fabian Society, Graham Wallas, Bertrand Russell and George Lansbury. It was this group that constantly talked of Wilson's administration as a "democratic" administration. Baker's dispatches to Wilson in Washington, deliberately referred to "your democratic administration."

The Paris Peace Conference foundered on the Constitution. Some 59 enlightened Senators, fully aware of the intentions of the Socialist, refused to pass the League of Nations Treaty, recognizing it as a One World Government document that sought to put the League above the United States Constitution. At that juncture, House is said to have told Sydney Webb that *the only was to get around the United States Constitution was to permeate all future United States administrations with key Socialists who would take a "bi-partisan approach to matters of major consequence."* Ever since those words were spoken, "bi-partisan approach" became a euphemism for a Socialist approach to matters of vital consequence to the American people.

In order to breathe life into the new "bi-partisan" idea, House held a dinner party at the Majestic Hotel in Paris on May 19, 1919 for selected Fabianists and American Socialist. Invited guests included Professors James Shotwell, Roger Lansing (Wilson's Secretary of State), John Foster and Allen Dulles, Tasker Bliss and Christian Herter, who was later to place Mao tse Tung in power in China. On the British side, John Maynard Keynes, Arnold Toynbee, and R.W. Tawney, all leading practitioners of Fabian Socialism and its standard bearers, also attended.

The group said that to get around the United States Constitution, it would be necessary to set up an organization in the United States under the direction of the Royal Institute of International Affairs (RIIA). The American branch was to be called the "Institute of International Affairs." Its mandate given by its London parent, was "to facilitate the scientific study of international questions." The Fabian International Bureau was to act as advisors to both the RIIA and its American cousin, which, in 1921, changed its name to "The Council on Foreign Relations" (CFR)

These three institutions were set up with three main purposes in mind:
1. Do and end run around the United States Constitution.
2. To use these organizations to influence and deceive the United States Congress and the public.
3. To divide opposition to Socialist causes in the House and Senate by the subterfuge of "bi-partisan study committees."
4. Destroy the separation of powers between the legislative, executive and judicial branches of government, as recommended by Professor Harold Laski.

Mandel House was the originator of "fireside chats," an essential propaganda tool by widely used Roosevelt, and he "suggested" most of the Socialist cabinet appointments. In many instances he consulted with Professor Charles W. Elliot of Harvard — that hotbed of Socialism which has played such a crucial, if secret, role in our history. This is not surprising, given the fact that Harvard was totally dominated by Fabian Socialist Harold Laski, whose frequent lectures at Harvard, set the tone for heavily Socialist leaning teaching methods.

Much of the views held by House, appeared in the "New Republic," a magazine much favored by American Socialists, including Wilson himself. House had many Socialist intimates among the Socialist Register. One of them, Joseph Fels, was prevailed upon by House to lend 500 English pounds to Lenin and Trotsky on one occasion when they were stranded in London before they met with Lord Alfred Milner. Baruch once said, "House has a hand in every cabinet appointment and all other important appointments." This was indeed an understatement.

It is believed that Wilson was fully aware of the activities of Socialist Nina Nitze who served as the chief paymaster for German spies operating in the United States. That did not apparently bother Wilson or House, any more than it was later to affect the judgment of Presidents Kennedy and Johnson, who appointed Nina's brother, Paul Nitze as Secretary of the Navy in both administrations and chief spokesman at various disarmament conference. Nitze is known to have tipped the balance of power in favor of Russia at each and every one of the disarmament conferences, at which time he represented the United States.

What Socialism Is: Why it Leads to Slavery 57

Again, according to documents in the British Museum, the financing of Hitler was done via the Warburg family on both sides of the Atlantic; in Europe, particularly through the Socialist Mendelssohn Bank of Amsterdam, Holland, Schroeder Bank in London, and Frankfurt, Germany, while the same bank handled the Hitler-financing scheme through its New York branch. The transactions were monitored by the Committee of 300 legal firm of Sullivan and Cromwell, whose senior partner was Allen Dulles of the notorious Dulles family. The Dulles brothers rode herd over the Senate and the State Department to ensure that dissenting voices of some who perchance might stumble upon the arrangement contracted in Hell, would be smothered before they could alert the nation.

These kinds of financial arrangements were common also to the runup to WWII. I came across some documents in the British Museum in London during my five-year study period relating to the way the Socialists worked both sides of the fence. Telegrams sent by the German Ambassador in Washington to his home office superiors in Berlin, stated that from 1915, J. William Byrd Hale was one of their very own, being employed by the German Foreign Office at a salary of $15,000 per annum.

Hale, one of the inner circle at Turtle Bay, an exclusive summer colony wherein resided the elite of the elite of American Socialists. Among them were Professor Robert Lovett and a large number of other Harvard Law School professors. House lived close by in Manchester. All were described by an adoring press of the time as "polished products of Harvard and Groton," but the press was so blinded by these glamorous persons that it failed to state that they were also Socialists out of the top drawer of the Fabian-American Society. Lovett adored the work of self-styled "old school Communist" John Ruskin, and William Morris.

Hale, a dedicated "Christian" Socialist, made his mark with Wilson in Mexico while orchestrating the theft of Mexican oil for his top Socialist colleagues. (See "Diplomacy By Deception" for a full account of this scandalous robbery of the Mexican people.) It transpired that Hale actually represented the German Foreign Office until June 23, 1918, this, while thousands of American Citizen Militia soldiers were dying "for the cause of freedom." Thereafter this "Christian" Socialist went to Germany as the correspondent for the American Press Service. His much slanted, pro-Socialist reports figured prominently in newspapers of the period which can be found in the archives of the British Museum.

Though these transactions the elite of the Socialist world grew fat and sleek. Not that there was anything new in this disgusting arrangements. In the runup to the Civil War, and it was during its entirety, Communism and Socialism made huge strides in America, a fact not mentioned in our history books and kept well hidden from the public in the massive Hollywood extravaganzas about this, the most tragic of all wars.

A common thread runs through the Fabian Socialist movement: a passionate desire to pull down and destroy everything. This is confirmed in pages 4594–4595, Congressional Record, February 23, 1927, under the title "General Deficiency Bill." This page in our history delineates the Socialists and Communists and their efforts to tear down the Confederated Republic of the United States of America. There is plenty of information how the Socialists cooperated with their Communist brothers, in the booklet, "Key Men of America."

Socialism is world revolution much more than was Communism, only at a slower pace and on a more sedate level. But the revolution desired by the Socialists is the same: spiritual anarchy, destruction of nineteen centuries of Western civilization, scattering of traditions, and an end to Christianity. If this is doubted by the reader, then a reading of Franklin D. Roosevelt's book, "On Our Way" will convince the skeptics that Socialism differs only from Communism in method.

Bolshevism was the violent, radical experiment that tried to rid Russia of Christianity: In the United States, other more subtle means are being employed, such as banning of prayer in schools, the so called "Separation of Church and State," and in the classrooms, where myriads of Socialist teachers are brainwashing students in a manner fit to promote the silent revolution the Socialist are carrying out. Bolshevism, Marxism. Socialism, all have the same common purpose, and they go hand in hand with "liberalism," "pacifism," "tolerance," "progressive," "moderate," "peace," democratic," "people's," and subterfuge issued to dissemble and disguise the true purposes of Socialism.

These terms are intended to dupe the unwary so that Socialism not be associated with revolution. But the purpose of Socialism and Bolshevism are the same: the destruction of civilization built upon nineteen centuries of tradition and Christianity. The goals of Socialism are:

1. The abolition of government.
2. The abolition of patriotism.
3. The abolition of property right. (While the Communists would banish it outright, the Socialist choose the stealthy sneaking course of taxing private property rights out of existence.
4. The abolition of inheritance. (Again, the Communists would banish it outright, the Socialist by means of inheritance tax laws).
5. Abolition of marriage and the family.
6. Abolition of religion, especially Christianity.
7. Destruction of national sovereignty of countries and national patriotism.

Woodrow Wilson knew of these aims, yet he did not recoil from them nor from becoming a tool of the international Socialists, embracing American Socialist programs with enthusiasm, for which he needed powers not granted to him by the United States Constitution. Wilson was not averse to using the sly methods of Socialist to attain his goals. For instance, he was successful in getting the United States into WWI by classifying it as a "patriotic duty" to defend America, which was never at any time threatened by Germany!

Wilson was not the first power-hungry president, although he was the first openly Socialist one. The dubious distinction of power-grabbing belongs to President Lincoln who was the first to come out with proclamations, now called Executive Orders. President George Bush followed right along in Roosevelt's footsteps, using the same unconstitutional methods to feather his nest, diving into every cesspool where there was money to be made at the cost of the American people.

A so-called "Republican, "Bush did as much to harm the "common people" of the United States as Roosevelt had done, and Wilson had done before him. *Beware of party labels.* George Washington called political parties "baneful and unnecessary" and modern history shows them to be divisive. Tyrants have succeeded because of political parties and their "divide and rule" mentality. The Constitution of the United States provides for impeachment of men like Wilson, Roosevelt and Bush. In fact, patriotic Congressman Henry Gonzalez filed six Articles of Impeachment against Bush during the Gulf War, but partisan politics stood in the way of the Article 2, Section 4, Article 1, Section 3, being used to bring George Bush to justice.

There were a multitude of causes to impeach Bush, not the least being his failure to adhere to the Constitution and obtain a properly-drawn up declaration of war. Next, his unconstitutional forgiveness of Egypt's debt of $7 billion, his bribery of Syria and other nations who joined his "Desert Storm" against the nation of Iraq: His continued misuse of all three branches of the services in violation of the Constitution, and calling himself the commander in chief of the armed services, which he was not, is also impeachable.

It is worth repeating that the Gulf War was illegal. It was fought without a declaration of war in defiance of the Constitution. Congress, largely conditioned by party sentiments, tried to write up a type of resolution — not a declaration of war — that purported to give the semblance of legality to Bush's action. But Congress added insult to injury to the American people in that they made the mistake of writing up their version of a declaration of war in consonance with the United Nations mandate given Bush, and not in consonance with the Constitution of the United States.

This was absolutely wrong: The United States never constitutionally joined the United Nations and a declaration of war by this One World Government body CANNOT be on the same instrument or even associated with a declaration of war by the Congress. Article 1, Section 9 of the United States Constitution denies and or limits the power of Congress to legislate. Congress does not have absolute power to legislate and can only do so in consonance with the Constitution.

The "neither fish nor fowl" resolution passed by Congress behind which

Bush tried on to take a semblance of legality for his illegal war, was outside of the pale and the ken of the United States Constitution and did not constitute a declaration of war. An analysis of the way Congress voted shows dramatically, that almost to a man, the hundreds of Socialists infesting the House and Senate voted for Bush to allow Bush to continue his flouting of the Constitution. Bush should have been impeached and tried. If the Constitution were followed in such proceedings, there is no doubt that he would have been jailed, as he rightly deserves.

The powers of the president are contained in Section II of the United States Constitution. Actions not in Section II are exercises of arbitrary power. The Socialists, starting with House, Frankfurter and Brandeis, and followed by Katzenbach et al, have it that the three branches of government are coequal. This is a falsehood-just another of the lies that go to make up the huge iceberg upon which this nation will be wrecked unless we alter course. Professor Harold Laski was the chief instigator of this lie, viewed as the first step toward weakening the separation of powers as mandated by the United States Constitution.

The three branches of government are *not* co-equal and never have been. The House and Senate created the judicial branch, and the House and Senate never intended to give them equal powers. Of course if this ever became known, the Socialist outflanking of the Constitution "by the legislative route" would be thrown out of the window. Perhaps the American people will wake up to the way in which judges gerrymander the Constitution before it is too late.

Congress has superior powers — one of which is through the purse. Another, simple way to get rid of Socialist judges is to enforce Article III, Section I which says that judges may not "receive for their services, a compensation which shall not be diminished during their continuance in office."

What this means is that U.S. Supreme Court judges cannot by law be paid in debased money, and a better example of debased "money" is Federal Reserve notes, commonly (and mistakenly) called "dollars" is not to be found. What a blow it would be to the inheritors of the Kelley doctrine if We, the People, closed the Supreme Court down for lack of money that is not debased.

Wilson should likewise have been impeached. His mad grab for power was at the instigation of Mandel House, the arch-Socialist enemy of the people of the United States who worked in the dark his sinister, scurrilous, evil plans to overturn and destroy the Confederated Republic of the United States of America. To this end House had Wilson appoint all manner of elite Socialists to key positions.

The goals of American Socialism have been well concealed in the past, particularly in the period leading up to WWII. That Socialism has achieved many of its objectives is clear. They did it by the formation of movements designed to break down the morals of America, as witness the startling growth of " free love" (love without responsibility) which has thus far cost the lives of more than 26 million murdered babies sanctioned by the Supreme Court's pro-abortion rulings, all

100 percent unconstitutional, as the Constitution is silent on abortion. Where the Constitution is silent on a power, it is a prohibition of that power.

President Clinton is a firm believer in infanticide and like the good Socialist he is, supports abortion with all of the might of his administration. It is interesting that the first time abortion clinics were thought of was when Mrs. Laski, wife of Professor Laski of the Fabian Society began to establish birth control clinics in England. Mrs Laski's tactics employed the methods of the notorious Communist commissar, Comrade Alexandra Kollontay.

When Socialists are confronted and exposed in advancing the cause of Communism by different tactics, they protest loudly. But the old saying, "wound a Communist and a Socialist bleeds" was never truer than it is today. What we have in the United States is a secret, upper-level parallel Socialist government known as the Council on Foreign Relations that was set up in 1919 by arch-Socialists Mandel House and Walter Lippmann, under the direction and control of the RIIA in London.

Many times we see stories in the press about open disagreement between Communists and Socialists. This is done to deceive the unwary and keep in line those who have been duped into believing that "progressive," "liberal," "moderate" really mean something other than what their Socialists meaning is. Thus they are able to keep in line a vast number of people who would otherwise recoil in shock if they knew they were promoting the aims of world revolutionary government. That our new president, accused of being a philanderer, a libertine lacking in morals, is acceptable to millions of Americans who are not Socialist, is a triumph for the methods of Fabian Socialism.

Their methods are so subtle that their goals are not always at first recognized . Lately there has been much discussion (much of it of low caliber showing the paucity of an understanding of the United Constitution among the majority of senators) about Line Item Veto supposedly the right of the president. This is pure Socialist anti constitutional propaganda, and a continuation of the process started by the Socialists during the Wilson presidency of surrendering the rights that properly belong to the legislature to the president. It is the goal of the Socialists to give the president powers that he has not got, nor is entitled to, so that they can proceed to steamroller the Constitution out of the way of their New World Order plans.

The Socialists want the president to have veto powers not granted by the Constitution in so-called "enhanced rescission." In typical Socialist fashion, they do not come right out and say "we want the president to be able to veto any parts of a bill that has passed the House and Senate." This is what is meant by line item veto.

This subterfuge follows Florence Kelley's directive that changes must be carried out, "by the legislative route" if they cannot be done by constitutional means. As we see elsewhere in this book, Professor Harold Laski devoted a great deal of his time to discussing with Felix Frankfurter and President Roosevelt, how to subvert the constitutional provision that the powers of each branch of government granted by the constitution cannot be transferred. Laski frequently lashed out at this stumbling block to promoting Socialism, via "the legislative route." The shocking hypocrisy of the Socialists is revealed in their insistence on the so-called "separation of church and state" idea being strictly enforced. Apparently, what is sauce for the goose is not sauce for the gander.

To turn this kind of power over to the president is an act of suicide — and quite possibly, treason. The real issue here is power, and how the Socialist can grab more and more of it via a servant of theirs whom they place in the White House. There is nothing more dangerous than the Socialist drive to turn over to the president powers reserved to the House and Senate. This would produce super Wilsons, Roosevelts, Bushs and Clintons and rush the United States headlong into a Socialist dictatorship — which we practically have already.

Line item veto powers would become a party politics wrangle, intimidate the lawmakers whom the people of the States have returned to Washington to do the bidding of the people of the States — not the Federal Government. Line item veto surrender of Congressional powers will ensure future tyrants even worse than George Bush whose private war for and behalf of the British crown, cost the lives of hundreds of Americans and $200 billion. Line item veto powers for the president would be a great triumph for Florence Kelley.

Line item veto powers for the president would throw the House and Senate into confusion, paralyze their efforts and generally hasten a breakdown of government in this country — all declared Socialist aims. Tensions and passions between the legislative branches would boil over and make Congress totally subservient to a belligerent president hell-bent on following the Socialist agenda. It would make of the Constitution of the United States a blank piece of paper, with checks and balances reduced to a smoking ruin.

This nation has suffered far too much already from Socialist excesses of presidents they have installed (Wilson, Roosevelt, Kennedy, Johnson, Carter, Eisenhower, Bush and Clinton.) These presidents have rushed the nation into deadly wars in which we should never have become embroiled, at the cost of millions upon millions of lives, not to mention the billions of dollars these wars generated, billions that went to the Wall Street and City of London bankers, the Bank of International Settlements, the World Bank etc., for which the people are still being taxed.

Line item veto powers plus the illegal so-called Executive Orders will make a future tyrant-president of the caliber of Roosevelt and Bush a king, as surely as if the title had been bestowed upon them. *To give the president constitutional power to line items veto bills of congress would require an amendment to the U.S. Constitution.* The three departments cannot legislate or by any other means transfer duties or powers to another division of government. The Founding Fathers wrote this provision to stop would-be tyrants from seizing powers by this method.

If we want an example of tyranny, we need look no further than the assault
on a Christian church at Waco by the Federal Government in total violation of the
United States Constitution. There were 87 people murdered at Waco. The
Tienenman Square "massacre" (a Socialist media description of the event) killed
74 Chinese. Yet Clinton was prepared to cross swords with China over its "human
rights" violations occasioned by the Tienenman Square uprising against the
Beijing government, but thus far has done nothing to bring the perpetrators of
Waco to justice. This is typical of the gross hypocrisy of a true Socialist.

Where in the United States Constitution does it say that the Federal
Government has the right to rush into the States and persecute a religious group?
It is not there! The Federal Government has no business meddling in the States,
especially when it comes to police powers. The 10th Amendment is perfectly
clear on this: police powers in health, education and police protection, belong
exclusively to the States. If the Branch Davidians *had* perchance committed any
crime that warranted police action against them, that action should have been take
by the *local police* and *no one else*. The Sheriff's Department at Waco failed lamentably in its duty to *protect* the Davidians inside their church properly.

The Federal Government once again displayed its arrogant attitude toward
the United States Constitution by violating Article 1 of the Bill of Rights of the
United States Constitution which states:

"Congress shall make no law respecting the establishment of religion or prohibit the free exercise thereof; or abridging the freedom of speech, or of the press,
or the right of people to peacefully assemble, and to petition the government for
redress of grievance." What happened at Waco was that the Federal Government
took powers it does not have and went to Waco with the express intention of prohibiting the free exercise of religious beliefs and freedom of expression. This is
secular humanism in action which has no place in our Constitution. The Socialists
are very hot on "separation of church and state" — when it suits their book. What
happened to "separation of church and state" at Waco? It was not there!

The Federal Government decided it could simplify religion, which is a complex subject that defies simplification. On page E7151, Congressional Record,
House, July 31, 1968, Justice Douglas put the matter this way;

"...It is impossible for government to draw a line between good and bad (the
secular humanism nostrum) and to be true to the Constitution, better to let such
ideas alone." Instead of listening to its own Socialist judges, the Federal government decided it has the right to decide between a "good" religion and a "bad" one.
Government agents on the ground at Waco took it upon themselves to oversim-
plify the complexity of religion. Experience through the centuries has shown that
religion cannot be simplified. Moreover it lies outside of political issues and it
was never supposed to be simplified.

The first 10 Amendments of the United States Constitution are a restriction on the Federal Government. In addition, Article 1, Section 9 of the U.S. Constitution denies the Federal Government any right to pass legislation on religious matters. The Primary powers of the House and Senate are found in Article 1, Section 8, Clause 1-18. Remember, the Federal Government has no absolute powers. The Federal Government has *zero right* to decide what is a church and what is a cult. Apparently, government agents on the ground at Waco, made this determination with the assistance of a "cult deprogrammer" of one kind or another. The whole idea of such action is repulsive, not to mention downright illegal.

For the Federal Government to have this power — which it does not — would be to grant it all power to destroy any and all religions — a plank in the Socialist program and one of the goals of world revolution. This power is not in the First Amendment to the United States Constitution, nor is it found under the delegated powers of Congress or of the primary powers of Congress in Article 1, Section 8, Clauses 1-18. When the United States Constitution is silent on a power, it is a *prohibition* of that power.

So where did the FBI and the ATF get their power that allowed them to attack a Christian church? Apparently from the President and the Attorney General, neither of whom has such powers, and, since they both admit responsibility for the dreadful deed at Waco, they ought properly to be impeached. More Americans died at Waco than did Chinese students at Tienenman Square. Did the jackal press of the United States call the Chinese students a "cult?" Of course not. Neither does the Federal Government have the right to call a Christian movement a "cult."

The United States Constitution was compromised by the actions of the Federal Government at Waco. The United States Constitution cannot be compromised. No government agency is above the Constitution, and the Federal Government agencies that took part in the Waco attack broke the law. They had no constitutional right to intervene in a matter that fell within the purview of the State of Texas. it was not in the purview of the Federal Government. The Federal Government talked of the Branch Davidian as "terrorists," but should not have had any say in making such a delineation. That was for the State of Texas to do.

Nowhere in the Bill of Rights has the Federal Government the authority to call a Christian church a "terrorist" organization. Authority for the attack at Waco is not found in Article 1, Section 8, Clauses 1-18 . It would have taken a CONSTITUTIONAL AMENDMENT to a Dow the Federal Government to launch an armed attack on the Branch Davidian Church at Waco. To properly understand the horror of Waco, one has to read the Declaration of Independence, wherein is found a recital of acts of brutality perpetrated against the Colonists by King George m Waco is King George III relived — only worse.

Congress (the House and Senate) has the power to right this wrong. They can order a full-scale Congressional hearing. Congress can also cut off funding for those Federal agencies that took part in the modern-day King George III attack on the citizens of the United States. Articles of impeachment are urgently necessary. The Congress has to take most of the blame. The Federal agents who took part in the storming of the Branch Davidian Church, probably thought they were acting under authority of the law, when they were not. Congress is supposed to know this, and Congress is supposed to correct the situation, lest it be perpetuated somewhere else. Birch Bayh, Socialist former Senator from Indiana, was used by the Fabian Society to undermine the Constitution of the United States, and he did so at every opportunity, as a reading of pages S16610-S16614, Congressional Record, Senate clearly establishes.

Where does it say in Article 1, Section 8 or the delegated powers of Congress that the Federal Government has the power to use military vehicles to attack a church? Where does it say that Federal agents are empowered to call a church a "cult?" This attack on the Christian Church Branch Davidian is a violation of the 1st, 4th and 5th Amendments and is a bill of attainder of United States citizens at Waco. Neither the Legislative, Executive or Judicial branches of the Federal Government has the right to call a Christian church — nor for that matter, any church simply by calling it a "cult." Since when has the Federal Government had the power to decide on these complex religious matters? *Since when can the Federal Government exercise a Bill of Attainder?*

What the Federal Government did at Waco was take a complex religious matter and turn it into a simple matter of a "cult" it did not like. The Executive Branch in Article II of the United States Constitution has no power to attack what the President and his Attorney General called "a cult." This is not the first time that the Federal Government has launched an attack on a religious group it did not like. It is no excuse to simply say that the President and his Attorney General take the responsibility for breaking the law.

On pages 1195-1209, Congressional Record, Senate February 16, 1882, we see that the Senate tried to act like God in appointing a five-man commission to prevent Mormons from voting simply because they were Mormons. *This was a gross violation of a bill of attainder.* The only saving grace about this ugly piece of history is that there was a debate in the Senate. The victims of the Federal Government at Waco had no such right. On the efforts to block the Mormons from voting and we find it on page 1197 — and this is highly relevant to the Waco attack, we read, "That right belonged to American civilization and law long before the Constitution was adopted."

This right existed in colonial times, like the right to bear arms, and these rights were made a part of the Constitution through a series of amendments, in addition to those in the original instrument. These stood for the protection of rights. They were merely a guarantee of rights *that already existed before the Constitution,* which was not the creator of the rights itself. What the Federal Government did at Waco was no very different from the type of action advocated by International Socialist Karl

Marx — which the Chinese Government observed at Tienenman Square. The citizens who died in the blaze at Waco were not given their Constitutional rights to a fair trail and due process of law as stated in the 5th Amendment.

Continuing to read from the Congressional Record, Senate, February 16, 1882, on page 1200: "For example no one, we presume, will contend that Congress can make any law in a Territory respecting the establishment of religion, or free exercise of, or abridge freedom of speech or of the press, or the right of the people of the Territory peaceably to assemble, and petition the government for redress of grievances. Nor can Congress deny to the people the right to keep and bear arms, nor the right to a trial by jury, nor compel anyone to be a witness against himself in criminal proceedings. These powers, in relation to the rights of person, which are not necessary here to enumerate, are in express and positive terms denied the General Government; and the right to private property have to be guarded with equal care."

What happened at Waco was unhindered *Socialism* in action, grossly flouting the United States Constitution. Since it is clear that neither the Congress (House and Senate) nor the Judicial branch, nor the Executive Branch (The President) had any Constitutional rights whatsoever to order an armed attack on the Branch Davidian Church at Waco, the next question is, what is the Congress doing about righting this gross violation of the Constitution and what is it doing to bring the guilty among the Federal Government to justice?"

In a Socialist/Marxist state, Waco would have been merely an exercise of government power. But the United States, thanks to its Constitution is not a Socialist/Marxist state; it remains a Confederated republic, notwithstanding the horrendous assaults upon it by the likes of Fabian Socialists Harold Laski, Felix Frankfurter, Hugo Black, Franklin Roosevelt, Dwight Eisenhower, George Bush, and now, President William Jefferson Clinton. Waco was a cynical exercise of powers not granted to the Judicial or Executive branches of government and appears on a level with the excesses of the past concerning religious intolerance.

Getting back to the attempts by Socialists to transfer powers from one branch of government to another. Even without Line Item Veto powers, we already had a king instead of a president. I refer to "King" George Bush, whose lust for power begat more power and more power until the nation was carried away on the flood tide of his mad power grab and landed in a war that was as unconstitutional as any in the history of the United States.

What has been entirely lost in the debate in the House and Senate as to whether to "give" the president such power is that being 100 percent unconstitutional, it would require an amendment to the United States Constitution. The Congress (House and Senate) does *not* have the authority to grant the president line item veto powers: This cannot be done by the Congress but only by way of a Constitutional amendment.

The Founding Fathers meant to prevent the Constitution being circumvented by the three departments passing powers back and forth. Article 1, Section 9 of the United States Constitution denies or severely limits the power of Congress to legislate.The Congress *cannot* pass its duties to the Supreme Court or the president without a constitutional amendment. This was meant to stop power-mad Socialist like Wilson, Roosevelt, Bush from rushing the country into one war after another, but even that did not stop power mad Wilson, Roosevelt and Bush from doing just that.

Clinton awaits his chance to start another war. He narrowly missed out against North Korea, but his turn may yet come before his single term comes to an end. Line Item Veto power is another step toward the Socialist goal of "making the United States Constitution of no effect." The Constitutional power of the president is found in Section II of the United States Constitution. He has no other power.

The Fabian Society carried on the war that was lost by the armies of King George III. They provoked the Civil War and all wars since then, in the hope of toppling the Confederate Republic of the United States. The Annals of Congress, Congressional Globes and Congressional Record provide a wealth of information and detail to confirm this opinion. On page.326, Congressional Globe, House, July 12, 1862, we find a speech by the Hon. F.W. Kellogg, "Origin of the Rebellion:"

"National pride has been gratified, also the increase of power, and the certain knowledge that in a half of a century more, the United States must be by far the most powerful nation on the globe. But the great powers of Europe have witnessed rapid growth with uneasiness; and defend America, which was never at any time threatened by the Germans!"

The mischief done by modern day American Socialists is tremendous. Jacob Javitts saw in what he called "civil rights issues" a golden opportunity to stir the racial waters by infiltrating Socialists in such key government bodies as the Equal Opportunity Commission. On the international scene, Javitts, using scare tactics at which Socialists are so good, was responsible for establishing so-called "international banks" and then getting Congress to fund them in an utterly unconstitutional manner.

Another big promoter of Socialism in this country was Judge Abe "Fixer" Fortas, who more than any other Socialist was responsible for "legalizing" a flood of obscene literature and pornography. This was designed to further weaken the morality of the nation. Fortas cast the deciding vote on the U.S. Supreme Court's 100 percent wrong decision to allow pornography under the guise of "freedom of speech." We are told by psychologists and psychiatrists that this led directly to a huge increase in crime as this kind of "entertainment" titillates the lower brain centers.

House and Senate members must bear their share of the blame for this and the shocking rise of unemployment and crime in tandem. The House and Senate by a two-thirds vote can overturn any Supreme court ruling, and they should have done this ten years ago and not wait for the situation to get out of hand, and then stand by an allow the Socialists in their midst to blame the problem on "guns." There are some really red-hot Socialists in the House and Senate. Representative Bill Richardson is a notable example: On pages E2788 E2790, Congressional Record, Wednesday July 31,1991, Richardson launched forth a paen of praise for one of the worst Socialists on earth: then Representative Stephen Solarz, who interfered in the affairs of Rhodesia, South Africa, the Philippines, South Korea and every non-leftist country under the sun. As if that were not bad enough, investigators looking into the House bank scandal, found Solarz had written the highest number by far of bad checks By comparison with Solarz, Benedict Arnold was practically a saint.

Other Socialist "saints" that have caused this country unlimited harm and caused a breakdown not only of our economic, political and judicial systems, but who have actively sought to advance the Socialist agenda to the detriment of the American people were: Harry Dexter White, John Kenneth Galbraith, Arthur Schlesinger, Telford Taylor, Robert Strange Mc Namara, David C. Williams, George Ball, Felix Frankfurter, Bernard Baruch, Arthur Goldberg, Alger Hiss, Judge Gesell, Ralph Bunche, Nicholas Katzenbach, Cora Weiss, Louis Brandeis, McGeorge Bundy, Henry Kissinger, Allen and John Foster Dulles, Sam Newhouse and Walt Whitman Rostow. Some of these, and other Socialist "warriors" will be found in the chapters, "Stars in the Socialist Firmament," with an account of their deeds.

Their plans and aims were to slowly, insidiously, induce the United States to adopt Socialism, in easy stages that would not be noticed by the people. The program was one worked out by the Fabian Society of London, as detailed by their lead players, Professor Laski, Graham Wallas and Kenneth Galbraith. These plans were laid out in such a manner as to coincide or dovetail with what "Liberals" were doing in America, especially in the fields of education, undermining the United States Constitution, the American system of political economy based upon sound money and trade protection tariffs.

These largely coincided with the International Socialist plans for an eventual One World Government — New World Order. For the Fabians of England to adjust their plans to an American timetable was a big undertaking. How successful they were can be measured in terms of the fact that between the 1920s and 1930, they almost succeeded in totally Socializing the United States.

3

SOCIALIST-CONTROLLED EDUCATION: THE ROAD TO SLAVERY

The one sector of life in the United States that has been completely co-opted by Fabian Socialism, is education. Perhaps in no other of their fields of endeavor to Socialize America did their indirect, stealthy, furtive methodology succeed nearly as much as it did in Fabian Socialism's long march to capture the educational system of this nation. The Socialists took over Yale, Harvard, Columbia and many other colleges, held to be of direct service to Socialism. They were to be the future educational centers and "finishing schools" for Socialists in America as Oxford and Cambridge are for the Fabian Society in England.

In these universities were developed a layer of top-level elite educators whose ties to British Fabianism were strong. Among the top in this elite group was Walter Lippmann and John Reed, who is buried in the walls of the Kremlin in Moscow. Socialist pressure on education expanded with Leftist/Socialist professors threatening to give conservative students failing grades for giving wrong answers — wrong whenever they clashed with Fabian Socialist ideas. In this manner have traditional American Christian conservative views undergone a terrible erosion. An enquiry lasting two years (1962-1964) in one California school district, showed the selfsame pressures operating in classrooms staffed with Socialist teachers, as was in use in universities across the nation. Parents were reluctant to complain, because in instances where complaints were filed with the school board, their children received bad grades and loss of credits.

As far back as the visit to the United States by Ramsay McDonald, the Fabian Socialists in London knew that a frontal assault on education in the United States was out of the question. At one of the most memorable of many Socialist meetings held in New York in 1905, at Peck's Restaurant, the Intercollegiate Socialist Society (ISS) was formed. This was the bridgehead that was to give the Fabian Socialist in America a highway into education.

The man the Fabian Society selected for the job of Socializing education in America, was John Dewey, Professor of Philosophy at Columbia University, New York. Dewey became known as the father of progressive (Socialist) education, identified with Marxist bodies such as the League of Industrial Democracy (LID), of which he was a president. Dewey first came to the notice of the Socialist hierarchy while teaching at the Lincoln School of Teachers College, a hotbed of Marxist-Liberalist education, supported by the General Education Board.

It was here that Dewey met Nelson Aldrich and David Rockefeller. Of the two, Dewey reportedly said that David was completely Socialized, committing to its philosophies wholeheartedly. The Un-American Committee cited Dewey as belonging to 15 Marxist-front organizations. A few years later, Rockefeller rewarded Dewey by making him Governor of New York and a member of the Council on Foreign Relations (CFR). Although Dewey went on to occupy mostly political positions, it was his indoctrination of Nelson and David Rockefeller into Socialisms and Marxism that did the most damage, as millions upon millions of dollars were thereafter donated to fighting "religious clause" school cases in the Supreme Court and undermining education and infecting America's school system with the Socialist virus.

The 10th Amendment of the United States Constitution reserves the police powers of education, health and police protection to the States. The powers of the Federal Government are powers delegated by the States. The first 10 Amendments to the United States Constitution are a prohibition of power, one of the strictest being that education is a matter for the States.

Until they were able to make progress via the legislative route as Florence Kelley (real name Weschnewetsky) had stated, the American Fabian Socialists had to go about undermining education in the United States in a typically Fabian Socialist way. The Intercollegiate Socialist Society (ISS) meeting at Peck's Restaurant was the first slow step taken to penetrate and permeate education without disclosing the direction it was to go. When we look back to the seemingly slow, almost halting formation of the ISS, it is hard to believe that the very same American Fabian Socialist movement who formed, it are today galloping along, dragging our education system along with them by the hair of its head.

There were others who thought just like Justice Douglas, Felix Frankfurter, Frank Murphy, William J. Brennan, Arthur Goldberg, Justice Hugo Black and Abe Fortas. In addition to being ardent Socialists, Douglas, Murphy and Brennan were high-ranking Freemasons. It was during the time 1910-1930 that the Supreme Court began taking an untoward interest is so-called "religious clause" school education case, from which it had shied away from at least for two decades. This was the era when the most damage was done to the American education system, enabling Socialism to make huge inroads which previously seemed to be out of the question.

While the Supreme Court had outlawed religious education — especially prayers from schools — their Masonic brethren had been very successful in penetrating and permeating schools with Socialist Mason literature. In 1959, Franklin W. Patterson persuaded the principal of a high school in Baker, Oregon, to use Socialist-oriented text books in the school. The same thing happened in North Carolina were Socialist-Masonic literature was distributed in every classroom of every school in Charlotte.

As House Banking Committee chairman, Louis T. McFadden said:

"In the matter of education the Fabian Illuminati have followed a theory which is none other than that suggested by the souls of Bavarian Illuminism, Nicolai, in the eighteenth century. Having secured posts in the school boards of the country, it became very easy for the Fabian Socialists to instill their educational, de-Christianized principles in the school curriculum. Their attack on religious teaching was subtle but deadly, as seen in the Education bill of 1902."

"They boast openly of having in their ranks several bishops and divines, the list being headed by Bishop Headlam, one of the earliest Fabians...Under Fabian educational schemes come the formation of the educational groups of the 'nursery,' the latter designed as a kind of a training school for very young prospective Socialists. (Then Governor Clinton of Arkansas modeled his Socialist "Governor's School" along these lines)...But by far the most important steps taken by the Fabians along educational lines was their inauguration in existing universities of 'Universities Socialist Societies.'...The culminating triumph of the Fabians in the realm of education was the creation of the London School of Economics and Political Science at the London University, where today one of the chief lecturers is the Socialist, Harold Laski..."

One can say of Socialist plans that they infected the realm education with a virus that they hoped would spread and radically change our social order. This "virus" would get into the spinal cord of "social studies" and "social sciences" turning all studies in a leftward direction. This was the basic premise of the National Education Association set forth in their 14th Year Book in 1936, from which position the Socialist educators have never wavered: "We stand for Socializing the individual."

In pursuance of this, in the 1920s the Socialists who swarmed over the United States like a cloud of locusts were intent upon carrying out as many of the ideas written up in the Communist Manifesto of 1848, embodied in legislation pertaining to education. They hoped to circumvent the constitution by what Florence Kelley called "legislative action." On pages 4583-4604, Congressional Record, Feb. 23,1927, under the title " General Deficiency Appropriation Bill, we find their methods exposed. "...The Communist groups must show children how to convert secret hate and pent-up anger into a conscious struggle...Most important is the struggle against the tyranny of school discipline."

John Dewey and his disciples tried to limit the learning of vocabulary in schools, knowing as they did that the depth of education is commensurate with one's vocabulary. Children should be taught vocabulary, even if it is only taught straight out of a dictionary. All government job applicants ought to be obliged to pass an *English* vocabulary test, and this could be extended to State job applicants. Even welfare applicants should be obliged to take a proficiency test in vocabulary in the *English* language. This would negate the effect of Socialism in education, and thwart Socialism's aim of turning out a mediocre majority of children who will grow up to become mediocre adults, "pushovers" for swallowing a diet of Socialism.

Another specialist tactic is to waste the Nations' substance through irresponsible spending so that "destructive" becomes the order of the day. This has the effect of steadily raising higher education fees. We see the cumulative effect of John Maynard Keynes policies in the number of students who are not going to college, and those who drop out as fees get too much for them to pay. In this way, the number of students with future leadership qualities is diminished, by intent and by design.

The general thrust of Socialist "education" is to keep intelligence to a minimum wherever possible, while promoting mediocrity. Of course this does not apply to their own chosen future leadership who are selected out of the best and brightest Socialists and sent to the "finishing school" at Oxford as Rhodes scholars. An excellent reference to education as a means of confounding Communism and Socialism, is found In the Congressional Record, House, June 26, 1884 on page 336, Appendix thereto:

"I believe the sheet anchor of our form of government is intelligence, hence I am an earnest advocate of popular education." Daniel Webster uttered this sentiment of which history has demonstrated the truth when he said. 'it is intelligence that has reared the majestic columns of our national glory, and this also can prevent them from crumbling into ashes.' The spread of intelligence is to be the Government — it will be not only protection against centralization of political and financial power on one hand, but our sure and safe defense against Communism, nilhism and revolutionary tendencies on the other."

"While ours was a comparatively frontier population, with sturdy self-reliance and individuality as a common characteristic, our dangers were not many, but with a dense population, accumulated wealth, and *comparative effeminacy,* new perils arise, and we must depend upon education and intelligence to counter these as far as possible, for, 'as thou so west so shall thou reap' applies to States as well as to men. Next to the Christian religion, the greatest civilizer of men is the school. Public schools, like everything else, are criticized, but until something better is devised, I am in favor of maintaining and extending them..."

This great speech was made by The Hon. James K. Jones of Arkansas, and shows just how far ahead our representatives were in the 1800s than those who are now in Congress. It also shows up in the clearest possible light why the Socialists feel so compelled to take charge of education for their own sinister purposes, and why the likewise feel the need to negate Christianity. It is clear that morality, education and religion go hand-in-hand, and the Socialists know it.

The Socialists managed to get one of their most important protagonists, Hugo Lafayette Black on the bench of the Supreme Court. Black, a Unitarian (Godless) church member and a Freemason, should never have been confirmed, because it broke all Senate rules. The serious situation posed by Black's nomination was raised by Senators William Borah (R.ID) and Warren Austin (R.NH). They pointed out that Black was constitutionally ineligible because he was a member of Congress when it enacted legislation raising the salary of Supreme Court Judges, and in consequence, he could not be promoted to a post that paid more money than he received as a member of Congress.

The Constitution is perfectly clear on this point: "No Senator or Representative shall, during the time for which he was elected, be appointed to any civil office under the authority of the United States, which shall have been created, or the emoluments where of shall have increased during such time." At the time of Black's nomination he was paid $109,000 as a member of Congress, while the Justices salaries were raised to $20,000 a year. Yet, in spite of this clear violation of the law, Roosevelt's Attorney General, Homer Cummings, ruled that Black's appointment to the Supreme was legal!

The Socialists-Masonics alliance needed Black on the Supreme Court because they knew that he was sympathetic to their cause and would always rule in their favor on "religious clause" education cases, and their faith in Black was amply rewarded. Black was in league with Samuel Untermeyer, Schofield, Gunnar Myrdal, Justices Earl Warren and Louis D. Brandeis, Roosevelt and Florence Kelley who were all working to bring education under the control of Socialism.

The supreme and organic law of the land is the law based upon the Christian Bible's teachings. By failing to obey it, the U.S. Supreme Court is in a state of transgression. Modern education, on the basis of Supreme Court rulings has broken Biblical law. Schools and colleges have become the most dangerous places to leave our youth unsupervised and unattended. One of the ways in which the Socialists obtained the upper-hand was the non-recognition of religious schools — and especially Catholic schools.

Here, the services of the *illegally appointed* Justice Hugo Black were invaluable in ruling against cases brought under the so-called "religious clause" by the enemies of the Constitution of United States. Black, known to be militantly anti-Catholic and anti-church school education in general, followed slavishly Masonic "principles" in his court rulings, in fact most of them were taken direct from Mason literature. The most noteworthy "principles" which on which Black based his rulings, were:

Principal No.1 "Public school education for all of the children of all of the people."

Principal No.5 "The entire separation of Church and State, and opposition to every attempt to appropriate public moneys, directly or indirectly, for the support of sectarian or private institutions." As we shall see in the chapters dealing with corruption of the Constitution, within two years of Black's nomination, the Supreme Court took a huge lurch to the Left and declared unconstitutional State funding of religious schools, on the utterly false premise of Jefferson's Bill for Religious Freedom, which was not in the Constitution, but restricted to Virginia. That is how the "wall of separation of Church and State," came to be born, totally unconstitutional based on deception and outright fraud.

The issue of "federal" aid for religious schools was raised again by Representative Graham Barden back in 1940. Barden was a Socialist-Freemason, and as we proceed, we shall see just how well Masonry and Socialism have combined to wreck education in America. The intention of the Barden bill was control over schools so that Socialism could be freely taught. This was confirmed by Dr. Cloyd H. Marvin, president of George Washington University in a letter dated May 11, 1944, addressed to the House Committee on World War Veterans. What Burden was striving to do was to eliminate the right of war veterans to attend theological seminaries, especially, Catholic seminaries, if they so chose. Barden had attended the Fabian Conference of Representatives of Educational Associations in 1941, which conference was a tool of both Freemasonry and Socialism.

According to Dr. Marvin, there should not be any private schools, because in his words, "we cannot maintain two systems to interfere with regular education policies." This was one of the clearest cases on record of Masonry as the driving force behind the Conference of Representatives of Educational Association. While ostensibly the bill under discussion was primarily about the G.I. bill, nevertheless its ramifications were very wide, because Rep. Barden attempted to put private religious schools out of bounds for those veterans who were attending college on the "G.I. bill."

Dr. Marvin was no ordinary educator. He was a longtime Socialists and 33rd degree Mason. At George Washington University he was able to exert a powerful influence because of the grant of $100,000 he received from the Scottish Rite of Freemasonry. Marvin found a friend in Justice Hugo Black, who owed his Supreme Court position to the Masons. After he left the Senate, the Socialists got Black's Senate seat filled by Lister Hill of Alabama, a regular Socialist crusader and staunch Mason. For years, Hill was able to block federal funding for private schools, especially religious schools. Hill was listed in the Congressional Directory, 79th Congress, 1st Session, August 1985, page 18, as a 32nd degree Mason.

Nowhere was Socialist pressure on education so strongly manifested than through the National Education Association, (NEA). With passage of the GI Bill there appeared a new attempt to wreck federal funding for private schools without strings attached, the strings always in the hands of the NEA. On January 10, 1945, the NEA sponsored new legislation that would not allow federal funding of private schools. The legislation was believed drafted by Justice Hugo Black. What the measure did was to accomplish through omission rather than direct exclusion, the desired goals of the NEA. It was a cleverly drafted piece of legislation. The same cleverness was displayed in 1940 in the drafting of so-called "separation of church and state" legislation.

Decisions by Socialist-Unitarian Justices who dominated the Supreme Court from 1935 to 1965, effectively barred Christian education curricula from public schools. In the war hysteria atmosphere of the 1940s, nobody saw fit to point out that any interference by the Federal Government in education was an outright violation of the 10th Amendment. The far-reaching so-called "separation of church and state" ruling of the Court was completely unlawful, not to found in the Constitution. There is no constitutional grounds for "separation of Church and State" which was used to destroy the basis of religious instruction in the schools.

The acceptance of this skewed piece of legislation, a strong attack on the Constitutional rights of We, the People, had a direct bearing on the quality of American education, which went into a tailspin, immediately after this fraudulent, unconstitutional ruling. American education was there after overrun by teaching all sorts of "rights" that did not exist, "women's rights," "civil rights" and "homosexual rights." Following the barring of religious instruction from schools and the introduction of "humanism" by John Dewey, a very substantial rise of violent crime followed almost immediately.

America, founded on Christianity, was abducted, held to ransom, violated, a victim of Socialist barbarity, battered and bruised, and barely able to crawl on its knees in the 1990s, about as far removed from the country that the Founding Fathers strove to make it as it was possible to get. In this savage assault on the Virtuous Republic of United States, Socialist-Masonic control of education from the 1st grade onwards, played the leading role.

It has been proved over and over again that children start learning in the primary grades, 1st, 2nd, 3rd. In middle class homes, where a higher value of learning prevails, parents will help their children with reading, but in the lower class families, parents invariably don't help their children, with the result that children who read badly are found to gravitate toward criminal activities. There are always exceptions, but the foregoing is recognized by educators not blinded by "minority" blinkers to be generally true.

In a rotten conspiracy entered into between the Socialist and President Harry Truman, the Plessy vs. Ferguson ruling, the "separate but equal" doctrine of education, was undermined by President Truman, pretending slyly all the while to favor it. The real issue was that neither Truman or anyone in the Federal Government had the right to interfere in matters of education, since as we have stated elsewhere, the 10th Amendment to the United States Constitution reserves the powers of education to the States. The Federal Government is prohibited in meddling in education, which belongs solely to the States.

One of the chief causes of the horrible decline of education in the Nation, can be found in the landmark case, Everson vs. Board of Education brought before the New Jersey Supreme Court, October 5, 1943. The case arose out of issues made by Rep. Graham Barden in 1940 about religious schools receiving government subsidies The Everson case was a revival of Barden's defeated bill. As I have previously indicated, the Socialists are tenacious in their efforts to overturn the Constitution of the United States, which they view as the principal stumbling block to their ardent desire to Socialize the people of this Nation.

The Everson case was about the State of New Jersey allowing the town of Ewing to pay the cost of transporting (voluntarily as opposed to mandatory) schoolchildren to all schools, including religious schools. The plaintiff, a Mr. Arch Everson, had objected to the funding of transportation for children attending religious schools. In this he was supported by the Masons, and the American Civil Liberties Union (ACLU), although the ACLU kept well out of sight during State court proceedings. Ostensibly, the objection came only from Mr. Everson in those proceedings. The Socialists needed to win the case in order to use it as a precedent-setting corner stone for future planned assaults on education "religious clause" cases they planned to bring if Everson was successful.

The matter was heard by the New Jersey Supreme Court which allowed the town of Ewing to continue funding transportation of children to all schools. Backed by the ACLU, which now emerged from hiding, and the Masons, Everson took his case to the Supreme Court. It was the chance of a lifetime for Black to demonstrate his ignorance of the Constitution and his prejudice against Christianity, while striking a blow for Socialism. The Supreme Court ruled against the State of New Jersey, with the ACLU coming out in the open as a so-called "friend of the court." The ACLU brief was virtually an in to to copy of a Mason citation made by Elmer Rogers many years earlier. Overlaid on the Mason citation, the ACLU brief was virtually a near-perfect fit.

The majority decision of the Court was written by Justice Hugo Black. Being packed with Socialists and Masons, the Court could hardly have ruled against the prejudiced viewpoint of its members, Christian haters violently opposed to the teaching of Christian beliefs in schools receiving so-called "Federal" aid.

Prior to 1946, the "wall between Church and State" had hardly ever been used in a legal argument. It was, after all, merely the words of Thomas Jefferson, a mere phrase, not found in the Constitution. But after the Everson case, which

Justice Hugo Black had been elevated to the Supreme Court specially to rule in favor of plaintiff Everson, the courts unleashed a torrent of verbal abuse against Christianity in particular, and against religious instruction in schools in general.

The courts outlawed prayers in schools; banned oral Bible readings, declared atheism and secular humanism as religions protected by the First Amendment and struck down the custom of allowing children to attend prayer services inside school property, all against long standing traditions, customs, such as singing Christmas carols, prohibited religious instruction by teachers, and as we shall see in the chapters dealing with Law, beyond the ken and the pale of the constitution. The Supreme Court took a phrase uttered by Jefferson, "wall of separation between Church and State" which has no constitutional standing, and inserted it in the Constitution, thereby turning the United States of America into a society in which the Christian religion was not allowed to play any role whatsoever in State affairs, certainly not what the Founding Fathers had intended.

So blatantly prejudiced was Black, that his fellow Justices had occasion to write about him in unflattering terms. In a diary entry dated March 9, 1948, Frankfurter wrote that Justice Harold O. Burton "hasn't the remotest idea how malignant men like Black and Douglas not only can be, but are." This was manifested in the Everson case, where Black demonstrated his prejudiced determination based on hatred of Christ, that religion not play a role in the life of our Nation. The rot started with Everson, continued with Brown vs. Board of Education and inevitably, Roe vs. Wade, which up until now remains the greatest victory and triumph over the Constitution of the United States and the American people, ever achieved by the Fabian Socialists. The Supreme Court went CROOKED with the advent of Black and has remained so ever since.

There was never a clearer case of a violation of the 9th Amendment than the Everson decision. The 9th Amendment forbids judges from putting their own thoughts into matters of law that are not spelled out in the Constitution. This is called predilection, and that is precisely what Black and his fellow justices did in the Everson case. They twisted and squeezed the Constitution to fit their own stinking prejudiced predilections and came out on the side of Socialist-Masonry, in utter defilement of the Constitution.

The Socialists were about to bring their Brown vs. School Board, Topeka, Kansas case before the Supreme Court. Justice Vinson had told Truman that the Brown vs. School Board case would be disposed of and that "separate but equal" education would remain in place. Vinson did this knowing full well that it was a not true. Thus when 33rd Degree Mason Socialist Chief Justice Earl Warren read the decision on the Brown vs. School Board case, there were gasps of surprise from the spectators, some of whom, being in the know, had come to hear the court uphold Plessey vs. Ferguson.

Few present in the court on that fateful day could have been aware of the tremendous blow that had been struck for "standardized," "Socialized" education in the most blatant violation of the Constitution up to that time. It is true to say that several attempts had been made in the past to circumvent the Constitution by "legislative action" as proposed by the Socialist, Florence Kelley (Weschnewetsky). A bill was introduced in 1924, with the intent and purpose of violating the 10th Amendment to the United States Constitution, in that the bill sought to create a Department of Education, which took its title from the Communist Department of Education in Bolshevized Russia. The idea was to "nationalize," "standardize" and "federalize" education in the United States as it was in the USSR.

What the bill sought to achieve was force every child in America to read the same, "standardized" text books, which would include a good leavening of Marxist, Socialist, Leninists text books, so that children would emerge from the school system as good little Socialists ready to march into the One World Government — New World Order. Leading Socialist of the Fabian Society had always said that to standardize education was the quickest way to break down the natural barriers against Socialism in America, arising from the big land mass, geographical, weather, local customs, local school boards. Webb had remarked that diversity was a problem for socialism, and diversity existed in America in abundance, which made the country difficult to penetrate with Marxism, Communist, Socialism.

That is why our Founding Fathers in their foresight and wisdom, made sure that the powers of education remained with the States and prohibited to the Federal Government. This system of States education was a safeguard against anarchy and nilhism from within the Nation. Although they failed in this instance, Socialists never gave up on their attempt to seize control of education, and their chance came with the treasonous conduct of President Jimmy Carter and seditionists in the House and Senate, who got an Education bill federalizing education passed, in violation of the 10th Amendment. As a result, the illegal U.S. Department of Education was created.

Carter will go down in history as a president who committed wholesale treason and sedition. "I will not lie to you" said Carter, and then set about implementing Socialist legislation that robbed the States of making their own decisions on education, and robbed the people of the Nation, of the Panama Canal. The 13th, 14th and 15th Amendments to the Constitution of the United States were never ratified, so any legislation passed by the Congress in pursuant of these amendments are outside of the ken and the pale of the Constitution, Socialist Dr. William H. Owen would have loved Carter. Owen was the president of the Chicago Normal College, Chicago, Illinois and president of the NEA, who was chosen to represent the NEA at the World Conference on Education, June 23, 1923, held in San Francisco. Included in his speech was the following "...In spite of what we write and say, the world does not believe that education as a form of social control is comparable with armies, navies, and statecraft...We should spend our time and efforts in sharing a constructive educational program that will demonstrate what education can do as a form of social control comparable with armies..."

The foregoing, demonstrates why it is so dangerous to leave education to the tender mercies of the Federal Government, especially with the advent of the Socialist Woodrow Wilson, whose administration collected Socialists by quantum leaps, until today, we have the Clinton administration riddled with Socialists, in fact, differing little from the Socialist Labor Party governments in England. Our Founding Fathers were wise enough to foresee the time when Socialist agents like Wilson, Kennedy, Johnson, Carter, Bush and Clinton, and Socialists like Owen, disguised as "educators" would try to steer our, Nation leftward through their seditious "education" programs, and so they made sure that the powers of education were prohibited to the Federal Government.

However, using the Supreme Court to get around the Constitution was a dangerous development the Founding Fathers could not have altogether foreseen. They knew treason mongers existed in their day and age, but they could not have had any idea that a man like Chief Justice Earl Warren would come along and make a mockery of the Constitution. It is said of Warren, that he made the 14th Amendment to the Constitution of the United States, mean "everything and anything." It was through this ugly subterfuge, of unratified amendments and a Supreme Court choked with judges with sedition on their minds, that the obnoxious Brown vs. Board of Education became "law," which it is not, but which the States are forced, nevertheless to obey.

Another ugly subterfuge and piece of outright deceit, was the use by Warren of totally prejudiced sociological data dredged up by Dr. Gunnar Myrdal, a Socialist reprobate whose economic theories had cost Sweden billions of dollars, and we shall return to this outright liar in due course.

The Department of Education was established to take control of education away from the States and replace American education with a system that would ensure children grow up in the Socialist format and become political leaders, in the Socialist way of promoting a new political order based on the Soviet system, which will lead to the One World Government — New World Order.

What the Warren Court tried to do with Brown vs. Board of Education, and other Supreme Court Justices have also tried to do, was separate the 1st Section of the 14th Amendment from the whole Constitution, so that it would mean anything they wanted it to read into it — classic predilection forbidden by the 9th Amendment. Any part of the Constitution HAS to be interpreted in the light of the total Constitution, which cannot be fragmented. The Slaughterhouse decisions made a mockery of Warren's Brown vs. Board of Education ruling, which, if he had observed it, would have shown Warren the error of his ways.

Because Justice Warren decided not to read the Slaughterhouse decision, he went and ruled on the Brown vs. Board of Education basing it on the so-called "Civil rights" act of 1964. We deal with this more fully in the chapters on the Constitution. In Brown vs. Board of Education, we have the Communizing of education in the United States. What is the difference between transporting children in forced busing out of their locality and transporting political prisoners to the gulags in Siberia, or the transporting of Colonists to England for trial, against which Thomas hurled his full fury?

There is no difference! Children, black and white, are transported against their wills to other locations. This is a violation of life, liberty and property as to due process of law, which Brown vs. Board of Education denied children and parents. In this alone, Brown vs. Board of Education is 100 percent unconstitutional. Why should parents and children suffer a violation of their 5th Amendment rights in order to fulfill the Socialist designs of the Socialist educators and their friends at court? Our children suffer "cruel and unusual punishment" by being bused out of their area to magnet schools, paring schools and the like, because of their race. There is no trial by jury available to them, no due process, simply a herding aboard buses under Communist-like, totalitarian "laws."

The children and their parents are citizens of the States FIRST: Article 1V Section 2, Part 1. The citizens of each State shall be entitled to all privileges and immunities of citizens in the Several States and U.S. citizens, second. The 14th Amendment is still a restriction on the Federal Government, even though it was not ratified, so the States kept their sovereignty and could not be imposed upon in matters of education by the Federal Government.

There was tremendous pressure on judges to rule in favor of the American Civil Liberties Union (ACLU) in cases involving religion in schools. The ACLU filed 23 such briefs and in the cases heard by Justice Felix Frankfurter, he always ruled in favor of the ACLU. One of the allies of the ACLU was Pastor Davies of the Unitarian Church of which Justice Hugo Black was a member. This is what Davies had to say about "religious clause" school cases:

"Like St. Paul's freedom, religious liberty with a great price must be bought. And for those who exercise it most fully, by insisting upon religious education for their children, mixed with secular by terms of our Constitution, the price is greater than others... The religions of the creeds are obsolescent, the basis of their claims expired with yesterday." Justice Hugo Black was 100 percent in favor of packing the Supreme Court of the United States with Socialist justices which is what Roosevelt and Truman certainly did.

Justice Hugo Black was a committed Freemason, and one must suppose that he held to Mason tents regarding education:

"Next to this, the form of learned literary society is best suited for our purposes and had not Masonry existed, this cover would have been employed and it may be much more than a cover, it may be a powerful, engine in our hands. By establishing reading societies and subscription libraries and taking these under our direction and supplying them through our labors, we may turn the public mind which way we will... We must win the common people in every corner. This will be obtained chiefly by means of schools, and by open, hearty behavior, popularity and tolerance of their prejudices which at leisure root out and dispel... We must acquire the direction of education, of church management — of the professional chair and of the pulpit."

What is truly astonishing is that if we take the writings of Beatrice and Sydney Webb and overlay them upon the Masonic views of education, we find they are almost always identical! The onslaught on American education was directed by the Tavistock Institute of Human Relations, the premiere brainwashing establishment in the world, and their "educators," Kurt Lewin, Margaret Meade. H.V. Dicks, Richard Crossman and W.R. Bion. These enemies of the American Republic were unleashed upon an innocent, unsuspecting general public, with disastrous consequences for education.

Among their "new science" sciences projects for American schools were the study of masturbation, homosexuality, transvestitism, lesbianism, prostitution, exotic religions, cults and religious fundamentalism.

The so-called "civil rights law" of 1870, which was supposed to enforce the 15th Amendment which was never properly ratified applied specifically to the Chinese brought over by the opium peddlers and the railroad magnates like the Harrimans, should not have any bearing today as the 15th Amendment was never properly ratified. To imply that "equal protection of the laws" in the Section 1 of the 14th Amendment, means that every person has the same level of intelligence — more than even the worst star-struck Liberal would hold to be true! But this is exactly and precisely what Brown vs. Board of Education attempted to do — level all minds to one mean or average level. This is at the core of Brown vs. Board of Education and it is egalitarianism in action.

Sedition in education is a reality as much of a reality "gun control" as the sedition practiced by Senator Meztenbaum and Representative Schumer. By perverting education, first through the establishment of a Federal Government department of education and second by Supreme Court action of the order of Brown vs. Board of Education, treason and sedition transpires. To destroy the American system of education and replace it with a Marxist/Leninist/Socialist system will result in the rot of the Nation from within. The secular humanist Justice Warren was guilty of treason when he allowed Brown vs. Board of Education to become "law."

The National Education Association (NEA) is a 100 percent Socialist-Marxist organization. Their first task was to remove from the schools the proper teaching of history, geography, civics and in their place, install social studies favoring Communism. The NEA is a Socialist organization that has been actively engaged in undermining education in the United States sine the 1920s. They were no doubt in the vanguard of those who brought Brown vs. Board Education case in 1954, "fixed" by Justice Earl Warren, in the Abe Fortas manner.

With the Socialist take-over of American schools, new curriculums were introduced, children being awarded credits in courses such as soap operas and nonsensical "environmental issues. "In all, Tavistock Institute drafted 4000 new science social scientists to work on turning American education away from traditional values. The result of their efforts can be seen in the huge upsurge of violent teenage crime, school crimes, rapes. These statistics mirror the success of the Tavistock Institute's methods.

Among the "educators" drafted by the Socialists were the Socialist Gunnar Myrdal and his wife, who hailed from Sweden. The Myrdals had a long history of fealty to Socialist/Marxist ideas. Dr. Myrdal had worked as an assistant to avowed Socialist Walt Whitman Rostow, at the United Nations Economic Commission for Europe in Geneva. Rostow's treasonous activities are recounted in other chapters of this book. Myrdal had worked in Sweden as Minister of Commerce before joining Rostow, in which capacity he did almost irreparable damage to Sweden's economy, in true big-spending Socialist style.

Myrdal was chosen by the Socialist Carnegie Foundation to conduct a study in race relations in the United States on a grant of $250,000. It was believed that since Myrdal had no experience with blacks, there being none in Sweden, his study would be impartial. What was not realized at the time.was that the whole thing was a set up: Myrdal was to produce a set of conclusions that would be used in the notorious Brown vs. Board of Education case. Myrdal produced a report filled with totally fraudulent so-called sociopolitical conclusions which said, in essence that blacks were getting a raw deal in education. *Myrdal's conclusions were riddled with gaping holes.*

Moreover, far from being a disinterested scientist, Myrdal was an avowed enemy of the Constitution of the United States, which he referred to as being, "a nearly fetishistic cult...a 150-year old Constitution (which is) in many respects impractical and ill-suited for modern conditions...Modern historical studies reveal that the Constitutional Convention was merely a plot against the common people....Until recently, the Constitution has been used to block the popular will."

Myrdal and his wife toured the United States under the auspices of the Socialist Benjamin Malzberger. Among the lesser of scores of disparaging remarks made by Myrdal was the one in which he described the American people as, "narrow-minded whites, ridden by evangelistic religion," and Southern whites he dismissed as "poor, uneducated, coarse and dirty." This was the man who wrote the "unbiased" sociological background report which it is said, made up Chief Justice Earl Warren's mind on which way to rule in the Brown vs. Board of Education case.

What was behind the great Socialist drive of the 1920 and 1950s to wreck America's education system? It can be summed up in a few words: The central idea was to "make new minds" for only through new minds could humanity remake itself — this according to one of the high-priests of Socialist education, Eric Trist, who added that the new mind would exclude belief in the Christian religion. And as Myrdal said, "what better place to start than in the schools?"

In bringing the Brown vs School Board case before the Supreme Court, the NAACP received ten million dollars from a variety of sources, including the Political Action Group, a Socialist-front organization, and Freemasonry. NAACP lawyers received extensive briefings from Florence Kelley and Mary White Ovington. Kelley was the originator of the "Brandeis Briefs" which consisted of hundreds of sociological opinions and often covered by no more than two pages of legal references. The Brandeis Briefs method was the way in which the Supreme Court was to rule in all future cases involving Constitutional matters

The Socially-corrupted American school curricula does not teach the Constitution, because if children were given instruction in it, they would have to be taught that the Constitution is there as a primary defense against the Federal Government and presidents like George Bush and Bill Clinton, who would aspire to become tyrants, if not subject to its constraints. *The aims of Socialist educators is to gradually erode the constitutional safeguards that guarantee life, liberty and property for all citizens and replace them with totalitarian Socialism.*

Only a Biblical-based education system is good. All other systems were devised by men and therefore must of necessity be imperfect. Our schools have fallen into the hands of profoundly influential people whose main purpose in life it is to turn them into a Socialist bulwark. In this they have the backing of the judiciary. The goal is to advance, slowly, in true Socialist style, toward a Socialist/Marxist government, by altering the thrust and direction of what is taught in schools. If the Socialists continue to make the kind of progress they have made over the past three decades, by the year 2010 we shall have a nation of young adults and middle aged citizens who will have no quarrel with the secret agenda of centralized power in a Socialist dictatorship, backed up by a national police force.

It is clear that one of the objectives that has already been reached by the Socialists is the lack of interest in reading. American children would be totally lost if they were placed, let us say, in the British Museum Library in London, or the Louvre in Paris. The great writers and artists would have little to say to them. Books are not the friends of children as they were in the early days of our history. Our education system has seen to that. Even Dickens is a stranger to the majority of American students.

The lack of true education is leading children and young adults to seek "enlightenment" in the movies, in rock music, which is how it was intended. The only way we can fight this insidious creeping paralyses is to intervene regularly and vigorously. The so-called "struggle against racial prejudices" in the 1960s greatly affected the minds and attitudes of our young people. The so-called demo-craticization of our schools and universities over the past three decades was a direct attack on their internal structures, which brought in its wake a loss of focus and direction.

The so-called "feminist" movement is a direct product of the Communist man-ifesto of 1848 and the twisted thinking of Gunnar Myrdal and the new science sci-entists of the Tavistock Institute. This has resulted in students questioning the gen-der of God. Likewise the distortion of "history" is very much in evidence in the 1990s. A group of school children was asked who the most evil man in the world was; without hesitation they answered, "Hitler." The same group knew nothing at all about Stalin, certainly not that he was the greatest butcher of humanity of all times who killed ten times as many people as Hitler is said to have caused to be murdered. Such a statement would bring looks of puzzlement to their faces.

The heroes of school children and students are not the great figures of histo-ry; rather their "idols" are the decadent, evil, unwashed, drug-ridden "pop stars." Beethoven and Brahms mean nothing to them, but they will at once show a real interest when the hideous sounds of "rock" music fill the air. On the other hand, Marxis known to most college students but they do not really know what he stood for. We have arrived at a point in education in our schools where "reform" is put above learning. In the 1990s, virtually every educational matter is attached to the word, "reform."

Nowhere has a greater transformation due to "reforms" taken place than in sex education. The Communists were determined that even the very youngest stu-dent be forced to learn about sex. Madame Zinoviev was in charge of the project in Bolshevik Russia, which she tried to transfer to the United States, but which was blocked in the 1920s by a Supreme Court *not yet packed with Socialist jus-tices,* and by the alertness of the Daughters of the American Revolution. The products of "feminist courses" now regard marriage as merely another contract. Sex has had the mystic taken out of it, so that today's college girl does not want to spend time forming an emotional relationship before indulging in "free love." We know that these ideas were prepared in Bolshevik Russia by Madame Kollontay and then transplanted to the United States by her.

Our badly-flawed educational system is turning out girls who are maladapt-ed toward society and the truth of the statement is borne out by crime statistics involving teenage girls. The drug culture is deeply embedded in the youth of the 1990s. Spiritual matters have been driven out of our schools. Today, our young students are the edge of the "Age of Socialist Enlightenment" where anything goes if it feels good.

Of all the sciences, political science is the oldest, its beginnings traceable to ancient Greece. Political Science covers the love of justice, and it explains why men want to rule. But political science is not taught properly in our educational institutions, which now teach a perverted form of it known as Socialism. If political science had been properly taught in our schools and colleges, Justice Warren would not have had such an easy time forcing Brown vs. Board of Education down our throats. Thus, by cunning, by stealth and deception did the Socialists work their way into the fateful Brown vs. Board Education ruling, which redirected education in the United States into Socialist/Marxist/Communist channels.

The Rockefeller and Carnegie Foundations funded a study-group composed of Margaret Meade, a new science anthropologist and Rensis Likert, to come up with a review of all educational policies governed by Biblical law. Meade used Tavistock Institute's reverse psychology technique to overcome what the report termed "a teaching problem." This report, which has had a devastating impact on education in the United States, remains classified to this day. One of the results of the Meade-Likert study was the emergence of the National Training Laboratories (NTL) with more than four million members. One of its affiliates was the National Education Association (NEA), the largest teachers organization in the world.

Thanks to the efforts of this organization and the hundreds upon thousands of Socialist teachers, secular, humanist education has come the full circle from its slow beginnings of 1940. By the 1990s the Socialists have mustered so many impressive victories in the Supreme Court that they are quite open about their intentions of altogether secularizing education. The new scheme, although not really new except in the choice of title, will drag American education down to the dust and leave our children among the most uneducated in the world.

Earlier, we mentioned the Tavistock Institute for Human Relations in Sussex University, England and the crucial role it has played in the economic, political, religious and educational life of the Nation. This organization was unknown in the United States until I published my works about it in the 1970s. Tavistock is under the direct control of the most powerful Socialist figures in Britain and is closely allied with British Freemasonry. It has the closest of contacts with the National Education Association, whose top management personnel were trained at the National Training Laboratories. This is the level at which "geopolitics" entered education at the teacher's level.

The "new" system is called, "Outcome Based Education" (OBE.) What OBE is going to do is teach our children that there is no need to learn to read and write properly, there is no need to excel in education; what matters is how they relate to each other and children from other races.

What is OBE? It is a system that punishes excellence and rewards mediocrity. *The OBE aims to make our children over into one level students where the ruling standard is mediocrity.* Why should this be so desirable? The obvious answer is that a nation in which the vast bulk of the population is educated at the lowest common denominator level, will be easy to steer toward a Socialist dictatorship. The basis for OBE was established with Brown vs. Board of Education, which in a very real sense, "pegged" education levels to the lowest common denominator.

What OBE will do is turn Christian American children into pagans, with no respect for their parents, and no love for country, children who will despise national identity and patriotism. The love of one's country is turned into something ugly, to be avoided at all costs. OBE teaches the Marxist concept that traditional family life is out of date. This is precisely what Madame Kollontay tried to force on the United States in the 1920s; it was what Socialists Bebel and Engels strove to introduce into mainstream education in America. Now, their wildest expectations are being fulfilled through OBE.

It is eerie, even uncanny, how OBE duplicates the writings of Bebel, Engels, Kollontay and Marx — almost a carbon copy of the haters of family life and the sanctity of marriage. It is uncanny how the system proposed in OBE is found almost word-for-word in the Communist Manifesto of 1848. We can only say that following the stunning successes of the Evers case and Brown vs. Board Education, Socializing education in America took off like a hurricane, and seemingly, today, there is no holding it back.

Justices Black and Douglas would have rejoiced if they were still with us, as would have Brandeis, Frankfurter and Earl Warren. OBE has seized control of the schools. Today, instead of having teachers, we have *change agents* who force acceptance of group views, which they, the facilitators, brainwash into the minds of the students. The "reforms" the facilitators carry out are turning children against their parents and their family values. The group leader in the class takes the place of the parent. There is always the notion that "inner reform" or "inner needs" must be catered to, and those "needs" mean anything the group leaders says they mean.

The old Socialist technique of "sexual education" is pushed far beyond anything previously encountered. In OBE there are group pairing with explicit sensuality training and promiscuity is actively encouraged. There is no attempt to foster a sense of history. Nothing is taught about the great leaders of the past who brought civilization to the world. The emphasis is on the present, "do it now" and "do it if it feels good." OBE is responsible for the tremendous upsurge in juvenile crime. The present and future generation of youth now being taught through OBE methods will become street mobs of today's "French Revolution," to be used for the same purposes, in the not too distant future.

There is no doubt that project OBE arose from the 1986 "World Curriculum" and from the book, "Brave New World," by Aldous Huxley in which he stated that a perfect world would be one without families, children without parents, in which a loathing and disgust were induced for the words, "father," "mother" and cared for by State social institutions, children whose allegiance would be only to the state. The quest for such a society goes back a long way, before "World Curriculum" and Huxley. The Communist Bebel wrote his version of how children ought to be regarded — as wards of the state. So did Marx, Engels, and particularly Madam Kollontay, whose work, "Communism and the Family" was the source of much of Huxley's "Brave New World."

Children would come via the test tube, and laboratories would match sperm to give a higher level of mentality, mid-level intelligence and lower intelligence. In their adult life these beings would be assigned various roles in a slave world, as I described in my book, "The Committee of 300." If this sounds too much for the reader to accept, then bear in mind that test tube babies are already with us. They have been accepted by society, not realizing the sinister purpose behind this ungodly development. Socialism needs a dullard mass and a small number of people of higher intelligence. The dullard masses will do the work in the slave-labor Socialist world, the intelligent class, the ruling. In such a world, we shall have "apartheid" such as would make the South African version look like a golden age of goodwill.

The reaction of readers to this information will be predictably one of skepticism. However, we need to examine *realities,* so let us see just how far OBE has come in matching Huxley, Kollontay, Engels and Bebel. House of Representatives bill, HR 485 is part of the Socialist agenda to "reform" education. President Clinton was selected to carry out a wide-ranging battery of reforms — and he is doing it with great speed and efficiency, knowing that he will be a single-term president. The Parents as Teachers (PAT) Socialist plan is already in action in 40 States. The so-called "Co-parenting Program" (COP) began with a pilot program in St. Louis, Missouri in 1981. The real intent of COP is to substitute parental authority with COP social workers, preferably in the pre-natal period.

Taking her cue from Aldous Huxley, Laura Rogers wrote a work she called, " The Brave New Family in Missouri" in which she stated that it has taken only *four years* for PAT to be accepted by the Missouri's State Legislature and that the PAT concept has spread to Europe and is being implemented in 40 States in America. Is this reality? Does it compare with what we have exposed in this chapter about educational "reforms?" The Socialists intend to "reform" education to such an extent that it will produce the very climate foretold by Huxley's "Brave New World." And they are doing it now, before our very eyes!

Under PAT, a so-called "educator" will attach himself or herself to a family — in the literal sense, and begin the process of changing attitudes of both parents and child or children to conform with Socialist ideals. How this is being done was explained by Rogers in her article, "The Brave New Family in Missouri:"

Step 1. The "parent-educator" will visit schools and homes "bond" herself to the family, under the guise of furthering the child's education.

Step 2. The child or children is given a computer identification number which will be permanent.

Step 3. The "change agent" will work toward changing the relationship between child and parents through a "mentoring program" such as happens in the Socialist Oxford University.

Step 4. "Parent educators" are required to report anything they deem "hostile behavior" or abuse by calling a "hotline" especially set up for this purpose.

Step 5. Judges will decided "hotline cases" and if the child or children are deemed at risk, the child or children may be removed from parental custody.

Step 6. If the mental health services recommendations of the "parent educator" are refused by the parents, such as what medication to be prescribed, the state can remove the child or children from parental custody. The child or children can be placed in a residential treatment center and the parents ordered by the courts to undergo "psychological counseling" for as long as the "parent teacher" deems necessary.

What the PAT program does, is set itself up as judge and jury in deciding who are fit and unfit parents! For this PAT uses what Rogers calls, "risk factor definitions" which have become the standard yardstick for measuring the fitness or unfitness of parents to raise children, and bear in mind, this criteria is being used at present in 40 States:

"Inability of parent to cope (which is not defined) with inappropriate child behavior (e.g., severe biting, destructive behavior, apathy)".

"Low-functioning parents." These are considered as potentially abusive parents. In this category the parent-teacher has a large number of options. Virtually *any* parent could come under the category of "low functioning."

"Undue stress that adversely affects family functions." This gives a virtually unlimited number of options to the parent teacher to cite as "abusive" danger signs, including low income.

"Other... This can include a wide variety of conditions such as allergies, heavy cigarette smoking in the house (does R.J. Reynolds know about this?), a family history of hearing loss..."

From the foregoing it is clear that Socialism in education has come of age in America. What Madame Kollontay, Engels, Bebel and Huxley found most desirous has now come to pass. Education is the way in which Socialism can be defeated, as so many of our statesmen in the 1800s made clear, but in the wrong hands, it is a mighty weapon which Socialism will wield without mercy to bring about their longed-for New World Order slave state. None of this would have been possible, but for the treason and treachery of the Supreme Court and especially the venomous attitude of Justices Douglas and Black, who should go down in history as two of the most vile traitors in the history of this Nation.

4

THE FEMALE OF THE SPECIES

All through history, women have played a decisive role. Before the 20th century, it was usually from the background, observing, giving advice and encouragement, never in an obtrusive manner, and seldom, if ever, publicly. But that was to change in the late 1800s, and the vehicle of change was the Fabian Society and International Socialism.

When the small, bespectacled Sydney Webb met the statuesque Martha Beatrice Potter, sparks began to fly. (Miss Potter preferred Beatrice, which had a better ring to it than Martha.) Both recognized in the other a peculiar genius for organizing and getting the day to day business done. Anthony and Cleopatra were more glamorous, the Queen of Sheba and Solomon more majestic; Hitler and Eva Braun more dramatic, but by comparison with the Webbs, their impact on the world was of a lesser degree. The damage done by the Webbs is still reverberating around the world, long after the other two somes have become mere historical figures.

Sydney Webb met Beatrice Potter in 1890. She was well endowed both physically and financially. He, by contrast, was short and small and had no money. Beatrice came from a family of Canadian railroad tycoons and she had her own income from her father. Perhaps what brought the Sydney and Beatrice together was their conceit, which they never bothered to hide. Beatrice had been angered and embittered by the rejection of her love-offering to "upper class" Joseph Chamberlain, which seems to be the fuel that kept her "class hatred" fires burning. Webb worked as a clerk in the British Colonial Office, considered a fairly low station in life in Victorian England.

In 1898 Beatrice and her husband turned their attention to the United States, going on a three-week "grand tour." During this time, the Webbs did not meet with rank and file members of labor unions nor any of the ladies slaving away in New York's garment district. Rather, they sought out, and were received by the elite of Socialism in New York, including Miss Jane Addams and Prestonia Martin, both right out of the Social Register.

This was a pattern that was to be followed by all Socialist/Bolshevik leaders in later years. In 1900, thanks largely to the work of Beatrice, the Royal Commission of London University ruled that henceforth, economics would be elevated to the status of a science. Beatrice lost no time in impressing Granville Barker, a theater man of note, and President Wilson's personal representative, Ray Stannard Baker, with this great achievement, at a lunch hosted by Beatrice and her husband.

The Webb-Potter partnership developed into marriage and set the fashion of a husband and wife team devoted more to Socialism than to each other in private, but for appearance sake, a very devoted couple. This was to prove a big draw card for attracting women into the ranks of social causes and politics, and can be said to be the birth of radical feminism. From Clements Inn, headquarters of the Fabian Society came the "Fabian News," published first in 1891. Beatrice was coauthor and her money paid for the cost of printing.

It came naturally to Beatrice that the best way to promote their ideal was through the elite of the land. While the ordinary people were good for Billy Graham-type "rallies" it was the elite who could get things done. In this regard, Beatrice never lost her snobbishness. As she saw it, they had to convert the elite first; the rest would follow. This was the pattern that Bolshevik leaders were to adopt in later years. One never saw Khrushchev staying at a dock workers cottage or having meetings with the rank and file of the trade unions during his visit to England and other West European countries. It was always to the elite to whom Khrushchev gave his rapt attention, Agnelli of Italy, Rockefeller of the United States, and so it was with all Socialist leaders.

It was no surprise that Beatrice began concentrating on the sons of the rich and the famous at Oxford University. How well she did her job can be judged from the number of high-society traitors, products of Oxford and Cambridge, who willingly betrayed the West in the cause of promoting their goal of a Socialist world revolution of whom Burgess, Mclean, Philby, Anthony Blunt, Roger Hollis are the best known, but certainly not the only ones. Underneath the mantle of social "reforms" was a deadly dangerous cancer eating away at Christian Western ideals, *and it was called Fabian Socialism.* One of its earliest converts of note was Walter Lippmann, whom Beatrice Webb "induced" to join the Fabian Society.

By 1910, Beatrice and her money had established several centers from where Fabian propaganda was disseminated. Writers, theater people, and politicians of the day were beginning to drift toward her circle. The general opinion was that Beatrice was running a nice, liberal, cultural movement, according to the "New Statesman." Millionaire Charlotte Payne-Townshend became a friend of Beatrice who was responsible for introducing her to George Bernard Shaw, after which Charlotte made an honest man of him. Now, both the male leaders could afford devote their entire time to promoting Socialism, thanks to the money of their respective spouses.

What has often been remarked upon is how these two women spent their lives attacking the very system that provided the money for their pursuits. Beatrice Webb was the guiding force in securing control of the Labour Party, just as in later years, another Socialist, Mrs Pamela Harriman, was to secure control of the Democrat Party in the United States and put in power a president whose Socialist agenda was designed to usher the country into a Socialist One World Government — New World Order.

Certainly Beatrice Webb worked tirelessly to wreck the economic policies and dismantle the social and economic order of an orderly England. What surprises me is that the Webbs were not arrested for sedition and treason, along with "Red" Professor Harold Laski. Had this happened, it might have saved the United States from Socialist oriented convulsions that are still going on. By now Beatrice numbered among her friends a Countess, and many of the famous ladies of London society at the time, including the wife of Sir Stafford Cripps. These devotees of radical feminism opened their homes to tea parties and weekend retreats in furtherance of Socialist causes.

Throughout her long reign, Beatrice Webb never wavered in her support of the Bolsheviks, which didn't seem to phase her long list of high-society contacts, including Sir William Beveridge who was to make a tremendous impact on politics in England and the United States.(The Beveridge Plan became the blueprint for Social Security in the United States.) When Beatrice died in 1943, her services to Socialism were recognized in a bizarre manner — Martha Beatrice Webb's ashes were interred in Westminster Cathedral — a strange place for an avowed atheist to find herself!

The tigress of the radical feminist, anti-marriage, anti-family movement that was given a window of opportunity to the world by the Fabian Socialists, was Madame Alexandra Kollontay. It is not known whether Beatrice Webb ever met Kollontay during her frequent trips to Moscow. Who was Madame Kollontay? On page 9972 of pages 9962-9977, Congressional Record, Senate of May 31, 1924 we find the following:

"Madame Kollontay is now Soviet minister to Norway, after a hectic career which included eight husbands, two positions as people's commissar, first as commissar of welfare, two visits to the United States (1915 and 1916), a German Socialist agitator, after having been deported from three European countries in 1914 as a dangerous revolutionist..." Then there is a further expose of this hard-core Communist world revolutionary radical feminist, on page 4599 of pages 4582-4604:

"...Recently there came to Mexico as the ambassador of the Soviet Union, one Alexandra Kollontay. She is said to be a leader in the world revolutionary movement for 28 years; that she has been arrested in three different countries because of her effort in 1916 and in 1917 she visited the United States speaking from coast to coast. She was under the management of Ludwig Lore, now a prominent Communist in the United States. The object and purpose of the visit of Kollontay to the United States in 1916 and 1917 was to incite the Socialists of this country and to hamper our activities if the United States entered through a system of resistance by what took place. Alexandra Kollontay is the world's greatest exponent of 'free love' and nationalization of children. She is in Mexico for that purpose and bodes no good to the people off the United States."

Kollontay' s book, "Communism and the Family" is the most violent and savage attack on marriage and the family ever written, surpassing the decadent evil of Fredric Engels' "Origin of the Family." Kollontay's radical 'free love' followers formerly called themselves the "International League of Peace and Freedom." But they have undergone a number of name changes to disguise the fact that their agenda is still the same as that of Alexandra Kollontay: to day they call themselves the National League of Women Voters and the National Abortion Rights League (NARL) They also have the audacity to go by the label of "pro choice advocates" meaning that they have a choice of whether or not to murder unborn children.

The goals of the Marxist/Socialist "liberal feminists" — better known as radical feminists — were outlined in the 1920s-1930s and they have not changed. The clamor for "women's rights" is for love without responsibility — i.e. abortion on demand. They and their incendiary Socialists in the House and Senate are in an unholy alliance with the jackals of the media, which began in the days of Florence Kelley.

Kollontay was the standard bearer of the crop of radical feminists with which this country is cursed today. The Overman Committee on Bolshevism of the United States reported as follows:

"The apparent purpose of the Bolshevik government of Russia is to make the Russian citizen especially the women and children, wards dependent on that government...It has destroyed the natural ambition and made impossible of accomplishment the moral obligation to provide care for, and adequately protect the child against the misfortunes of orphanhood and widowhood...They have promulgated decrees relating to marriage and divorce which practically establish 'free love.'" Senate Document page 61, 1st Session, Pages 36-37 Congressional Record.

The foregoing fits perfectly the aims and objectives of Fabian Socialism. Radical feminism, rampant and running wild across the United States today is a Socialist teaching. The Fabian Society's Socialist pattern allowed for radical feminism, indeed, encouraged it while at the same time cloaking it in a veil of domesticity. While Beatrice Webb and her associates were not able to establish open abortion houses, it is worth repeating that Mrs. Harold Laski, wife Professor Laski, of one of the great names in Socialist circles, was the first one to push the idea of birth control counseling centers in England.

Dr. Annie Besant was well-known to Beatrice Webb through Liberal Party circles in London. Besant was the successor to Madame Blavatsky and inherited her Theosophy Society, whose adherents were to be found among the rich and the famous in elite circles of power in Victorian England. Besant played no small role in instigating unrest via the drawing room, her first venture being an attack on industry in Lancashire, a large industrial center in England.

As the head of Co-Masonry allied to KKK "Clarte" (no connection to the KKK in the U.S.) and the Grand Orient Nine Sisters Lodge in Paris, Besant was very active in promoting what she called, "social democracy" but all the time she was under the control of the Grand Orient Lodge in Paris, from whom she received the title of Vice President of the Supreme Council and Grand Master of the Supreme Council for Britain. It is here where the convergence of Freemasonry, Theosophy and the Fellowship of Faiths becomes clearly recognizable.

H.G. Wells was a believer in Besant's notions, probably, because like Besant, he was a member of KKK "Clarte" as was Inez Milholland. Both Socialist ladies worked hard for the cause of women's suffrage, which Sydney Webb astutely saw as the wave of the future when it came to getting votes for the Labor and Liberal Parties.

Whatever Besant became, she owed to Madame Petrova Blavatsky, who, in turn, owed her rapid rise up the social ladder to Herbert Burrows who promoted her "talents" through the Society for Physical Research, a select club for the rich, the aristocracy and the politically powerful in Victorian London circles. These circles were patronized by H.G. Wells and Conan Doyle (later Sir Arthur Conan Doyle.) Wells described Blavatsky as "one of the most accomplished, ingenuous and interesting imposters in the world."

Blavatsky was initiated into Carbonari Masonry by the undoubted leader of that Lodge in Italy, the great Mazzini. She was also close to Garabaldi, and was with him at the battles of Viterbro and Mentana. Two men who greatly influenced her life were, Victor Migal and Riavli, both Freemason revolutionaries inside the Grand Orient Lodge. She died in 1891, a hardened and confirmed Socialist.

Susan Lawrence was one of the first three Labour Party candidates elected to Parliament as a result of the work done by the suffrage movement, spearheaded by Fabian Society warriors Ellen Wilkinson and Emily Pankhurst. Lawrence became famous for her statement, "I don't preach Class War, I live it." Margaret Cole developed her instinct for radical feminism by working as are searcher for the Fabian Society. She was later able to put what she learned to good use when she served in the British Ministry of Labour, while her husband, G.D.H. Cole, rose to great prominence in a succession of Labour Governments. Like the Webbs, the Coles maintained an outward appearance of domestic bliss, but theirs was a marriage of Socialist convenience.

One of Beatrice Webb's star pupils was Margaret Cole, who wrote "The Story of Fabian Socialism" in which the goals of radical feminism are given a coating of sugar to attract the flies. Cole was responsible for much of the penetration and permeation of Fabian Socialism in America. It is believed by Fabian Socialist researchers that the nullifying of the Lusk Report through the veto of New York Governor Al Smith perfectly fits Fabian Socialism's dictum: "Get someone-Socialist to do the dirty work for you." Cole was a member of the delegation of International Confederation of Free Trade Unions at the United Nations.

Over in the United States, one of the most important of the female Socialists was Florence Kelley. Her real name was Weschenewtsky. Nobody seemed to know much about her, except that Kelley had studied Lenin and Marx in Switzerland, the international haven for revolutionaries. She liked to call herself a "Quaker Marxist," sometimes a "Marxist Quaker." One thing that the Fabian Socialists did know was that Kelley was leading the "reform" charge in the United States. At times she overshadowed her more famous friend, Eleanor Roosevelt, persuading Roosevelt to join the Socialist National Consumers League (NCL) of which she was one of the founder members.

The NCL, a dedicated Socialist institution, was an organization bent on getting the Federal Government involved in health, education and police powers that belonged to the States under the 10th Amendment of the United States Constitution. Kelley proved a genius in this regard. She is credited with formulating the so-called "Brandeis Brief" strategy which consisted of burying a thin legal case in masses of irrelevant documents so that the case was decided, eventually, not on law, but on Socialist-slanted sociology and economic "juridical notice." Since the judges were not trained in sociology, they were not the people to judge the merits of the SOCIOLOGY of the case before them, so that such cases were generally decided in favor of the Socialists.

Elizabeth Glendower, an extremely wealthy socialite often had Kelley as a house guest along with Brandeis and the top Socialist writers of the day. Kelley is known to have struck up a close friendship with Upton Sinclair, whose early literary works were made up of bundle after bundle of Fabian Socialist "position papers" which were sent to Socialist university students for distribution on campuses around the nation. In spite of her denials, Kelley was a ceaseless opportunity-seeker in promoting the cause of world revolution.

Mrs. Robert Lovett, whose husband held the position of professor of English at the University of Chicago, was a close ally of Kelley. The Lovetts, Kelley and Jane Addams ran a Socialist induction center named Hull House, which was frequented by Eleanor Roosevelt and Frances Perkins. Many Hull House members traveled to England to take part in the Fabian Society Summer Schools program. Kelley was good at making converts to Socialism, and was a tireless missionary in the service of American Socialism.

Socialist women came on the scene in the United States at the close of the Civil War. Communists were very active in the runup to the war and in its immediate aftermath, a fact that is not mentioned by establishment history books, and these Socialist "feminists" were very successful in penetrating and permeating legitimate women's organizations concerned with the well being of their families.

This was relatively easy for trained Fabian Socialists, given the custom of the time of putting women on a pedestal of respect, deserving of male protection. Some of the leaders of the "carpet baggers" were deeply-committed Socialists or Communists. When the question of women's suffrage was being raised by women Socialists, men felt it was not well advised to expose women to the rough and ready of politics, but they did not know their tough female Socialists.

Others were fully aware of how the Socialists and Communists were recruiting militant, aggressive females and training them to go against mainstream feminism. The attitude of the period is well expressed on pages 165-170 Appendix to the Congressional Globe, "Suffrage Constitutional Amendment." The Hon J.A. Bayard said of Socialism in 1869:

"The next exception is that of sex. I will not argue this position either with the Communists or the Socialists, nor with the women's rights party, because of the folly of this species off a naticism, though, it has made great progress lately, is not sufficiently widespread to need elaboration or refutation. Inordinate vanity and love of notoriety may have tempted some women to unsex themselves, both in their dress and their pursuits; but women's hearts and the instincts of maternity will keep her true to the greatest of her duties in life, the culture and the formation of the character of her offspring..."

That it was the age of chivalry, which has been thoroughly destroyed by Hillary Rodham Clinton, Bella Abzug, Eleanor Smeal, Elizabeth Holtzman, Pat Schroeder, Barbara Boxer, Dianne Feinstein and their close relatives, is found on page 169 of the Appendix to the Congressional Globes (Speech by Senator Bayard):

"I feel proud and gratified that in this country, our own America, there is a chivalrous devotion to sex which has not been equaled in any other country. I yield to none in my deference to sex, and a desire to secure and protect women in all her rights; *but a suffrage is not a right...*" It is interesting how much the Socialists used legitimate concerns felt by feminine society and turned them into a vehicle for Socialist causes, to telling effect. It is due to the natural consequence of such penetration and permeation by clever Fabian Socialists that the United States Congress became the stamping ground for a hardened, unfeminine cadre of women who turned chivalry on its head in their fierce desire to see Fabian Socialism take over the United States.

Some of the so-called "women's rights" Socialist fronts were the following:
General Federation of Women's Clubs.
National Congress of Mothers and Parent-Teachers Association.
National League of Women Voters.
National Federation of Business and Professional Women.

Christian Temperance Union.
Association of University Women.
National Council of Jewish Women.
League of Womens' Voters.
National Consumers League.
Women's Trade Union League.
Women's International League.
Girl's Friendly Society America.

These organizations were a party to a court action brought by Mrs. Florence Kelley and several leading "feminists" (Socialists) in July of 1926. They were trying to get a bill passed, "Maternity and Infancy Act," which violated the 10th Amendment to the United States Constitution, but the Supreme Court, free of the control exercised over it today (which began with the Roosevelt era) saved the nation from a Socialist bid to completely take-over the United States. President Carter took most of the material in Madame Kollontay's book, "Communism and the Family" for his education bill

It was always the intention of the Socialists to nationalize the children of America. Socialist Shirley Hufstedler, who at one time headed the unconstitutional U. S. Department of Education took her cue from Madame Lelina Zinoviev, wife of Gregory Zinoviev. Hufstedler was seeking to "nationalize" and "internationalize" American children to fit them for their future role as race-mixers in a One World Government.

This was also the intention of Frances Perkins, a trained social worker who led the so-called "feminist movement" in the United States for many years. Perkins was Governor Franklin D. Roosevelt's New York State Commissioner of Labor. She counted Eleanor Roosevelt as one of her closest female friends, and Kelley was close to Roosevelt during his three-term stay at the White House. One of Perkins' first assignments was founding the International Association for Labor Legislation along with Eleanor Roosevelt and her protege, Harry L. Hopkins, with whom Perkins worked closely to bring in work relief for the unemployed in New York State.

The original plan came from a Socialist group known as the Association for Improving the Condition of the Poor. Perkins and her friends pushed all the right buttons and pulled out the right stops to get their "reforms" passed by the New York State Legislature. Hundreds of booklets and pamphlets were distributed throughout schools and universities to elicit support for these "beneficial changes" while kept writers churned out articles which were snapped up by the jackal press. Scores of "polls" were run to create "popular sentiment" for labor "reforms" that could only "benefit the whole country."

Perkins wore many hats, and was noted for her tireless energy and devotion to the Fabian Socialist movement in the United States. When Roosevelt moved from Albany to Washington, Perkins went with him. She was the first women to be named to a cabinet post in the history of the United States. Her influence with Roosevelt was only slightly less than that of Eleanor Roosevelt.

Perkins remained with Roosevelt, from the very first to the very last day of his three terms in office, during which time she introduced a veritable flood of Socialist legal personnel, economists, statisticians and analysts into the Federal government. When John Maynard Keynes went calling on Roosevelt and tried to explain his economic theories without much success, it was Perkins who sold them to Roosevelt. Perkins swallowed the "multiplier" theory, making the near immortal observation that "with (Keynes's) system, with one dollar you have created four dollars."

Perkins concocted the scheme to rig the 1940 Democrat Convention, which gave Roosevelt his third term, although the "credit" for this has generally gone to Harry Hopkins. Early in the days of Roosevelt's Governorship of New York, Perkins was the lobbyists for the National Consumers League and the Women's Trade Council in Albany, New York.

Her contacts among leading Socialist intellectuals of the day is said to have numbered in the hundreds and she was a favorite of Felix Frankfurter. Another of her male supporters was Harry Hopkins, who was to rise to tremendous heights in the Roosevelt era and do tremendous harm to the United States. Perkins brought a host of Socialist economists and labor specialist professors with her to Washington, from where they poured out a veritable torrent of Socialist material, much of it still taught in universities today. More than any other women — including Eleanor Roosevelt, Perkins influenced Roosevelt to get the United States into WWII.

Perkins is credited with writing the nation's unemployment insurance and old age pension legislation. At the request of President Roosevelt, Perkins worked behind the scenes to bring these two socialist dreams to reality, using Prestonia Martin's " Prohibiting Poverty" as a guidebook. Perkins received much help from John Maynard Keynes, who visited the United States in 1934 as a Fabian Socialist ambassador of goodwill. Keynes and Perkins agreed that Socialism had a priceless opportunity to make great strides during the tenure of Roosevelt.

Like almost all of the New Deal, which was taken virtually verbatim from Graham Wallas' book of the same name, "Prohibiting Poverty" was widely used to formulate a system for setting up compulsory social insurance (Social Security.) Perkins had sought and obtained a great deal of input from Sydney and Beatrice Webb, who pointed out to Perkins and Roosevelt, that the Fabian Society had drafted the Labor Party's 1918 election plank and had a lot of influence in writing the Beveridge Plan which became the basis of Britain's Social Welfare.

Thus, "The New Deal" by Graham Wallas, the Beveridge Plan, and Sydney

Webb's proposals written for the Labor Party in 1918, and the economic "tax and spend" principles of the Fabian Society's John Maynard Keynes, were with adaptations and minor adjustments the basis of Roosevelt's "New Deal." The role played by Frances Perkins in bringing this to pass cannot be overstated. People often ask me, with deep doubt in their voices, "How could the British possibly influence, let alone run a country like the United States, as you aver?" The Social Security Act of 1936 was the work of Sir William Beveridge, Professor Graham Wallas and Fabian Society director, Sydney Webb, touched up and rounded off by Frances Perkins. A study of how this was achieved and the role played by Frances Perkins answers the question of all Doubting Thomases far better than any words of mine could ever do.

The Social Security Act of 1936 was pure Fabian Socialism in action. It was unprecedented in the history of the United States and also 100 percent unconstitutional. I spent a good deal of time researching Congressional Records of 1935-1940 and beyond to see if I could find anything that would have made this piece of outright Socialist legislation constitutional, but to no avail.

The manner in which this Socialist heist of the American people was carried out is a case history of how the Socialists will go to extraordinary lengths to get their patently absurd laws sanctified by the Supreme Court. Perkins facing this dilemma, saw no way out of it. Roosevelt needed the Social Security Act to become law so that he could use it to get reelected. Thanks to the intercession of Harry Hopkins, Brandeis and Cardoza, Perkins found herself seated next to Socialist Justice Harlan Stone, a leading Liberal, at a Washington dinner party, at the height of the crisis.

Secretary Perkins told Justice Harlan Stone that she was up against the Constitution and needed away to fund Social Security that would pass muster the Supreme Court. In breach of every judicial etiquette, if not a gross violation of the law, Justice Stone whispered in Perkins' ear, "the taxing power of the Federal Government, my dear, the taxing power of the Federal Government is sufficient for, everything you want and need." Perkins took Justice Harlan Stones advice, and that is how today we come to have Socialist Social Security in a Confederated Republic. There is no doubt at all that Justice Stone ought to have been impeached, but no charges were ever brought against him.

Perkins kept the Justice's confidence, telling no one but Roosevelt who immediately used this grossly illegal stratagem to fund every single one of his Socialist New Deal programs. Later, Harry Hopkins was let into the secret, and he was allowed to take credit for the phrase, "tax and spend, tax and spend."

Perkins was a confidant and friend of Henry Morganthau, Justice Hugo Black, and Susan Lawrence, the formidable Member of Parliament and top Fabian Society executive. Perkins was one of the leading personalities in the attempted takeover of the United States by Socialists in the 1920s — a deadly scheme that was modeled along the lines of "Philip Dru-Administrator" the book written by Col. Edward Mandel House.

According to what Susan Lawrence told Jane Addams, it was by "one of history's strangest freaks, the elaborate system of checks and balances devised in the American Constitution has resulted for the moment at any rate, in the complete personal ascendancy of Franklin Roosevelt." However, a quick look at "Philip Dru-Administrator" shows that rather than due to happenstance, it was elaborate planning and a careful heed of Colonel House's technique that placed Roosevelt in the top slot, ready to seize control of the Democrat Party.

When the time came, Frances Perkins was right there with her former employer. A product of Hull House, a professional social worker, Perkins has been described as the Socialist's best opportunist. Perkins moved easily in the circles of British Fabian Society "aristocracy" and she learned her lessons well at the hands of Lilian Wald, Jane Addams and Eleanor Roosevelt. When the moment for her edification came, she was ready. If there were two main women conspirators in the 1920s they would be Kelley and Perkins. The latter's devotion to Socialism was what caught the attention of Mary Rumsey, the Socialist sister of Averill Harriman.

Mary Harriman Rumsey was the earliest of a band of enthusiastic New Deal proponents who urged the adoption of the Fabian Society' s blueprint, adapted to fit American conditions. Rumsey came from one of the top elitist families in the United States in the 1930s. Her close association with Eleanor Roosevelt helped to sharpen her already deeply committed Socialist activism. Rumsey was a tireless reader of the writings of Sydney Webb, Shaw, Haldane, Muggeridge and Graham Wallas.

Her life-long friendship with Frances Perkins developed after they met through Eleanor Roosevelt and quickly discovered their common passion for Socialist causes, which Rumsey was quick to insist be followed by her illustrious brother, Averill Harriman, who became a devout Socialist and intimate of a succession of Bolshevik leaders. Rumsey's Socialist endeavors took her all over the United States and Europe, and in England she was feted by the Webbs and the blue blood aristocracy Fabian Society members.

What was often remarked at the time was how this women whose social graces marked her clearly as from the top drawer of society, came to be inciting women trade union leaders and working in among women trade union rank and file where she was seemingly quite at home. Clearly Fabian Socialism had left an indelible imprint on the life of Mary Rumsey, reputed to have been among the top five richest women in America.

Mary Rumsey's long friendship with the genteel Miss Jane Addams, "ladylike to her fingertips" as a social columnist of one of the New York papers once wrote, was yet another of those anachronisms that seemed to flout conventional classification of Socialists on both sides of the Atlantic. Addams was the driving force behind Hull House, that Fabian Socialist "think tank" where the female elite of the day were introduced to Socialist beliefs. When Beatrice and Sydney Webb visited the United States in April of 1898, they were guests of Miss Addams. The former "clerk in the Colonial Office" was said to have been bewitched by the command of the English language displayed by Addams, and "her beautiful dark eyes."

A spinster all of her life, Addams commanded the respect of men like Colonel Edward Mandel House, H.G. Wells. Arthur Conan Doyle, and Sir Arthur Willert, a leading British Fabian newspaperman.

Addams was heavily involved in the founding of the One World Government Church, a Socialist compromise with religion, which was set to become the official "religion" of the One World Government, whose history we detail elsewhere herein.

Addams was a true Socialist "pacifist" who was awarded the Nobel Prize for her efforts to promote "international peace." Addams founded the Women's International League in conjunction with Mrs. Pethwick Lawrence, who was a member of the "upper crust" of British society and a notable London society figure at the turn of the century. Like Addams, she was a member of KKK — "Clarte" and Co-Masonry. Note the high-society names, not the kind that one would associate with anarchists and revolutionary bombers, yet the damage done to the United States by these notable female devotees of Socialism, in many instances, transcended the impact of the radicals.

Addams was received by two American presidents and was an enthusiastic backer of the Wall Street bankers who had invested in Lenin and Trotsky, and a stockholder in Lenin's Russian American Industrial Corporation and the Communist Federation Press. Addams was connected with the American Society for Cultural Relations with Russia, which distributed Fellowship of Faith publications, mostly to bookstores specializing in Socialist/Communist literature.

Her close friendship with Rosika Schwimmer was important, because Schwimmer had the ear of Count Karloyi, the man who handed Hungary on a bloody plate to the foul beast, Bela Kuhn (real name Cohen) who murdered hundreds of thousands of Christians in Hungary, before he could be expelled. Addams was the Socialist who arranged a lecture tour for the bloody, fiendish Count Karloyi.

The female devotees of Fabian Socialism were rich, powerful with the right family connections that ensured that their strongly-Socialist ideas had an appreciative audience. The impact of Socialist women like Webb, Perkins, Rumsey and Mrs. Pethwick Lawrence, Addams, Besant, on a series of key events in the United States and Britain has not ever been fully described nor properly understood today. These aristocratic looking and sounding ladies would have contrasted very markedly with the Boxers, Feinsteins Abzugs and Schroeders of the "women's rights" movement in the United States. Of all females in political activism in the

1980s-1990s, only Margaret Thatcher would have been at home with Jane
Addams, whose frequent visits to London, while not netting her an invitation to
No. 10 Downing Street, made her the darling of the Fabian Society and its lead-
ers, Beatrice and Sydney Webb.

Addams' manners and refined speech hid an interior as hard as nails and a
spirit that refused to back down, even against great odds. Although never admitted, Addams was the one who profoundly influenced Robert Mors Lovett, the
man chosen to lead the Fabian Socialist push in the United States. A more unlikely leader for Socialist causes was not to be found. Reserved and aloof, Lovett was
transformed into a firebrand after meeting with Addams at Hull House. In many
way, Lovett's campaign for socializing America was one of the most important
battles ever fought by Socialist's "greats." Harry Hopkins, the man who started
more runaway forest fires for Fabian Socialism in America than any other single
individual in the Socialist ranks, owed his job to Addams, who strongly recommended him to Roosevelt in 1932.

Addams topped the list of female Socialist and was awarded the Nobel Peace
Prize for her pacifist activities on behalf of the Socialist agenda for the United
States. She carried on her Socialist crusade under the umbrella of the Women's
International League for Peace, which she founded in Chicago, and which became
a Communist front for "peace," dearly loved by the Bolshevik leaders. Addams
made a detailed study of Fabian Society publications, especially those distilled
from Madame Kollontay's books attacking marriage and the family, and most of
her time was devoted to Socialist anti-family causes in the United States.

Although they were never close, Dorothy Whitney Straight (Mrs. Leonard
Elmhurst) was an admirer of Addams. The Whitney-Straights like Addams, were
straight out of the top drawer of American high society. Dorothy Whitney-
Straight's brother was a partner in J.P. Morgan, which gave the Whitney-Straights
carte blanche entre into the smart set in Fabian Socialist circles in London, New
York and Washington. The Whitney-Straights financed the American Fabian
Socialist publication, "New Republic" (Dorothy was its largest stockholder) to
which Walter Lippmann was a regular contributor as well as the leading Socialist
professors at Oxford and Harvard. Professor Harold Laski was one of the favorite
"New Republic" writers. Dorothy Whitney Straight was an enthusiastic backer of
President Woodrow Wilson.

After her marriage to Leonard K. Elmhurst, Dorothy moved court from her
Long Island estate to Dartinton Hall, Totnes, Devonshire, England, "where her
heart was" as she told friends, in order to be closer to the center of Fabian
Socialist power. There she mixed with the "greats" of British Socialists, like Lord
Eustis Perry, Sir Oswald Mosely and Grahame Haldane. In 1931 Dorothy and the
Webbs were busy with their plans to introduce the New Deal to the United States
in anticipation of the coming of Franklin Roosevelt. In order not to arouse suspi-

cion, at Dorothy's suggestion, the plan was called "Political and Economic Planning" (PEP) although Moses Sieff, one of the original members was unwise to mention PEP as being "our New Deal" in a speech he delivered to Fabian Socialists in London in 1934.

From the very first, PEP was a subversive organization bent on undermining the Constitution of the Republic of the United States, and no single member worked to that end in a more tireless manner than Dorothy Whitney Straight. Of her endeavors, Congressman Louis T. McFadden had this to say:

"May I point out to you that this is a secret organization with tremendous power? The definition of their organization is as follows:

A group of people who are actively engaged in production and distribution in the social services in town and country plan, in finance, education, in research, in persuasion, and in various other key functions within the United Kingdom...."
McFadden called the group a " brain trust", which, he said, *"is supposed to influence the present United States policy of trade tariffs.* Neither you nor I are particularly interested in what takes place in England, but what should interest us both is that there is a strong possibility that certain members of the brain trust around our President are in touch with this British organization, working to introduce a similar plan in the United States...I am assured by serious people, who are in a position to know that this organization practically controls the British Government and that this highly organized and well-financed movement is intended to practically sovietize the English-speaking race."

The huge damage done to trade barriers so wisely erected by past presidents of this country to protect the well being of her citizens is recounted elsewhere in this book. McFadden accused the American counterpart to Dorothy Whitney Straight's English "brain trust" of consisting of Professors Frankfurter, Tugwell, and William C. Bullit (the man who sabotaged the White Russian Army's almost certain defeat of the Bolshevik Red Army). Of them McFadden said, "I think there is no doubt that these men belong to this particular organization with distinct Bolshevik tendencies, and that this plan will be developed in the United States..."

In this Dorothy Whitney Straight had the always-available counsel of Felix Frankfurter who had been a frequent visitor to her Long Island estate before she moved to Devonshire. The fabulous wealth of the Whitney-Straight family was what financed not only the "New Statesman" but also PEP and scores of other Fabian Society front organizations and their activities.

Dorothy held court at her lavish Devonshire estate like the royalty she longed to be a part of. In addition to Frankfurter, frequent visitors were J.B. Priestly, a writer of note, Israel Moses Sieff, Richard Bailey and Sir Julian Huxley, Lord Melchett and Malcolm McDonald, son of Ramsay McDonald. Although these names may not be well known to Americans, they are the names of men who were at the top of the Fabian Socialist ladder. But one American who did recognize these names was Congressman Louis T. McFadden, Chairman of the House Banking Committee.

McFadden had long suspected Dorothy Whitney-Straight of being a traitor to her country, and during a speech in the House, McFadden wanted to know what Dorothy and her entourage were planning and how it would affect the United States. He queried why one Moses Sieff, would be talking about the "New Deal" as "our New Deal." McFadden revealed the strong connection between British Fabian Socialists and American Socialists and Communists whom he knew to be actively working to bring down the Republic of the United States: "The political economic plan (PEP) is now secretly operating in England." What was the goal of Dorothy Whitney Straight's PEP?" According to McFadden, it was something their secret publications had revealed to its "insiders:"

"The method of work is to bring together as a group a number of people who are concerned professionally with one or another aspect of the problem (how to break down the Constitution of the United States) under discussion, as well as a few non-specialists who can ask the fundamentals questions which sometimes escape the experts.

This technique enables the PEP to bring to bear on a problem the combined experience of men and women working in different spheres including business, politics, the Government and local authority services and universities..."

"...The names of those who form the groups are not disclosed...This rule was adopted deliberately from the first and has proved of great value. It enables people to serve who would not otherwise be able to serve; it ensures that the members can contribute freely to discussion without being bound by official views of any body with which they may be identified... It is a strict condition of anonymity that this broadsheet goes to you. It is essential in order that the group may prove effective as a nonpartisan organization making its contributions outside the field of personal and party polemics..."

It has been shown to me by intelligence contacts that 90 percent of the Congressional (House and Senate) staffers work in this manner. The hearings of the Senate Committee on Judge Clarence Thomas were an amazing revelation of how this Socialist "penetrate and permeate" tactic is still widely used inside every branch of Government in America, in the Church, in education and in places wherever vitally important decisions regarding the future of the United States of America are made.

The rule of Fabian Socialist secrecy successfully sheltered the often treasonable activities of PEP from the eyes of the American public. It was through PEP and many of the other highly secretive Fabian Socialist organizations that Socialism was almost successful in taking over the United States in the 1920s-1930s. Modeled on the British Fabian Society PEP model, the American version was called the National Planning Association (NPA) and Felix Frankfurter was the man chosen by Dorothy Whitney Straight Elmhurst to get it up and running in the United States. Thanks to an alert Supreme Court as yet untainted, many of NPA' s programs were thrown out. Dorothy Whitney-Straight was not perturbed by this and urged her fellow Socialists never to give up on their goal — the upending of the United States. She was truly the more dangerous of the female species of the Fabian Society.

Although not a personal friend of any of the high society Fabian Socialist ladies, the name of Laura Spellman must be included here, if for no other reason than to point out the extraordinary good fortune Socialism always seems to have in gaining unlimited access to very substantial funding. The Laura Spellman Fund kicked off with a capital of $10,000,000, but in practice there was no bottom to the Spellman well when it came to promoting Socialist programs in the United States. Usually these were called "reforms" in true Fabian Socialist style.

One of the "reforms" was that of undermining the United States Constitution. When Senator Joseph McCarthy was so close to blowing the lid off Socialist and Communist penetration of the United States Government, the Laura Spellman Fund gave unlimited grants to those who conducted research into the backgrounds of Martin Dies and Sen. McCarthy, and who were able to come up with anything that would discredit them. Thus the Spellman Fund was in an indirect manner, responsible for the dangerous attack on the Constitution of the United States which had reached frightening levels, and which Dies and McCarthy were threatening to expose.

The political prostitute, Senator William B. Benton, who led the charge against McCarthy was provided with all the support that Spellman money could buy when he demanded that Sen. McCarthy be expelled from the Senate. Benton's name will forever be synonymous with Aaron Burr and wanton treason and sedition. Benton was closely associated with the Fabian Socialist New Deal and his firm, Benton and Bowles got lucrative contracts from the British Labor Government. Benton was also closely associated with the Rockefeller National Bureau of Economic Research (devoted to pushing Laski's economic welfare state) and Owen Lattimore, one of the worst traitors ever found in this country. This is the Benton who incredulously, asked McCarthy if he felt no shame about his investigation of the Army, which was essentially to root out Socialist treason mongers in the United States Government.

Later, when it merged with the Rockefeller Brothers Fund, Spellman donated $3 million to Harold Laski's London School of Economics which opened the doors for Socialism's entry into the highest circles of the Government of the United States. Laura Spellman's money went into an intensive drive to introduce Marxist "educational" and "economic" programs into American schools and universities. Millions of dollars went into these Socialist programs, whose far reaching consequences we will probably never be able to measure, and which forever altered the shape and direction of education in this country.

The one overriding obsession of these female Socialists was the destruction of the American tradition of the family. As Sir Paul Dukes, one of the leading specialists on Bolshevism in the 1920s said: "The central tragedy of the Bolshevik regime in Russia is an organized effort to subvert and corrupt the minds of children...It has always been a Bolshevik principle to fight the institution of the family. Madame Kollontay's writings can leave no doubt on that score, even in the mind of the skeptical. The idea was to remove children at avery early age from parental care and bring them up in colonies."

The damage done by Eleanor Roosevelt has been told many times over and does not need to be retold here. Suffice to say that the so called feminist movement to which she devoted so much time in the 1920 and 1930s is thriving and has never been stronger than it is in the United States in 1994. Eleanor was the first to openly sanction lesbianism through her illicit relations with Lorena Hicock, whose love letters are to be found in the Hyde Park home of the Roosevelts. Perhaps the one event that showed us just how militant and powerful this Socialist activist group has become was the Anita Hill-Clarence Thomas struggle before a national audience of millions. What is worth noting is the number of so-called "women's rights" and "feminist" organizations that have sprung and mushroomed since the days of Eleanor Roosevelt.

The names of individual Socialist leaders and their "feminist" organizations are legion like the demons mentioned in the Bible. It is not my intention to single out each and every one of them for special mention-that is beyond the scope of this book. Therefore, I am obliged to draw attention to only the top people in the female Socialist hierarchy, who have followed the Socialist rule, penetrate and permeate. The stunning success of male Socialists in penetrating every branch of the United States government, and local and State government, permeating private institutions and organizations, would have been proudly hailed by Perkins, Kelley and Dorothy Whitney-Straight.

They would have loved Barbara Streisand, a raucous-voiced "entertainer" whose counsel reaches right into the Clinton White House. It is a measure of how the United States has been dragged down to levels never imagined by the great statesmen of the past — Washington, Jefferson, Jackson — that Streisand actually "sleeps over" at the White House when she is in town. Streisand and Bella Abzug are like two peas in a pod. Strident, combative, deeply committed to Socialist/Marxist ideals, both live in luxury while pretending to speak for the poor.

Abzug got herself appointed to the House of Representatives, essentially on the Jewish bloc vote, and once there, she began to make her gratingly loud voice heard, especially in the so-called "abortion rights" issue, which I might add in passing has no basis in law as it its outside the ken and the pale of the Constitution and is therefore, null and void.

Abzug went around the halls of Congress literally screaming at anyone who was against radical "free love" feminism. In this she was assisted by one of the worst frauds in the feminism business, Norma McCorvey, the "Jane Roe" of Roe vs. Wade. McCorvey wasn't even pregnant at the time the issue was raised. She was touted as a "great scholar" by the Abzug crowd when in fact her degree came from the unaccredited New College Law School in San Francisco, the same feminist organization that gave Anita Hill her law degree!

Some, although not all of the radical feminist organizations are the following:
The Margaret Bent Lawyers Achievement
The American Civil Liberties Union
National Women's Law Center
New College Law School
Ad Hoc Committee on Public Education on Sexual Harassment
Alliance for Justice
Center for Law and Special Policy
National Organization for Women (NOW)
Organization for the Advancement of Women
Planned Parenthood
National Abortion Rights Action League (NARL)
Women's Legal Defense Fund

The majority of these radical women's rights organizations want to use the Constitution to protect them while they go about their business of Socializing the United States — a legacy handed down to them by Felix Frankfurter. From time to time they utter pious platitudes about protection of individual rights, ninety nine percent of which are not found in the Constitution, while advocating the overthrow of the very Constitution by which they are protected.

The Socialist "Maternity and Infancy Act" introduced by Florence Kelley, the forerunner of Bella Abzug was lifted straight out of the Bolshevik system which Madame Zinoviev outlined for the world nationalization of children. What Bella Abzug and Pat Schroeder call "women's rights" amount to nothing less than female anarchy and is not found in the Constitution of the United States. Most of what these female Socialist aspire to, comes from Alexandra Kollontay's "Communism and the Family, Bebel's "Women and Socialism" and Engel's "Origin of the Family." So-called "abortion rights" come from this Bolshevik literature.

The Overman Committee on Bolshevism in 1919 came to the following conclusion:

"The apparent purpose of the Bolshevik Government is to make the Russian citizen and especially women and children wards dependent of that government...They have promulgated decrees relating to marriage and divorce which practically establishes a state of 'free love'(abortion). Their effect has been to furnish a vehicle for legalization of prostitution by permitting the annulment of marriage bonds at the whim of the parties." (Senate Document No. 61 1st Session pages 36-37, Congressional Record. In Roe vs.Wade, the U.S. Supreme Court Justices violated the Constitution through lurid figments of their imagination. So-called "women's rights activists" have left no stone unturned over the past two decades in seeking to enshrine "rights" in the Constitution which are simply not there.

The Anita Hill-Clarence Thomas case was a remarkable demonstration of the vast power these women's rights groups have gained since the days of the Roosevelt administration. The Senate, is filled with Socialists of the worst stripe, Kennedy, Metzenbaum; Biden being its standard bearers. There is a public perception that needs to be corrected: The Senate does not have any court powers: it cannot put anyone on trial. Its powers are confined to an investigative role. It has no prosecutorial role. Looking at the Anita Hill-Clarence Thomas affair, it was a quickly apparent that the Senate evidently completely forgot this restriction of its powers.

The chief instigator of the confrontation was not Hill herself, but a group of abrasive, aggressive women who saw an opportunity to make capital out of the overblown "sexual harassment" issue which had become their cause-celebre. The fact that this group was able to persuade the Senate committee and a large segment of the legislators that Hill was a victim of "sexual harassment" even though she had waited ten years before coming forward to make her charges, is an indication of just how powerful "women's rights" advocates have grown.

If one women could be singled out for this deplorable state of affairs that would have been Nan Aaron. If any man could be singled out for blame, it would have been Justice Warren Burger, the Socialist's dream of a judge who could always be relied upon to twist and squeeze the constitution and add his own predilections in total defiance of the 9th Amendment to the United States Constitution.

It is well worth a special mention that none of the Socialist judges who did the greatest damage to the constitution had any experience as judges before they were appointed to the Supreme Court. *Louis Brandeis, John Marshall, Earl Warren, Byron White and William Rehnquist were not judges before their SOCIALIST credentials elevated them to the Supreme Court, from where they did the bidding of key Socialists infesting every level of government.*

Gathering the formidable female Socialists together for an attack took a few days, but after that, Kate Michelman, the abortion rights baby-murder champion, Nan Aaron, Judith Lichtman, Molly Yard, Eleanor Smeal, Patricia Schroeder, Barbara Boxer, Susan Hoerchner, Gail Lasiter, Dianne Feinstein, Susan Deller Ross and Nina Totenberg, a marijuana smoking muckraker in the best traditions of the Fabian Socialist muckrakers of the 1920s, were in full cry. Of these, perhaps the most vicious was Totenberg, who had once been fired for plagiarism. Given to use the of foul language, Totenberg represents the worst of what is wrong with the so-called "feminists." In this she is ably backed by Senator Howard Metzenbaum, the best example of the worst of what is wrong with the Senate.

The first assault on Thomas came with a leak that was engineered by Aaron, Hoerchner and Lichtman who talked Hill into putting her alleged sexual harassment complaint in writing and sending it to the FBI. Hoerchner had been the first to call Hill in Oklahoma, not with standing that the two had no contact for more than seven years. Hoechner was like George Bernard Shaw in that she was not shy about approaching anybody, even strangers whom she felt might benefit her.

What these aggressive "feminists" feared was that Hill might not might come forward voluntarily to confront Judge Thomas. In that case, as the saying goes, "we will have to bring her out" using the techniques learned from the homosexual lobby whenever one of their number was reluctant to own up to his homosexuality.

By that time, Thomas had already undergone five days of questioning, with Metzenbaum pulling his usual stunt of delaying confirmation to see if any results would come from his muckraking squads. Finally, under terrific pressure from Catherine McKinnon, a feminist activist legal "scholar," and principally through Lichtman, Hill broke, and was forced to make the charges the female radicals wanted, and which were immediately leaked.

The rest is history, a fascinating account of the savageness of the female of the Socialist species who would go to any lengths to make a "kill," though in this case their quarry, Judge Clarence Thomas, was able to outrun them. The entire operation, from the time that Hoerchner contacted Hill, and until the confirmation of Thomas, was run along the lines of psychopolitics, the strategy that had served Socialism so well in England.

Unfortunately, radical Socialist "feminism" is here to stay. There will be no let up in the activities of Amazons like Patricia Schroeder and heavy-weights Boxer and Feinstein. We shall witness these radical feminist legislators introduce all sorts of legislation not in consonance with or pursuant of the Constitution. We have already seen how Feinstein had a so-called ban on "assault rifles" accepted by the Senate. The fact that Feinstein's bill violated the Constitution in no less that three major places did not phase this female gladiator one little bit. What has to be done is to train legislators in the Constitution, get them elected, and then coach them on how to counter and overturn any further encroachment of our liberties, using the Constitution as the principal weapon. For this we need a foundation similar to the Fabian Socialist Society.

5

SUBVERTING THE CONSTITUTION VIA THE LEGISLATIVE ROUTE

It was Florence Kelley (Weschenewsky) who said that the United States Constitution was to be subverted by what she called, "the legislative route" and since her pronouncement, Socialists have gone overboard in carrying out her directive. So far has this trammeling of the Constitution gone, that in 1994, there is hardly a day passes without a judge, somewhere, reading his predelictions into the Constitution and making decisions that are outside of the pale and the ken of the Constitution.

In the late 1920s and early 1930s, the American Socialists groups said that the interpretive role of the judiciary was to be used to get around restrictions in the Constitution. The Socialists were also responsible for dreaming up so-called "executive orders" as a way to legislate in a direct manner where it was not possible to enact legalization sympathetic to Socialist causes.

Although the Ninth Amendment to the United States Constitution was written with the express purpose of preventing judges from making their predelictions become law, by and large judges at all levels have ignored this restriction imposed upon them, and more and more, they are making laws that are clearly unconstitutional. Examples of this are so-called "gun control" laws, and restrictions on abortion protester groups.

Kelley came into prominence when she translated into English the rabid Socialist Engels' "Condition of the Working Class in England in 1844." This was the usual Socialist attack on capitalism. Engels wrote several books, one of them a slashing attack on religion and another, "Origin of the Family" a diatribe against the sanctity of marriage. Engels toured the United States in 1884, and made no attempt to heed the warning of Edward Bellamy to avoid confrontations that projected an image of Socialism as the home of sexual deviants, revolutionaries and anarchist. Apparently Americans in the 1800s were far better informed about Socialism than are Americans of the 1990s.

It was not by happenstance that Kelley elected to receive her Socialist education in Switzerland, the long-time home for revolutionaries, anarchists, sexual deviants. Danton and Marat came from Switzerland to start the French Revolution. Lenin spent a considerable amount of time in that country before venturing out to London. Kelley started her crusade to subvert the United States Constitution by joining the New York Nationalist Club, from where she launched her crusade to get the federal government to pass laws that would control wages and conditions in factories.

In pursuit of this goal, Kelley either formed her own fronts or joined other already in existence, such as the National Consumers League which she tried to give Marxists overtones. Kelley called herself a "Marxist-Quaker" and she was also an American Fabian Socialist. We shall learn more about Kelley in succeeding chapters. She became a close friend of Harvard's Professor Brandeis, from whom she learned a great deal about methodology to circumvent the Constitution, by the "legislative route."

Kelley worked with great energy to prepare the way for the "Brandeis Brief" that were to become the hallmark of Socialist judges. What the "Brandeis Brief" was in essence a sheet or two of legal opinions attached to huge bundles of carefully-chosen Socialist propaganda on economic and social issues. Needless to say, neither Brandeis nor his fellow judges were in the least bit qualified to interpret these slanted Socialist doctrines, so they were simply accepted as fact and written into judge's rulings. Around 1915, Kelley searchers world wide to gather information favorable to Socialism, which made up the bulk of the material that comprised "Brandeis Brief" court documents. It was a mammoth task, ably performed, one which was to change the way in which American jurisprudence operated.

"Brandeis Briefs" was a great triumph for Kelley and her "legislative route" to altering and circumventing the Constitution. On the instructions of Mandel House, President Woodrow Wilson named agreed, was to ensure the support of "Progressive Republican" Brandeis for the coming involvement of the United States in WWII. It is worth restating what has already been said, "progressive," "moderate" Republicans means that the person using these labels is an out-and-out ardent Socialist,

Another milestone in the history of Socialist triumphs over the judicial system of the United States came with the New York State Lusk Laws. So-called "immigrants" from eastern Europe poured into New York in the 1800s, bringing with them combative attitudes and lots of revolutionary experience. Many of these new arrivals worked in the garment trade. It was to investigate the revolutionary anarchist behavior of this large group from East Europe, that in 1919 the New York State legislature appointed Senator Clayton R. Lusk to head a committee of enquiry.

One of the strongest "immigrant" support centers was the Rand School. A stronghold of American Fabian Socialists, Rand provided legal support for the garment workers trade union and a whole slew of other trade unions which Rand was instrumental in founding. Rand School lecturers and instructors read like a Fabian Socialist Whose Who. Lusk descended on Rand complete with search warrants and escorted by State Troopers, confiscated records and files.

The reaction by the Socialist legal fraternity was swift. A prominent lawyer, Samuel Untermeyer — who in 1933 declared war on Hitler — and who had great influence around White House inner circles, sought and obtained an injunction against Lusk, who was forced to return the files and records he had impounded. This was an early demonstration of the awesome power of Socialism in the United States. Nevertheless, following Sen Lusk's report, the New York legislature passed what became known as the Lusk Laws, which required all New York State schools to be licensed. The object of the exercise was to close Rand School.

But the New York State legislators were not to be successful. In the decade 1920-1930, few were familiar with Socialism as a virulent disease that could strike when and where it chose. Prominent Socialist attorney Morris Hillquit aroused such a violent agitation against the Lusk Law among the powerful garment workers and other Socialist-dominated trade unions, that it was vetoed by Governor Al Smith. From this beginning grew a powerful political alliance that was to put Socialist Franklin Delano Roosevelt in the White House.

Once again, the Socialists had demonstrated that their stealthy sinister, scurrilous policy of infiltrating their chosen disciples as advisors to those in power, was the way to go. Years later it was discovered that Governor Smith a staunch Catholic, had been "advised on issues of social justice" by Father John Augustin Ryan, an avowed Socialist planted on Smith by a Socialist-dominated National Catholic Welfare Council. It was on the advice of Ryan that Smith vetoed the Lusk Law bill.

A devout follower of Sydney Webb, Ryan went on to become known as "the padre of the New Deal." In 1939, a dinner in his honor (none of the rank and file members of the garment workers and other labor unions were invited) was attended by Justices William O. Douglas, Felix Frankfurter and Henry A Morganthau. Rand School continued to function without interruption even though it was not licensed.

What upset the Socialists in the 1920s when they were attempting a virtual takeover of the United States, was the fact that the Federal Government did not have absolute power. Only kings have absolute power and they issue proclamations. President Lincoln did not free the slaves in his emancipation proclamation. He knew it to be unconstitutional. "Blackstone's Commentaries With Notes" by the great constitutionalist St. George Tucker, a professor of law at the University of William and Mary who served in the American Revolution, states the position very clearly:

"The right of issuing proclamations is one of the prerogatives of the crown of England. No such power being expressly given in the federal constitution, it was doubted, upon a particular occasion whether the president possessed any such authority under it..." The Socialists decided that in future, proclamations would be called "executive orders" but they remain legislation by fiat, forbidden by the United States Constitution.

The first ten amendments to the United States Constitution are a restriction on the Federal Government with perhaps, a small exception contained in the 5th Amendment. Article 1, Section 9 of the Constitution does not permit the federal government to legislate outside of its delegated powers which are contained in the Primary powers of Congress.

Frustrated by Bill Of Rights restrictions on federal government powers, the Socialists went on the offensive "by the legislative route." What they could not achieve through the House and Senate was achieved via the courts, which is why we have so many unconstitutional laws on the statute books. There is no doubt that had the Socialists not been blocked by the Constitution, they would have overwhelmed the country between 1920 and 1930.

Unhappily, since the 1970s, the Congress and the president have opted to implement Social programs in greater numbers each year. One example of this is, "A Bill to Establish National Voter Registration" offered by Senator Robert Dole, the Senate minority leader. Dole's bill is 100 percent unconstitutional, and it is a sad day for the United States when we see the minority leader of the United States Senate acting in such a thoroughly irresponsible manner. The details of Dole's bill can be found in pages S5012 — D5018, Congressional Record, April 24, 1991, No. 61, Vol. 137.

Dole's bill is wrong because it flies in the face of Article 1, Section 4, Part 1 of the United States Constitution which states: "The time, place and manner of holding elections for senators and representatives, shall be prescribed in each State by the legislators thereof; but the Congress may at any time by law make or alter such regulations, except as to the places of choosing Senators." The debates on this issue go back to the earliest days of our Confederated Republic.

The words, "may" does not mean "must" or "shall." The word "manner" simply refers to the type of ballotused. The words "alter" and "regulate" does not mean control over State elections by the Federal Government which Dole should be aware of if he has read the Congressional Globes and Annals of Congress. Dole tries to get the Federal Government embroiled in matters that are reserved to the States. This is a common expedient resorted to by all Socialists.

Wilson started the this kind of rot, and his mantle was picked up by Roosevelt, Kennedy, Johnson Eisenhower, Bush and now Clinton. As if in tandem, the Supreme Court has gone so far to the left that one might well wonder why it is not called the Socialist Supreme Court of the United States. One of the chief purveyors of Socialist doctrines was Justice Harlan Stone who advised Constitution butcher Roosevelt on how best to pay for Socialist programs, through Frances Perkins.

The main conspirators working to wreck the United States Constitution at that time were undoubtedly Colonel House, Justice Brandeis, Justice Felix Frankfurter, Bernard Baruch, Florence Kelley and Sidney Hillman. The Brandeis Briefs were mainly responsible for pointing the Supreme Court in the wrong direction. As explained elsewhere, the Briefs were masses of sociological position papers highly favorable to Socialist causes, covered by the thinnest of legal opinion. Thus was "sociological law" born, which has been a curse and a baleful evil around the necks of the American people ever since it was instituted in 1915.

Apart from the attack on the Constitution via the courts, the Socialist resorted to the strategy of sending their "advisors" to act as spokesmen for U.S. foreign policy, even though they were not representatives of the government nor elected to office by the people. Colonel House and George Maynard Keynes are two classic examples of how American Socialists flouted the Constitution with apparent impunity by exercising "spheres of influence."

House was openly for the utter destruction of the United States Constitution and Brandeis expressed his Socialist "reforms" of the Constitution in his book, "Wealth of the Commonwealth." So that they could conspire, scheme and connive to bring down the Constitution, House lived a short two blocks away from Roosevelt and both were in hailing distance of Sir William Wiseman, British intelligence MI6 station chief for North America.

The ACLU was the most active of all Socialist organizations in attacking the Constitution. The growth of its sinister influence can be found in the number of chapters in California alone, and the fact that it was able to challenge the McCarran Internal Security Act.

6

BRIGHTEST STARS IN THE AMERICAN SOCIALIST FIRMAMENT

As the heading of this chapter suggests, we will name some of the brightest stars in the American Socialist constellation out of thousands upon thousands of Socialist leaders of which Socialism is comprised. Among them are found some of the most dangerous subversives ever known in the history of this country. We were always warned to look out for "Communists" in Washington, and this succeeded in taking our gaze off the real cause for concern; the Socialists.

Socialist ranks are filled with key educators, particularly at the level of professors and college presidents. They are in the diplomatic service, in the United States State Department, in the House of Representatives and the Senate. The Justice Department overflows with those who are ready to do anything to promote Socialism. Key banking positions are filled by them, they control the money of the nation and there are thousands more in key positions in the military. Some of the most powerful international corporations act as change agents of Fabian Socialism.

Fabian Socialists are in the communications business, occupying key posts, and likewise in the news media, print and electronic. They make public opinion to suit the events of the day, seducing the public and creating opinions which the public has been conditioned to accept as their own. In short, Socialism is so entrenched in the United States of America that it would be difficult to dislodge, unless the whole support of the whole people were first obtained. Fabian Socialists have so penetrated and permeated the Christian Church, that today, it is utterly unrecognizable from what Christ intended. Fabian Socialists are Justices on the Supreme Court, using their predilections to get around Constitutional safeguards; they are Freemasons. The police system is riddled with Socialist, mainly in the top echelon officer class.

Perhaps the better known of Supreme Court Justices who have greatly assisted Fabian Socialists causes in the past are Justices Harlan Stone, Felix Frankfurter, William O. Douglas, Hugo Black, Louis Brandeis, Abe Fortas,

Warren Burger and Earl Warren, and we shall return to these stars in the Socialist firmament in due course. In other equally important areas, a host of professors have acted as advisors to Presidents of the United States; others have changed the American system of political economy from what the Founding Fathers intended it to be, to a Babylonian system that has illegally placed the purse strings of the nation in hands of Socialist aliens.

A more select band of Fabian Socialists became controllers of five United States presidents; a situation which was not envisaged by the Founding Fathers, and in consequence, one which created an especially dangerous camarilla which gradually led to the highest political office in the nation becoming penetrated and permeated, with great corruption following, which we are now seeing in full measure in the Clinton Presidency.

The one name that most readily comes to mind in this context and which typifies Socialism in America in the minds of serious researchers, is Colonel Edward Mandel House. "Colonel" was an honorary title, granted to him by "reformist" Governor Hogg as a reward for getting him elected Governor of Texas. House met Woodrow Wilson, the first openly Socialist future President of the United States in 1911. It was House who ensured Wilson got the nomination at the Democrat convention in Baltimore a scant year later.

As mentioned elsewhere, there is a strong suspicion that House was really Huis, of Dutch descent. His father, Thomas William House was the agent for the London Rothschilds. House Sr. was the only one in Texas to come out of the Civil War with a huge fortune, thanks, some historians say, to his Rothschild and Kuhn, Loeb connections. The name "Mandel" — a distinctly Dutch name — is said to have been given to Edward, because one the Kuhn's bore the name "Mandel."

Young Edward was sent to school in England, where he came under the influence of wealthy Liberal thinkers of the day, themselves strongly under the influence of British Fabian Society teachers. One of those who befriended young House was the Fabianist George Lansbury. Upon the death of his father, House found himself independently wealthy, which allowed him to devote his time fully to Socialist studies, particularly in "gradualism" or, "making haste slowly."

Because of the great influence of the wealthy and the powerful in the Fabian Society circles, House learned the lessons well and went on to take over the Democrat Party in the United States from the top down. The rise of House as a key player in American affairs, was undoubtedly due to the recommendations made by the Fabian Society elite and Sir William Wiseman, British intelligence MI6 North American station chief. Throughout the Wilson presidency, Wiseman and British intelligence carefully rode herd over the president, always through the good offices of House.

The coded communication between House and Wilson — known only to the two men — as confirmed by Professor Charles Seymour, president of Yale, was supplied courtesy of MI6. According to confidential documents I saw in several places in London, Wiseman eaves dropped constantly on House-Wilson conversations, as befitted his status as Wilson's ultimate controller.

We know that much the same, highly successful "model" was later used by Bruce Lockhart, the British M16 agent selected by Lord Milner to be Lenin and Trotsky's controller in overseeing the Bolshevik Revolution in the interests of free trade and British banking. MI6 strategy for United States used Hegelian principles in convincing Fabian Society leaders to help to induce "free trade" with the United States, something that had been barred, first by President George Washington in July, 1789, and kept in place by Presidents Lincoln, Garfield and McKinley.

William Jennings Bryan was at one time considered by MI6 as a possible free trade candidate, but was rejected because it was perceived that by his radical statements, the American voters would not accept him as presidential material, an assessment that proved to be highly accurate. Wiseman had given House a detailed profile of Wilson's career, first as a professor at Princeton from 1902 to 1910, and then, as Governor of New Jersey. Wiseman felt that Wilson was just the man House needed to carry out Fabian Socialist policies in the United States. With all of the background checks completed, House was instructed to meet with Wilson at the Hotel Gotham in New York, in November of 1911.

From then onwards it was "all systems go" with House setting up shop in unpretentious, rented quarters in a somewhat run-down East Thirty-Fifth street location in New York City. The House "office" began to look like a command center, with a switchboard and a direct line to Sir William Wiseman, who was occupying an apartment directly above him. After Wilson was elected to the White House by a minority vote (6,286,000 as against the combined Taft-Roosevelt count 7,700,000) the House-Wiseman switchboard had direct access to the new president via a coded telephone link.

There were many prominent Socialist visitors to the House office, including Bernard Baruch, to whom MI6 gave the incriminating Peck letters — later to be used to blackmail Wilson into changing his anti WWI stance. Wiseman was a favorite of the President and became one of Wilson's "confidential" messengers between London, Paris and Washington, which to a certain extent, showed that Wilson really did not understand just how much he was under the control of agents of a foreign government.

Wilson was chosen by MI6 to bring down United States barriers against "free trade. "His mentor, Col. House, had taught Wilson to regard trade barriers tariffs as a bar to good global business and a primary cause of prices having risen sharply alongside alleged "inflation," all just so much Socialist hot-air propaganda. House spent endless hours briefing Wilson on the inherent "evils of tariff barriers that benefited only the rich and the powerful vested interests at the cost of the working man." Then Wilson was ready to make his false claims:

"...We were living under at a tariff which had been purposely contrived to confer private favors upon those who were co-operating to keep the party that originated it in power..."

The Clinton administration was to use the almost identical spurious arguments to make out a case for bringing down the last of the tariff wall that had protected the young nation for so long and made its commerce and industry, its living standards, the envy of the world. Following close on the heels of Wilson's inauguration in March of 1913, the battle to topple United States trade barriers was joined. Yet, even one of Harvard's top professors in economics dismissed the presumptions that trade barriers were bad for the common people as being without substance.

House had done his job well: It was not for nothing that his friends called him "a pronounced radical whose Socialism opened the door to Communism," this in reference to the role House played in securing the release of Trotsky after Wiseman had intervened on behalf of the pro-Bolshevik Revolution plotter, Lord Alfred Milner. House was by his own account, an ardent admirer of Karl Marx and a hater of the United States Constitution.

One of the toughest assignments given to House by Wiseman, concerned the "neutrality" stance adopted by the Wilson administration toward the war raging in Europe. Allegedly "pacifists," the Fabian Socialists were used by MI6 to get Wilson to change his mind, via blackmail (the Peck letters) and a climate for war was created by outright lies upon lies told to the American people. In this endeavor, MI6 co-opted the services of Walter Lippmann, to whom we shall be returning.

As WWI was ending, House was selected by his British MI6 and Fabian Socialist controller Sydney Webb to be the mouthpiece for Wilson at the Paris Peace Conference, allegedly on the basis of the masterful House report speedily produced after just two days "in seclusion" at Magnolia, his summer home in Massachusetts. But the facts spoke otherwise. What was to become known as "Wilson's Fourteen Points" which was to have established a One World Government League of Nations "to take charge of all nations and overrule their sovereignty" (including the United States) was actually a Fabian Society document first drafted in 1915 by British Socialist leader, Leonard Woolf.

Entitled "International Government" the Fabian Society treatise was presented to the British Government for acceptance. The British Government later passed it to Wilson, who did not bother to open it before forwarding it to House in Massachusetts. This then, was the "Fourteen Points" which House was supposed to have drafted with the help of Professor David Miller. This incident points up the close, domineering relationship that existed between the British government, House and Wilson.

Wilson presented his "Fourteen Points Plan" to the Paris Peace Conference, which promptly rejected it. A bitterly hurt Wilson returned to the United States, the long-standing friendship between House and himself beginning to come apart at the edges. It was a signal triumph for the Constitution: Neither House nor Wilson had breached it in Paris. There after, the two men drifted apart, their seemingly endearing friendship wrecked on the Constitution of the United States of America.

In keeping with the Fabian Society's teachings, House was always a forward-looker. In 1915 his attention had been drawn to Franklin D. Roosevelt, Wilson's Assistant Secretary of the Navy. House arranged through discreet circles for a copy of "Philip Dru" to find its way into the hands of the dashing Roosevelt. It is said that the book had a profound effect on the already committed Socialist Roosevelt who was destined to succeed Wilson. In 1920, House told friends, "I am certain he (Roosevelt) will be the next president of the United States." Roosevelt's record as Governor of New York and the innovative (Socialist) programs he introduced, left no one in doubt about the direction he would take America if elected to the White House. In this respect, then former Governor Clinton of Arkansas is a carbon copy of Roosevelt in Socialist methodology.

When Roosevelt was elected the event was hailed by Socialists large and small on both sides of the Atlantic as an act of "providence." As is usually the case, such acts of "providence" do not bear close scrutiny, and this one was no exception. Once again, the astute political observations of Colonel House were about to bear fruit. Roosevelt was to launch and boost Socialism to new heights in America, a fitting successor to President Wilson. That Roosevelt owed his presidency to House was never disputed; only kept out of the public view, lest the timely act of " providence" be shown to have a human face.

A friend of Roosevelt's mother, House was quick to notice the good Socialist legislation passed by the Governor of New York State. The friendship that developed was also partly the work of Frances Perkins. House had recommended Roosevelt to Wilson for the post of Assistant Secretary of the Navy in the Wilson administration, and handed Roosevelt the "fireside chats" radio approach to winning over the American people and coached Roosevelt on how to create unconstitutional "executive orders," i.e., proclamations which only kings and queens have the right to issue.

House will go down in history as the man who changed the way presidents make their decisions and carry them out, by surrounding them with informal advisors, who, not being public servants, are hard to get a handle on. The informal advisor slippery Socialist system has done more damage to the nation than the people could ever begin to imagine. This aspect, more than any other of House's achievements, set him aside as the leading warrior of Socialism in the first quarter of the 20th century.

Roosevelt was presented to the American as an affable, likable highly competent man with a "wonderful smile" etc etc. How much truth was there in this propaganda? Apparently not very much. In 1926 when House thought Roosevelt would be the next president, the man with a "wonderful smile"was not even able to earn enough to take care of his family. Roosevelt ran as a candidate for the New York Senate on a Ku Klux Klan ticket. His much publicized "polio" was actually encephalomyelitis, which fact was hidden from the public. Propaganda specialists turned his "infantile paralysis" into a plus by portraying Roosevelt as a man of high courage, determined not to let "polio" stop his career. The only problem? It was all completely false.

Perhaps nothing is quite so much identified with Roosevelt as the "New Deal" and Harry Hopkins. The "New Deal" Socialist program was cleverly couched as a "relief" program for workers who were stricken by the Depression. In fact, the "New Deal" was the book "A New Deal," written by Stuart Chase, a British Fabian Society member which did not attract much attention, although Florence Kelley who liked Chase and his Socialist ideals, rated it as an important work.

Chase proposed that three major steps be taken by Socialists in America:
1.   To obviate accidental inflation and deflation, the dollar was to be "managed,"
2.   The national income to be forced-redistributed through increased income and inheritance taxes,
3.   A vast public works program was to be instituted, particularly in electrification works (based on the Soviet model) and large scale housing projects.

Roosevelt adopted the project in-toto and it became the "New Deal" which was adopted as the Democrat election plank in 1932. The "New Deal" was couched in obfuscation, and a panic-stricken public, seeing in it their salvation, gave the Democrats an overwhelming election victory in 1932.

Roosevelt soon became vulnerable to such unelected advisors as the Rockefellers whose malodorous presence was usually concealed by the likes of Drew Pearson and Walter Winchell among others. Later, when the Rockefellers became bolder, Roosevelt appointed Nelson Rockefeller as Coordinator of Inter American Affairs. During his time in office, Nelson squandered more than $6 million of the taxpayers money on what were strictly, Rockefeller enterprises in Latin America.

When Roosevelt went to the White House, he took a whole panoply of unappointed advisors with him, including more professors than Wilson had surrounded himself with. The rationale behind this was that the American public was less likely to suspect "Socialists" lurking behind academic facades than appointed officials, and this proved to be the case during Roosevelt's earlier years in office. With this purpose in mind, and bearing in mind that long-range planning was a key element among the Fabian Socialists, Harold Stassen was planted on the University of Pennsylvania, Edward Stettinus on the University of Virginia and General Dwight Eisenhower was planted on Columbia University.

Secret "advisors" were also responsible for getting Roosevelt to retrieve

Standard oil property taken over by the Japanese using American troops for this purpose, the so-called Stimson doctrine. This doctrine was repeated by President George Bush in the Gulf War which was fought to retrieve British Petroleum oil property seized by Iraq. The way that Alger Hiss was introduced into the Roosevelt administration is classic Fabian Socialist text-book material. In 1936, Hiss was invited to serve in the State Department by Professor Francis Sayre, Wilson's son in law. Sayre had long been recognized as a valuable Socialist property.

Sayre assisted in the preparation of legal documents for the defense of Sacco and Vanzetti two notorious Socialists accused of murder. Working with Sayer were Professor Arthur M. Schlesinger, Professor Felix J. Frankfurter, Roscoe Pound, Dean of the Harvard Law School and Louis Brandeis. Arthur Schlesinger Jr., was educated at Cambridge University in 1938, where he was very warmly welcomed with open arms by the Fabian Society. This was at the time when all efforts by law enforcement agencies and the Congress to arrest and deport a wave of anarchists who had come to the United States in the 1890s was mockingly called "overreaction to the Red scare."

Sayre was one of those who defended Hiss, long after it was apparent that Hiss was deeply involved in espionage against his country. When Adolph Berle of the State Department tried to warn Roosevelt about Hiss' activities, he was brusquely told to mind his own business. Likewise, Roosevelt refused to listen to intelligence reports about the activities of Owen Lattimore, and insisted on appointing him as his personal advisor to Chiang Kai Shek, which left Lattimore in the enviable position of easily betraying the Nationalists to the Communists. The Chinese Nationalist forces were further betrayed by Roosevelt appointee Lauchlin Currie, who ordered Army supplies intended for the Chiang Kai Shek's Nationalist forces dumped into the Indian Ocean.

Harry Hopkins became to Roosevelt what Edward Mandel House had been to Wilson. A protege of Frances Perkins, Hopkins began his career as a social worker, who got close to Roosevelt through his wife, Eleanor, and is wrongly credited with the New Deal slogan, "tax and spend, tax and spend." Hopkins came into his own in the Depression as Roosevelt's nominee for handing out so-called "federal" relief, i.e. welfare. A scarecrow of a man who clothes hung on him, and totally lacking in social graces, Hopkins would have looked sadly out of place in a room with John Maynard Keynes. What Hopkins knew about was corn. His greatest asset was selecting people with "clout" and insinuating himself into their circles.

It was this talent that made Roosevelt put Hopkins in charge of the 1940 Democrat Convention. Hopkins, despite his unlucky appearance, was able to rack up the support of the most powerful politicians of the day. Roosevelt is known to have personally approved an article by Arthur M. Schlesinger Jr. printed in the "Partisan Review" in which Schlesinger attacked those who were investigating the true causes of the Civil War. This should not surprise the well informed. As previously mentioned, Communism and Socialism were much more prevalent in the run up to that war, and more so during and immediately after the Civil War, than orthodox history allowed. This fact was deemed undesirable by Schlesinger and his fellow Socialists, who wanted the public to believe the established historian's account of the causes of the war — which, without exception — did not mention the part played by Communism and Socialism.

It was Arthur J. Schlesinger Jr., who called anarchists Sacco and Vanzetti "two obscure immigrants about whom nobody cared." Arthur Schlesinger Jr., did extensive work for the ACLU on behalf of these two anarchists. Schlesinger went on to write scores of articles for the "Fabian News" in which he pushed Socialists ideas. In one such article published in the "Fabian International Review," Schlesinger quite openly said that it was the intention of the American Socialists to gain outright control of the military and foreign policies of the United States.

The judges who twisted and squeezed the constitution to make their predilections fit the goals desired by Socialists, and who found their schemes blocked by the immutable Constitution are the brightest stars in the Socialist firmament, for without their willingness to corrupt themselves and defile their oath of office, none of the far reaching "popular" Socialist "reforms" that were so important in changing the course and direction of the mighty United States, would have been successful.

The process of electing good, robust Fabian Socialist judges to the United States Supreme Court really began with the Wilson administration and the appointment of Justice Louis D. Brandeis as one of the most important Fabian Socialist properties. As an examination of the record of Brandeis reveals, the Fabian Socialist hierarchy at home and abroad, chose wisely. Brandeis did more to undermine the Constitution and steer difficult Socialist legislation around and past it, than even Florence Kelley could have hoped for.

Professor Louis Dembitz Brandeis (1856-1941) fitted perfectly the Socialist idea of a Justice who would look favorably upon a "new constitution" as spelled out by Edward Bellamy. It was Bellamy who proposed a "new declaration of independence" based upon an evolutionary interpretation of the Constitution of the United States with a Judiciary that would institute "sweeping changes" and bring an end to the roadblock of separation of powers of the three branches of government. Bellamy called the Constitution, one devised by the well meaning, but sadly outdated Founding Fathers.

President Wilson himself was greatly in favor of wrecking the Constitution of the United States which he had faithfully sworn to uphold, and in Brandeis he found a kindred spirit. Brandeis had sat at the feet of the Fabian Society philosopher, John Atkins Hobson, believed to be the originators of the "Brandeis Brief," although Kelley always claimed the credit. Hopkins certainly originated the future strategy of surrounding incoming Presidents of the United States with

Socialist professor advisors, a strategy that has worked remarkably well in the Socialist war on the Constitution, initiated by Felix Frankfurter, Louis Brandeis, Harold Laski and John Maynard Keynes. These four Fabian Socialists changed the course and direction of the United States to the total detriment of We, the People, in a manner far beyond what Hitler, Stalin and Ho Chi Minh could ever have achieved.

Early in his legal career, Brandeis teamed up with the formidable Florence Kelley, without whose help he would not have been able to make use of a stratagem dreamed up in the think tanks of the London Fabian Society and perfected by British Socialist Hobson, that later bore the title of "Brandies Briefs." Kelley, with her devotion to the Socialist cause of getting around the Constitution by what she called "the legislative route" midwifed the new-born "Brandeis Brief" baby, that was to almost make her dream of ushering in total Socialist control of the United States became a reality.

Brandeis had a niece by the name of Josephine Goldmark who was Kelley's biographer and she explained how the Brief was prepared in 1907. It was not a complicated process, but one that took a great deal of time and energy to complete. All manner of sociological datas were assembled and appended to a one and a halfs page of legal argument. As the British Army drill sergeants used to say, "bullshit baffles brains" and that is exactly what the Brandeis Briefs did when presented to the Supreme Court in 1909.

Another notorious Socialist, Felix Frankfurter, called the new scheme, "the most majestic concept in our whole constitutional system" which allowed justices to read their own predilections into the Constitution in cases before them, that is predilections forbidden by the 9th Amendment to the Constitution of the United States. Nevertheless, this method became standard practice, which helps to explain why so many Supreme Court decisions have been in so many instances, unadulterated "B... S..."

Frankfurter attended the Paris Peace Conference, but left for home when he realized that the New World Order was not going to be ushered in there and then. A compatriot in conspiracies of the Socialist kind with Professor Harold Laski, Frankfurter would bide his time in true Fabian Socialist manner, and strike hard when the time came. Of all the American Socialists who admired Graham Wallas, the British Fabian Socialist professor at the London School of Economics, Frankfurter stood at the head of the line.

The failure of the New World Order to materialize at the Paris Peace Conference was largely due to the American public, who were disgusted with the rash of radicals who had appeared with the coming of the Wilson administration. The American people must be credited with having had a good deal of common sense in those days. That is not to say than things are so different now. But we must take into account the makeup of the population at that time, largely of

Western European origin, united by the English language, the Christian religion and their understanding of the American Revolution and its far-reaching consequences of national unity, which has been completely adulterated by Socialist policies.

Moreover, in 1919 there was no unlimited use of opinion polls, to make up people' s minds for them. What we have in the America of the 1990s is a totally different picture: a drastic change in the population makeup from overwhelmingly Western European Christian to a hodgepodge of every race on earth, Chinese, Indian Asians, Vietnamese, Eastern Europeans, Hispanics etc, in which the White Christian race is fast being submerged. In 1919 a unified people were demanding action against the subversive elements rearing their ugly heads across the American landscape, and they got it in 1919-1920, when Attorney General Mitchell Palmer ordered a series of raids to stamp out centers of sedition.

Brandeis immediately showed that his sympathies lay with the Socialists who were trying to overturn the United States Constitution, by joining a brief filed by Frankfurter and Walter Lippmann which sought an injunction against searches of the hundreds of Socialist subversive centers. The police officers conducting the raids were verbally abused by Lippmann, who appeared at the scene of some of the raids, with a whole pack of Socialist writers.

Not that Brandeis had an easy ride through the Senate confirmation process. Inasmuch that the senators in 1915 knew a great deal more about the United States Constitution than they do today, Wilson's choice for the Supreme Court was hotly contested, but to no avail. The Democrat Party majority saw to it that this dangerous, passionate revolutionary was appointed. The damage done to the United States Constitution by this ardent, passionate Socialist is still being tallied. Neither Hitler nor Stalin could ever have caused so much havoc.

Brandeis was one of the first Justices to become involved in New Deal politics. His friend Florence Kelley gave him a copy of a book by Stuart Chase, simply entitled "A New Deal" which Chase thought would be good for the future of British and American Socialism's plans, a view with which Sydney Webb and the hierarchy of the Fabian Society concurred. On the urging of Brandeis and Kelley, "A New Deal" quickly replaced the 1932 Democrat plat form, and in 1933, became Franklin D. Roosevelt's "New Deal."

It is interesting to note the views of Chase, who was not averse to violent anarchy and Socialist revolutionary action:

"It (revolution) may one day be necessary. I am not seriously alarmed by the sufferings of the creditor class, the trouble the church is bound to encounter, the restrictions of certain kinds of freedom which may result, nor even by the bloodshed of the transition period. A better economic order is worth a little bloodshed..."

But Stuart Chase relented in the end when he saw that the American people could not, would not, be duped into taking part in a Bolshevik-style revolution, supposedly for their own good. Instead, he advocated a collective-style government through national control by a central government, along the lines of Webb's "Labour and the New Social Order." Chase was a mild-mannered, yet very dangerous radical, whose ideas are in the main largely incorporated in the structure of a One World Government-New World Ordff now being ushered in.

The organizations and personalities who paid for and sponsored Chase's book were loosely connected to Moscow's ex-officio ambassador Ludwig Martens. Maartens was very close to the far Left Socialist magazine, "the Nation," and Edward A. Filene, who reportedly met the cost of printing the book in the United States through the Twentieth Century Fund, a Fabian Socialist financial angel. Chase was very friendly with both Kelley and Brandeis, and once described the Bolshevik Revolution as having been "absolutely necessary." When Franklin Delano Roosevelt stepped into the White House "A New Deal" became the "New Deal," one of the most far-reaching piece of Fabian Socialist legislation ever to darken the pages of American history.

Roosevelt's pathway to the White House was considerably smoothed by Felix Frankfurter. Born in Vienna, Austria, this almost dwarf-like, dome-head child was brought to the United States at the age of twelve. Frankfurter used his obvious intelligence to champion every Socialist cause that was at variance with the Founding Father's concept of the United States. One of the avenues of approach to Socializing the United States was through the American Civil Liberties Union, (ACLU) of which Frankfurter, Rose Schneiderman and Roger Baldwin were founders, and which was established for the sole purpose of making mischievous use of the Constitution to defend Socialist enemies of the Constitution.

The ACLU was founded with the avowed intention of "twisting and squeezing" the Constitution to protect the enemies of the United States bent upon its destruction. There can be no questioning the truth that the perverted practice of using the Constitution for the benefit of the enemies of the Republic came out of the domed head of Frankfurter. Out of the mind of this "Gnome of the Courts" was born the belief, propagated by the likes of Lippmann, Schlesinger and a host of Harvard law professors, that it was somehow unpatriotic to defend the United States against its avowed Socialist enemies, of which Frankfurter stood at the head.

Leader of the Socialist enemies of the United States as he was, Frankfurter thought it was publicly acceptable to protect the anointed one who would soon be in the White House. At the instigation of the Fabian Society, Frankfurter set up a think tank of noted Socialists to advise and help Roosevelt over difficult bumps and humps in the Socialist road to the White House. Arising for his concerns that "New Deal Roosevelt" do the right things at the right time, Frankfurter met with Roosevelt in a private meeting immediately after Roosevelt's inauguration ceremony.

In this endeavor, Frankfurter was greatly assisted by Harold Ickes who put together a large band of spies to cover Washington and other large metropolitan centers. This group became known as "Harold's Gestapo" though "Cheka" would have been more appropriate, since they were able to exert tremendous pressure on local and State officials to vote for Roosevelt. Ickes remained a close confidant of Roosevelt and was responsible for breaking the unwritten law established by President George Washington that presidents were to serve only two terms.

Also in attendance was Fabian Socialist Fred C. Howe, whose name was later to become a household word in Socialist circles on both sides of the Atlantic. Together, they chose the personnel who were to occupy key positions in the Roosevelt administration, especially in the State Department. This set a pattern which was to become a part of the scenery, whether a Republican or Democrat sat in the Oval Office. For instance, in the Reagan administration, 3,000 key positions were filled by Heritage Foundation nominees. Ostensibly a "conservative" think tank, the Heritage Foundation was run from behind the scenes by Sir Peter Vickers Hall, a leading member of the Fabian Society and a committed Socialist.

Although Cordell Hull was the nominal Secretary of State in the Roosevelt administration, it was "Felix and his boys," among them the traitor Alger Hiss, who were in command, a situation which Hull tolerated for 12 years. As Frankfurter was to admit in later years, his idea came from the British Privy Council system of advisers to the prime minister of England. In any event, two years after Roosevelt had entered the Oval Office, Ickes, Wallace, Hopkins and Frankfurter were the string pullers who acted from behind the Rand School of Social Sciences, the very one the New York authorities had tried to put out of business as a center of Socialist and Communist subversion against the United States.

Frankfurter, a leader in the field of Socializing the United States, proved his worth by getting public service utilities into the hands of municipalities which led up to the Tennessee Valley Authority Project (TVA). Passed off as an anti-depression move, the TVA was in reality one of the first advances toward socializing projects of this magnitude — a huge victory for American Socialists and their British controllers. As Mark Starr wrote: "As Socialism collectivism, public ownership and control becomes necessary in the United States, they will be adopted in specific instances and cases. It may be called by some other name, but, as in the case of the Tennessee Valley Authority, public ownership will be applied..."

Frankfurter continued to encourage leftwing penetration of government and one of the several front organizations he sponsored was the World Youth Congress Movement. A number of individuals associated with this Fabian Socialist enterprise were described as dangerous Communist subversives by a Senate Subcommittee on Internal Security. But perhaps his most damaging blow was his support of his protege and life-long friend, Dean Acheson, whom he insinuated into Johnson's inner circle of advisors.

The Dies Committee investigating Communism in the United States said that Professor Harold Laski, John Maynard Keynes and Felix Frankfurter were the entente terrible of American Socialism, an idea that was scoffed at by Roosevelt when it was drawn to his attention. But there could be no doubting that the legal language for all New Deal legislation was drafted by Frankfurter. It should not be over looked that it was Frankfurter who recommended Dean Acheson, and Oliver Wendell Holmes to serve Roosevelt, and two more treasonous subversives would have been impossible to find, the one serving in the State Department, the other on the Supreme Court.

More than any other single Socialist, past or present, whether in England or the United States, there is general agreement that the greatest of them all in preparing the way for Socializing America was undoubtedly the dome-headed near-dwarf, Felix Frankfurter. Of him it can be said that he did his utmost to break down the protective tariffs erected by Washington, guide the Federal Reserve into position and push Wilson into committing to England's WWI.

A close associate of Walter Lippmann, Paul Warburg, Thomas W. Lamont and the key Socialist leaders of the day, Frankfurter was well placed to work his appalling treason against the United States which had given him and his family sanctuary when they were virtually forced out of Europe. If ever there was a prime candidate to fit the saying, "he bit the hand that fed him," that candidate was Justice Felix Frankfurter, who almost single-handedly, perverted the Constitution and got close to rendering that great document a blank piece of paper.

Frankfurter wrote the majority of Roosevelt's "fireside chats" radio broadcasts, one of the most successful tools for penetration and permeation ever devised. He had a hand in Roosevelt's decision to send Harry L. Hopkins to England to lay the groundwork for the greatest heist on earth: the so-called Lend-Lease Act. But probably the most tremendous damage that Frankfurter was to do was his gradual (in true Fabian style) intrusion of the Court into the legislative branch of government, thus beginning the insidious practice of the gradual diminution of the powers of the Congress and increasing those of the Supreme Court and the President. Frankfurter was the man who almost made Professor Laski's dream of breaching and destroying the separation of powers come true.

That this was 100 percent unconstitutional did not seem to bother the little gnome of the Court. Thus, thanks to the treachery and sedition of Frankfurter, which he carried on throughout his life, the British Fabian Society was at last beginning to see some light in the dark tunnel they were construction under the walls of the separation of powers, identified by Laski as the most serious obstacle to Socialism's progress in the United States. Frankfurter maintained close contact with the wrecker of Western economies, John Maynard Keynes, and arranged for publication of "The Economic Consequences of Peace" in which Keynes predicted that capitalism in Europe was dying.

While Frankfurter wrote vigorous papers dissenting and decrying law enforcement raids by Attorney General Mitchell Palmer that began to take place on seditious movements in the United States, it was Lippmann who did the "on location" attacks. Lippmann was a leading member of the Roosevelt "brain trust" group that pelted the President with Socialist proposals. Congressman McFadden accused Frankfurter of being one of the original formulators of the National Industrial Recovery Act. McFadden stated, "it required 15 years of hard effort on the part of Mr. Baruch and his associates (one of them being Frankfurter) to foist this act upon the American people, and it was only through the sufferings over a period of great stress that he was enabled to do it..."

"...However, Baruch, Johnson, Tugwell, Frankfurter et. al. seem to be the most brazen in their efforts (in behalf of Socialism) in this country. Frankfurter has been furnishing most of the legal brains for the outfit...they have sought to compel, browbeat and bulldoze the business interests of this country to engage in private contract so that they would have the power to require business interests of the Nation to do their wishes regardless of the Constitution. The 'new deal' lawyers have no hesitation in appearing in court and asserting that private citizens can contract away their Constitutional rights. It has been through this method that they have broken down State lines..."

It is a well-known fact that Frankfurter virtually assumed the position of employment agency for the Roosevelt administration. Among the most dangerous of the Socialists recommended to Roosevelt by Frankfurter were the notorious Rexford Tugwell, and Governor Al Smith of New York.

Frankfurter's close ties to Harold Laski was the subject of intense interest in Socialist circles in London and Washington. Laski was a regular house guest at the Boston and Washington homes of Frankfurter. As fellow Socialists, the men had a profound effect on each other and both worked tirelessly to weaken the separation of powers mandated by the Constitution. Their letters to each other were addressed, "Dearest Felix" and "Dearest Harold." Being at the very heart of Fabian Socialism in London, Laski was able to keep his "dearest Felix" fully posted about the latest Socialist thinking, which Frankfurter then conveyed to Roosevelt, whose door was always open to him. The two "privy counselors" became the most influential shapers of Roosevelt's Socialist policies during his three terms in office.

The deciding factor in the United Nations Treaty came from Frankfurter, Laski and Keynes, although drafted by others, and it represented another brick removed from the wall separating constitutional powers. Historians of the period 1942-1946 say that the United Nations treaty was the first of many big moves into the legislature by the executive, a shocking trend that continues to grow by leaps and bounds with Clinton's Presidency. Keynes visited Roosevelt in 1934 and laid out his now thoroughly well debunked "multiplier," which supposed that every dollar spent by the Federal Government on relief was a dollar handed to the retailers, the butcher, the baker, the farmer and the candlestick maker-which is not the way it worked in practice.

"Lenin was certainly right. There is no subtler no surer means of overturning the existing basis of society than to debauch the currency. The process engages all other hidden forces of economic law on the side of destruction and does it in a manner which not one man in a million is able to diagnose."...John Maynard Keynes.

Although credit is given to Keynes as the originator of the "multiplier" theory, it belonged to one of his students, R.F. Kahn who invented it while a student at Kings College. In the summer of 1934, the Fabian Socialists decided to move their "economic genius" Keynes, to the United States. His book, "The General Theory of Money" had been read by Roosevelt, but not understood as Roosevelt confessed to Frances Perkins, who was responsible for the introduction of the two men: "I didn't understand his whole rigmarole of figures," Roosevelt confided in Perkins. Spending the country out of a recession was the underlying theory behind the Keynesian economic philosophy, which might account for his popularity with successive Socialist governments in England and the Democrat Party of the United States.

Keynes was looked upon with awe, and something akin to the respect one would afford a Mystic whose prognostications about the future were always right. Yet the truth is, Keynes, if the bedazzled would only have investigated his claims, was wrong at least 85 percent of the time. Keynes had the manner of an English gentleman in bearing, dress and speech. It is said that he was able to charm any woman into bed with him, if he so chose. Perhaps it was his education at Eton and tenure at Kings College, Cambridge that had imbued him with the mannerism that both sexes found so appealing.

Keynes got his alchemist-like secret that would make paper money multiply itself endlessly, from R.F. Kahn; had it been left with Kahn, nobody would have given it the slightest credence. But in the hands of an immaculately tailored, tall and handsome Cambridge Don, with an amazing knowledge of art, food and wine, the "multiplier" nostrum became big news. Even so, one wonders how, in spite of the special tutoring he received from Professors Marshall and Pigou, Keynes could only make 12th position-near the bottom of his small economics class. In 1911 Keynes became the editor of the "Economic Journal" and Secretary of the Fabian Society's "Royal Economic Society" one year later. When I think of Keynes I cannot help but think of the earthy, sage, homespun philosophy of my British regular army drill sergeant, which is well worth repeating: "Bullshit Baffles Brains."

That is really the essence of Keynesian economics: money would simply multiply itself into infinity, like some kind of a chain letter promise of a huge reward for little effort. To those few who queried what would happen at the end of the chain letter line, Keynes snapped, "we all have to die some day." Incredible as it may seem in retrospect, this is the Keynes "economic system," in reality just so much gibberish, that was accepted by international bankers and leading politicians of the Western world.

Was Keynes a kind of a Nostradamus, a Gregory Rasputin, or was he truly sincere about his economic principles? Could it have been that, added to what he had been endowed with by nature, his father, Neville Keynes, a Cambridge professor whose forte was to level constant attacks on the free enterprise system, also contributed to his son's stunning success that left John Maynard Keynes a millionaire, with a seat in the House of Lords?

John Maynard Keynes began his career as a civil servant, in the manner of Sydney Webb, but while the great Lord Bertrand Russell often sneeringly referred to Webb as a "clerk in the Colonial Office," he never applied this remark to Keynes. Perhaps this was because Keynes was in Russell's charmed circle at college, which proves that Socialists are just as class-conscience and snobbish as any other group.

From his early beginnings with George Bernard Shaw and the Fabian Socialists, Keynes was well thought of, especially since he was the one who "called the moral bluff of capitalism" according to Sydney and Beatrice Webb, the founders of Fabian Socialism. Although a member of the Liberal Party, Keynes enjoyed enormous respect from the Conservative Party and the Labour Party as one who could look into the future, financially speaking. "A real oracle reader" as the "Fabian News" wrote. Perhaps his "oracle-reading ability" is what caused Keynes to push for the founding of the International Monetary Fund (IMF) in which he played a big role.

Like so many of the One World Government (OWG) institutions, the IMF was simply a vehicle for draining money from the American economy and farming it out to countries that had excellent natural resources as collateral. What the unwary governments did not know, and indeed, had no way of knowing, was that the IMF would not only abscond with their natural resources, but also control and then destroy their national sovereignty. Rhodesia, the Philippines, Angola, Brazil are good examples of what happens when the IMF is let in.

By 1919, Keynes had charmed his way into the confidence of Colonel Mandel House, General Pershing and Walter Lippmann. Keynes expressed himself forcefully, declaring that "capitalism in Europe is dead." These contacts were to earn him a position of some importance with House, and later, with Harry Hopkins, an alliance that led to the founding of the Council on Foreign Relations, (CFR) first known as the Institute of International Affairs, in reality, a branch of the Fabian Society. According to the Congressional Record, House, October 12, 1932 page 22120, Keynes presented his book "The Economic Consequences of

Peace" in the United States as a destabilizing effort and to popularize Marxist economic theories.

Roosevelt received the Keynesian ideas with enthusiasm, as they gave him a leg to stand on when it came to getting $4 billion from Congress for so-called "public works" projects — in reality make work jobs that did not "multiply" federal dollars as Keynes had promised. Keynes developed a friendship with Henry Cantwell Wallace, both men favoring the elimination of the gold content of the dollar and a "managed currency. " Keynes continued to make a big impression at Harvard, where he was frequently in the company of Frankfurter and Laski. While Frankfurter provided the legalese for the Socialist New Deal, Keynes provided its economic basis, as usual, a total pipe dream, which when taken to its conclusion would wreck the economy of any nation.

The "English Socialists" like the soothsayer-charlatans of the Pharaonic priesthood, had indeed spun a web of their Mysteries around President Roosevelt who remained in their thrall until his death. If one were to search for the High Priest of the New Deal era, surely John Maynard Keynes would be the natural choice. His ability with the English language was remarkable in that he could make even the very elect believe that two and two made five.

The arrival of Keynes on the Washington scene was preceded by a full-page advertisement in The New York Times of December 31, 1933, which took the form of an open letter to President Roosevelt, filled with ideas totally foreign to American economists. Nevertheless, the Madison Avenue propaganda did the trick and is likely what paved the way for his 1934 visit to the United States. The long friendship with Lippmann and other leading Socialists stars in the firmament of the United States, opened all doors for Keynes.

Although Roosevelt did not understand the implications of what he was doing, on the advice of Keynes, his administration decided to take the United States off the gold standard in conformity with a similar action taken by the British Government. Keynes "multiplier" theory was adopted by Roosevelt, after Keynes told him not to be concerned by "that crude economic fallacy known as the quantity theory of money." This was music to the ears of the New Dealers, who felt they had been given the green light by the greatest economist in the world to embark on a reckless program of spend and spend, as if there were no accountability on the morrow.

Thus it was that with the 1936 publication of "General Theory of Employment" Keynes sought to ensure continued government spending based upon the belief that government is responsible for full employment and if that is not forthcoming, then welfare must take up the slack. Keynes was the chief advocate of deficit spending and Roosevelt was happy to oblige him. But for all that, Roosevelt was unable to spend his way out of the depression.

As for the great American public, all this was way over their heads. "Leave it to the experts" the media chorused, "it is too complicated for us." And that is exactly how the Socialists got away with the great fraud of deficit spending based on the bogus "multiplier" that never did work. The inestimable damage done to the United States by this Fabian Socialist economic leader is still being measured. "People are known by the company they keep " is an old, true and tried maximum. Among his friends Keynes numbered some of the worst traitors in the history of the Nation; Lauchlin Currie, Felix Frankfurter, Walter Lippmann, Bernard Baruch, Colonel House, Dean Acheson, Walt Whitman Rostow, Fancis Perkins, Abe Fortiss, Eleanor Roosevelt, whose evil deeds are as numerous as the stars in the night sky, too numerous to be fully covered by this work.

The great Congressman Louis T. McFadden made short shrift of Keynesian economics when he had Marriner Eccles, chairman of the Federal Reserve testify before the House Banking Committee of which he was the chairman.

McFadden, a longtime opponent of Fabian Socialism attacked Frankfurter and Keynes for their connections, particularly through the Foreign Policy Association of New York, noting that Paul M. Warburg was one of its founders. He also correctly chastised Henry A. Wallas, appointed by Roosevelt as his Secretary of Agriculture on the recommendation of Frances Perkins as belonging to the seditious Freedom Planning Group, the Fabian Socialist sponsor of the New York Foreign Policy Association. McFadden correctly identified Moses Israel Sieff with the group, quoting Sieff's advice, "Let us go slowly for awhile and wait and see how our plan carries out in America." Sieffran the British Marks and Spencer chain stores and was a multi-millionaire Socialist.

The "our" plan which Sieff referred to was one drafted by the Fabian Socialists in London that would place all land and agriculture under government control, which Professor Rexford Tugwell had previously advocated. Tugwell was the third member of the "terrible threesome" of Stuart Chase and Raymond Moley, teaching at the notorious, seditious, Rand School of Social Science. All three were confidants of Henry Wallace, who with the help of Tugwell, wrecked the thriving agricultural industry just coming into its own in 1936, by a policy of plowing under crops and killing farm livestock.

Tugwell was an ardent admirer of the Bolshevik Revolution, which he said was "having fun remaking the world." Trained at Columbia University, Tugwell was the first Socialists to apply Fabian Socialist theories to government practice. Tugwell had a finger in every New Deal pie baked by the Roosevelt administration. One of his major undertakings was to gut tariff protection against imported goods.

The New Deal plan had been enthusiastically received by Roosevelt, who said, " If we look at this thing from the broad national viewpoint, we are going to make it a national policy if it takes 50 years... The time is now ripe, overripe, for planning to prevent in the future the errors of the past and to carry out our social (Socialist) and economic views to the Nation."

One of those who was pleased to follow this injunction was Arthur Schlesinger Jr., whose wide range of Socialist activities, which included managing Adlai Simpson, first national chairman of Americans for Democratic Action (ADA) one of the deepest Socialist anarchistic, seditious, subversive organizations in the United States, for whom he wrote most of their propaganda material. It was Schlesinger who was responsible for putting John F. Kennedy over as a Socialist candidate, no mean feat, as it meant convincing pure Socialist ADA members to vote for one who typified everything they opposed.

A star performer in "penetrate and permeate," Schlesinger's role in secretly subverting Lyndon Johnson and getting him to promote ADA causes in the 1950s was a big feather in his cap. The whole story of how Schlesinger kept key ADA members from bolting after Kennedy announced that Johnson would be his running mate at the Democratic Convention in 1960, would fill a book. One can imagine the consternation of leading ADA Socialist David Dubinsky, on being told that Johnson, whom he had hated all of his political life, was to be Kennedy's running mate.

Had Schlesinger not succeeded, it is very likely that Johnson would have rejected Kennedy's offer. As it was, it was touch and go, as Johnson preferred the Senate majority leader post. Apparently, it was only after Schlesinger revealed to Dubinsky how he had made a closet Socialist out of Johnson in the 1950s, that Dubinsky rallied ADA support for the nomination. Schlesinger's successes continued over into the Johnson presidency, even though he was not in Johnson's "upper-level cabinet" (unappointed advisors — privy counselors). Arthur Schlesinger was one of the most dangerous unseen enemies this country has ever had.

Dean Acheson personified the underhand, penetration and permeation standard seditious practice of a well-trained Socialist. Acheson came from the Committee of 300 law firm of Covington, Burling and Rublee, who serve as lawyers for the great Committee of 300 accountants, Price, Waterhouse. He was also in the inner circle of J.P. Morgan, Andrew Mellon, Tommy Lamont (the man who pressed for American recognition of the bloody butchers Bolshevik regime), the Kuhn Loeb family and Felix Frankfurter. Acheson was your typical well-connected Socialist, seditious Wall Street lawyer, who went on to become Under Secretary of the Treasury and Secretary of State under President Roosevelt.

It was Frankfurter who recommended Dean Acheson for a position in the United States State Department. Among Acheson's more public acts of betrayal and sedition against his country in the service of Socialism, was his fierce struggle to get all possible assistance for the Bolshevik regime at a time when the White Russian Armies were defeating and putting to flight the Bolshevik Red Army, which is fully described in my book, "Diplomacy By Deception." In WWII, Acheson urged that no action be taken against Stalin for occupying the Baltic States. His betrayal of Nationalist China is already well known and need not be recounted here. To top off his career off treason and sedition, Acheson's support for the North Korean and Chinese forces during the Korean War was an open act of treason. But instead of being arrested, charged with treason and hanged, the highest honors were heaped upon him.

Dean Acheson's compatriots in Socialist crimes were Dean Rusk and Walt Whitman Rostow, who learned their Socialism as Rhodes Scholars at Oxford, the "finishing school" for future world Socialist leaders. Rusk was the opposite of Keynes in appearance, round faced, plump and balding, he looked more like some low-level functionary in the Bolshevik regime than Secretary of State in the Kennedy/Johnson administrations. Yet, his appearance belied his vicious Socialist character and his unstinting efforts on behalf of Red China and Stalin through the Institute for Pacific Relations (IPR), and directly, through a large number of State Department agencies.

It was Rusk who set up the "private sanctuary" staging area for Red Chinese troops in Manchuria, in collusion with the British government. General Douglas McArthur was forbidden to attack the sanctuary, where Chinese troops were massing, prior to crossing the Yalu River to attack the American forces. When MacArthur submitted a plan worked out by his staff and U.S. Air Force General George E. Stratemeyer, that would have destroyed China's fighting abilities and set them back for decades, it was the signal for Rusk to hastily summon President Truman to attend a conference at Blair House in Washington, D.C.

November 6, 1950, the Chinese forces were advancing rapidly across the Yalu. Stratemeyer's planes were bombed up and ready to go. But back in Washington, Rusk told Truman that he could not give the order for MacArthur to strike the Red Chinese troops. According to documents I saw, Rusksaid, "we have a commitment with the British not to take any action which might involve attacks on the Manchurian side of the river against the Chinese WITHOUT CONSULT-ING WITH THEM." Rusk had also called for an emergency meeting of the United Nations Security Council, ostensibly to get a U.N. resolution ordering China to pull its troops back. In reality, this was a treacherous, treasonous ploy by Rusk to give the Red Chinese troops time to cross the Yalu River, while holding up crucial attacks planned by MacArthur. If ever there was a seditionist, a traitor, a man who had no compunction in betraying his country, that man was Socialist Dean Rusk.

The third partner in this trio of seditionists was Walt Whitman Rostow, who once said: "It is a legitimate American national objective to see an end of nation-hood as it has been historically defined." (Rostow, "The United States in the World Arena.") In spite of having been declared a grave security risk by the State Department Intelligence Agency and the Air Force Intelligence Agency, Rostow remained in a most powerful position as the unelected representative of American Socialists, with an open door to Eisenhower, Kennedy and Johnson. Rostow had been stationed at the Massachusetts Institute of Technology by the Committee of 300, from where he plotted and planed strategy that he believed would bring about "the end of nationhood" for the United States.

That this monstrous traitor had a free rein in Washington, should forever silence those who believe that Socialism is merely a benevolent institution to help the needy, the unemployed and the poor. In December of 1960, Rostow flew to Moscow to see Vasily Kuznetsov, the USSR's deputy foreign minister. Kuznetsov had been complaining to Acheson and Rusk that the United States was building a first strike capability, pointed at his country.

Rostow told him not to worry, the situation would be corrected. And it was. Thanks to the intervention of Robert Strange McNamara, then Secretary of Defense, almost the entire Skybolt, Pluto, X-20 Dynasoar, Bomarc-A, Nike Zeus missiles defense system and the B-70 nuclear bomber production was drastically cut back or eliminated. There was no corresponding decrease on the Russian side. Apart from anything else, McNamara's treachery cost the United States $5.4 billion. A higher degree of treason would be hard to find, and in a Socialist treason and sedition lineup, McNamara would be in the top ten.

As a reward for his perfidious treachery, Rostow was appointed by President Johnson to the National Security Council in 1964. At the time of Rostow's appointment, Johnson praised this evil seditionist, saying that "he has the most important job in the White House, apart from the President." This was the same Rostow who had never wavered from his goal to one day end the nationhood of the United States.

Rostow was responsible for arranging for U.S. ground forces to be sent to Vietnam, after an intensive lobbying effort to get our troops into the Mekong Delta. But the Joint Chiefs of Staff told the president that ground troops should not be committed to South Vietnam, as they were sure to get bogged down and eventually, would not be able to extricate themselves from the region. Like all of the leading Socialist camarilla in Washington, Rostow did not give up on his plan and continued to press for a troop commitment.

Rostow used General Maxwell Taylor to get direct access to John Kennedy. Unfortunately, a green and inexperienced Kennedy accepted Rostow's scenario and in January of 1960, ten thousand American soldiers were sent to Vietnam. Through the treachery and treason of Walt Whitman Rostow, the Fabian Socialist method of penetration and permeation had infected the highest office in the land.

There has never been a war like the Vietnam War, where our soldiers tried to fight with both hands manacled behind their backs, the keys held by Robert Strange McNamara, Walt Whitman Rostow and Dean Rusk. No nation's military had to fight according to the rules laid down by an out and out traitor — Robert S. McNamara. This man should long ago been tried for treason and hanged. According to McNamara's "rules of engagement" our soldiers had to wait until they were surrounded and being shot at before they were allowed to respond.

Was there ever *treason* like this? Senator Barry Goldwater called McNamara's rules of engagement, "layers of restrictions, illogical and irrational," which also prevented our bomber pilots from attacking clearly visible, strategic targets. Instead, our bombers had to unload tons and tons of bombs on so-called "supply trails" which they could not even see, and which did absolutely no damage to strategic targets, in most instances, hundreds of miles away. It was a complete exercise in futility and a shocking waste of money.

Back home, the Socialists in control of the news media fought a running battle for public opinion — on the side of the North Vietnamese Communist regime. American soldiers were the "bad guys," while the Viet Cong could do no wrong. It is my fervent hope and prayer that these three enemies of the United States, Rostow, Rusk and McNamara may yet somehow be brought to trial on charges of treason. Hanging is too good for them.

If I were asked to give an opinion on which of the Socialist stars did the most damages to the Constitution and the concepts for a great American Republic, I would have to think long and hard, because there is a veritable host to choose from. But in the end, I would have to place Walter Lippmann near the top of the ladder, who joined the London Fabian Society in 1909, making him the oldest American Socialist.

In 1917, Lippmann was selected by British intelligence MI6 to visit Colonel House every two weeks to counsel him on how to get Wilson reelected and push him away from neutrality, which "opinions" often appeared in the Socialist magazine the "New Republic" on whose board Lippmann sat. It was not generally known that Lippmann was the leader of an informal group that set war policy for Wilson and mapped out his post-war strategy. The group was headed by Dr. Sydney Mezes.

Lippmann actively pursued a policy of securing private donations to foster Wilson's 14 Points which was hoped would result in the founding of the New World Order through the League of Nations. Lippmann was able to secure the services of 150 Socialist professors to propagandize and collect money and data for the coming Paris Peace Conference, among whom was the notorious Socialist, the Reverend Norman Thomas. In effect, thanks to these professors and the slickness of Lippmann, their ideas were fervently expressed by Woodrow Wilson who did not seem to mind that he was acting as a mouthpiece for international Socialism.

Lippmann became closely associated with "Radical Red" John Reed whose Bolshevik ideas for America had to be toned down, until Reed eventually rushed off in a huff to join the Bolsheviks in Moscow, but not before he and Lippmann had founded the Harvard Socialist Club. Reed was the subject of highly-imaginative Holly wood movie glorifying Bolshevism and stressing what an honor it was for Reed to have been buried by the Kremlin Wall after his long service to Communism.

Like Felix Frankfurter and Louis Brandeis, Walter Lippmann grew up in affluent circumstances. His career at Harvard has been correctly described as "brilliant" but of his membership of the Fabian Society in 1909, Lippmann confessed to it, meant more than anything he had achieved at Harvard. Thus, as in so many instances, it is apparent that good Socialists are not made, they are born that way. The Fabians in London had watched Lippmann's career at Harvard, and in the words of Harold Laski, "He was an ideal candidate to carry out our policy of penetration and permeation of the United States at all levels."

This Lippmann did with skill which showed a flair for deceptive practices and from 1932 to 1939 he devoted his time and energy in penetrating and permeating the leading American business houses, legal practices and banking circles. It was Lippmann who established a new class, a "moderate" Republican which was to serve Clinton so decisively in leading the United States down a Socialist road to slavery in a One World Government — New World Order New Dark Age.

The term, "moderate Republican" helped those who were ready to commit treason and sedition in the House and Senate to avoid being tagged as Socialists/Marxist/Communists. Among the most successful of these Machiavellian chameleons are Senators Roth, Cohen, Kassenbaum, Chaffee, Danforth who made it possible to make the Communist Manifesto of 1848 in the shape of the so-called "Crime bill" part of United States law.

Lippmann was the first American to adopt applied psychology for political situations, a tactic which he learned at the Tavistock Institute for Human Relations In Sussex, England. His unswerving support of Socialism was typified by his close friendship with Thomas "Tommy" Lamont, the J.P. Morgan banker who played a big role in prevailing upon the United States government to recognize and establish relations with the bloody. Bolshevik butchers in Moscow. Lippman acquired immense power through his syndicated press columns, which were carried by all of the major newspapers and magazines.

Lippmann went on to become a close friend and confidant of Presidents Kennedy and Johnson, and his Socializing of them resulted in the adoption of Socialist platforms, the New Frontier and the Great Society, taken straight from books written by Socialists, and adopted practically in toto as Democrat Party planks. Lippmann is credited with implementing the "make haste slowly" policy of the Fabian Socialists in the United States:

"In a general way, our object was to make reactionaries standpatters, standpatters, conservatives; conservatives, liberals; liberals, radicals; and radicals, Socialists. In other words we tried to move everyone up a peg. We preferred to have the whole mass move a little, to having a few altogether out of sight." (Source, Congressional Record October 12, 1962.)

This highly illuminating insight into how Socialist "gradualism" works should be studied by all who are concerned about the future of the United States, and we need to start schools that will teach how to combat this creeping menace, which unless stopped, will eventually paralyze our nation. The success of these tactics can be seen in the Clinton presidency, where one major piece of Socialist legislation after the other has been forced through on the basis of gradually converting opponents of Clinton to believers in his program.

Clinton's Socialist NAFTA, the Crime bill, and his bill imposing the biggest tax increase in the world on the American people are prime examples of how this creeping paralyses works, and also *how important it is to have traitors in Republican ranks who are whole heartedly for Socialism, but who are labeled "moderate Republicans."* By the Lippmann method, the psychological approach to politics he learned at the Tavistock Institute of Human Relations, the American people are being led, slowly but surely, one step at a time, as if dream walking, to accept with a murmur, the most radical and heinous changes in education, in economics, religion and politics in the United States, without seemingly being aware of what terrible changes have been made, and are in the process of being made.

The application of social psychology by Lippmann, greatly speeded acceptance of Roosevelt's "New Deal" Socializing of the United States, which was carried further by Kennedy and Johnson's Socialist New Frontier and Great Society. Lippmann was the most adept in a long line of adept Socialists who used the word "democracy" on every single occasion it was possible to introduce it, without letting on that in Socialist parlance, "democracy" really mean the increasing inroads of Socialism into the educational, economic and political life of the nation through government regulation of business. "True democracy," that is to say, unbridled Socialism was ushered in without the populace being aware of it. We see this policy in full swing in the Clinton administration, with the majority of the people not yet aware that the "democracy" Clinton has in mind is unadulterated Socialism.

Lippmann's tenure as president of the Intercollegiate Socialist Society established at Harvard in 1909 was the best foundation for his future in Socialism that money could buy, and stood him in good stead when he came to found the Socialist magazine, the "New Republic" in which his opinions were later to be aired about the Vietnam War. Lippmann and other Socialist writers told the American people through newspaper articles that if the United States tried to win the Korea, we would run up against China, and be defeated.

This was a calculated lie, as China was not in any sense of the word fit to wage war against the United States, and had a war resulted between the two nations, China would have been soundly defeated, a fact conveyed to Truman and the Pentagon by Gen. Douglas McArthur and General Stratemeyer. The lies about the invincibility of China continued with the Vietnam conflict, which Henry Kissinger and Dean Rusk kept going for at least two more years after the Vietnamese said they wanted to end it. Thus was the socialist goal of depleting the United States Treasury in the amount of $5 million per day, not to mention the 50,000 casualties suffered by the United States armed forces, fully realized.

Socialism was carried out by the policy advisors who surrounded Kennedy, Johnson and Nixon, advisors of the Dean Rusk — Robert McNamara kind who led the United States down a pathway of defeat in Korea and Vietnam, and whose latter-day replacements of the kind who surround President Clinton, will not hesitate to do exactly the same thing if it ever comes to war against a future enemy.

One of the future stars in the Socialist firmament over America whom Lippmann met at Harvard University, was Robert Strange McNamara. A product of the penetration and permeation Socialist method of John Maynard Keynes which settled Fabian doctrines in the Department of Economics in Harvard, McNamara taught at the Business School as an assistant professor in Business Administration from 1940 to 1943. He was later seconded to the Army Air Force and thence to the Ford Motor Company. Following his near-disastrous tenure at Ford, he was promoted to a position newly established at he head of the Department of Defense.

McNamara was impressed by the new Socialist gospel which was sweeping the campuses of the universities of the United States. The American political economy, the well-tried economic policies laid out in American economic system of tariff protection and sound money based on bimetallism, were swiftly being purged and replaced by the economic claptrap of John Maynard Keynes and Harold Laski . There was no Socialist leaders more anxious to carry out these un-American economic and political economy Socialist theories than McNamara. The one thing that emerged from the frantic rush to do away with the American economic model, was that the Keynesian model verged dangerously close on the economic theories of Karl Marx, an observation that was never allowed to be brought up in the press, radio or television.

More than that. McNamara was eager to sell out the military, and he did it by using the evil influence he had over President Johnson. There was never a time so dangerous for the security of the United States as when Socialist star Robert S. McNamara prowled the corridors of the Pentagon, canceling and countermanding one program after another, until the United States was well below par with the Soviet Union. McNamara even got Johnson to cancel the production of plutonium for the nuclear program via an illegal Executive Order.

Illegal, in the sense that only kings and queens can issue proclamations, which is what an executive order is. In earlier times in the history of the nation, both McNamara and Johnson would have been tried and found guilty of treason, as well they should have been.

In 1964, at a most crucial phase of the struggle to bring Stalin into line, McNamara canceled the nuclear battle plans of NATO, without so much as by your leave or ever having consulted with the NATO allies. It said of this amazing fait-accompli for victory by the Soviet Armed Forces, that the Soviet generals drank vodka and partied through the night in the Kremlin, in sheer disbelief at their good fortune. French rightwing leaders reaffirmed the wisdom of De Gaulle in having pulled out of NATO and establishing an independent nuclear deterrent for the French nation. The French renewed their vows never to be misled and disarmed by the United States, as they would have been had France not pulled out of NATO.

One marvels that the small in number, United States Communist Party, and a nominally non-existent Socialist Party was able to pull of such a massive victory for Fabian Socialism. Future historians will surely rub their eyes in amazement, wondering what had happened to the ancestors of those who dumped tea in Boston Harbor, and what happened to the descendants of Andrew Jackson, a man who not only clearly recognized the Socialist menace, but actively fought it tooth and nail all of his life.

Just what happened to the American people between the founding of this nation and the advent of the Socialists to power? The real answer is to be found in the population mix, which was now so adulterated as to only faintly resemble the original colonists. In a silent revolution, the Socialists rent this country from one end to another, and little by little, so demoralized the nation that it became easy prey for the forces that had been lying in wait for its downfall, ever since the War of 1812.

Constantly turning to the British Fabian Society for inspiration, slogans and programs, the Democrat Party in effect became the Socialist/ Marxist/Communist Party of the United States. Johnson's "War on Poverty" for instance, was originally written by Labor Party Prime Minister Harold Wilson. In his address to the international Socialists, Harold Wilson made it clear that the intention of Socialist in Britain and the United States was to divert funds for defense to funds to eradicate want. Disarmament, Wilson said, was what it all about, so that "want" could be banished from the earth.

Leading Socialist Michael Harrington, a member of the American Socialist Party, ten years later picked up the Wilson pamphlet and produced a book, "The Other America: Poverty in the United States." Puffed by the kept press, radio and television, Harrington's book was an instant success. The Socialist loved it. Nobody saw fit to mention that Harrington had merely taken Harold Wilson's notation a step further and applied them to the American scene. John F. Kennedy was sent a copy of the book and wrote Harrington that he was deeply impressed with it.

It is these stars in the Socialist firmament over the United States who have wrought greater havoc than any invading army could have hoped to accomplish. It is the Socialist who have prostituted and deformed our electoral system, until today, there is no telling just how much fraud and deceit goes to make up the final tally of votes. In this the Democrat Party is head and shoulders above the Republican Party.

It has come to this: What the candidates say is almost inconsequential these day; it is who gets out the most voters that counts. When a Republican candidate faces off against a Democrat contender, the international press begins to bay at the heels of the candidate as if he were running in England, Italy, France, Germany, Poland and the Scandinavia countries. It is quite astonishing to find the Socialist press in these countries closing ranks behind the Democrat candidate, almost without exception.

Worse than this, the arm-twisting and threats that accompany an election make a fair result nigh unto impossible. The Democrats are very good at this kind of activity. Businesses are intimidated, contracts threatened, funds withheld from neighborhood programs; the election process today has little to do with the number of voters who register and vote: it has come down to who can mount the most clout, who can intimidate and blackmail more successfully, who can lie to the American people without being exposed as outright liars.

For this, Madison Avenue types are hired at great cost. If a president makes a slip and says the wrong thing, the "fixers" jump in and assure the voters that it was THEY who had not heard aright. There is zero honesty left in politics as we come to the close of the 20th century. As Walter Lippmann explained in rare moment of candor following the 1964 elections:

"For the real business of the campaign was not to map out a course for the future. It was to beat and crush rebellion against the established line of domestic and foreign policy which was laid down (by the Socialists) in the generation which followed the great depression and the second world war."

There are many other bright stars in the Socialist firmament, past and present, and in the Notes section, we mention their names, although not as fully as we would have liked. To jump over the years and come up to the present, perhaps the brightest star of all in the Socialist firmament as we come to the close of the 20th century, is President William Jefferson Clinton.

Like so many of his predecessors, Clinton was insinuated into the American political scene in order to penetrate and permeate and lay the base of his presidency. Few imagined that a relatively small-time politician from a relatively unimportant state, would be the best agent of change that Fabian Socialism had thus far been able to come up with. We will skip the formal, known details of Clinton, and try, instead to look past the conventional information about him which hardly needs repeating.

Instead, we shall try to give our readers some of the information that has been kept under wraps and which has not yet seen the light of day, in spite of Clintons host of powerful detractors who would like nothing better than to kick him out of Washington.

Except for some time spent in London, where he acted as a leader of Socialist agitation against the Vietnam War, and a period at the Socialist finishing school

(Oxford University), Clinton had little experience in politics outside of Arkansas. Yet he was nevertheless able to maintain a remarkably tight grip upon the State of Arkansas.

In this he was ably assisted by his friends Tyson and Stephens, two of the richest men in the State. Clinton was recommended for promotion and referred to Jay Rockefeller and Pamela Harriman by "King" Stevens. Harriman and Rockefeller are the leaders of the Socialist Party of the United States, better known as the Democrat Party. In Clinton Mrs. Harriman saw a man with potential, so Clinton was shipped off to be groomed by the Bilderbergers as a future world Socialist leader. Harriman and Rockefeller were not disappointed, as Clinton turned in an impressive performance, and upon arriving back in the United States, he got the nod from the Democrat Party as its candidate of choice for the 1992 presidential election.

There was some concern expressed about the skeletons in Clinton's closet, but his boyish good looks and keen mind were thought to be enough to overcome anyone boorish attempts to refer to them. And so it was that on January 20, 1993, Clinton became the 42nd President of the United States. That a more unlikely personality had control of the largest and most powerful nation on earth stunned his detractors — and there were hundreds of detractors in the highest places of power in the country — who tended to overlook Clinton's exceptionally keen mind and dwell on his homely background, not to mention the charges of sexual indescretions that began to surface.

The Socialists were jubilant. Their choice had made it to the White House; henceforth Socialist programs could now be speeded up and the country would not be allowed to recover from one crisis before the next descended upon it. A new era of hijacking of State powers was about to begin, the great Socialist heist was about to slip into high gear. The Socialist hierarchy had laid out a timetable of four years for Clinton to fulfill his mandate. Clinton was to be a single term president, yet the programs that he would be called upon to ramrod through the Congress would have the most terrifying consequences for the United States for the next 1,000 years.

How awfully close to failure the well-laid plans for William Clinton had come to failing has never been disclosed except in reports in World In Review (WIR). It was like this: Mrs. Clinton had become more than disenchanted with her husband, because of his philandering ways and his numerous extra-marital relationships. Being of the best Socialist "feminist" material, Mrs. Clinton, who kept her ancestry well hidden, came to a point where she decided to go it alone. Hillary Clinton (there was no mention of "Rodham" then) duly parted ways and left her errant husband to ponder over his marital misdeeds.

It was shortly before Clinton was approached by Pamela Harriman and Jay Rockefeller, that he found himself without his wife. This was a bad setback; obviously, a man with martial troubles was not suitable to occupy the Oval Office. Harriman made a beeline for Hillary, and explained the situation: If she returned to her husband, she could count on being the next "first lady." Never one to pass up an opportunity for advancement, Hillary agreed to mend relations with her spouse, on condition that there be no more extra-marital affairs. This was agreed to, and the race was on. The rest is history.

What is not history is the background of William Jefferson Clinton, which to this day, has been hidden from the American people. Clinton was born in Hope, a small town in Arkansas and the family moved to Hot Springs, which was an "open" town with houses of prostitution and other big city "delights." It was this convivial "anything goes" atmosphere in which Clinton was raised that some say was responsible for him having trouble with the truth.

According to what a former Arkansas State Senator, Judge Jim Johnson stated, one Nora Waye, a former partner of Clinton's step-father claimed that Clinton was hardly anything that the establishment media had built him up to be. Waye gives some for instances:

"When you think about Bill Clinton's aversion to the truth you wonder if this is because of the lackadaisical background that he has in this area. He lied about being a Rhodes Scholar. He never completed that (course) and yet he said he was a Rhodes Scholar." In this Waye is seemingly prejudiced. Anyone who is selected as Socialist Rhodes Scholar and who goes to Oxford, even if he does not complete the course, is allowed to call himself a Rhodes Scholar.

Very serious allegations have been made against Clinton of abuses of power, drug-related matters and insider trading by his wife. These allegations have been made by Larry Nichols, who was a close friend of Clinton in the 1970s. According to what Nichols said, he "did a lot of projects for Clinton from a marketing perspective." Nichols went on to make a series of allegations which he says have never been investigated. Most of these center around massive cocaine dealings out of Mena, in Arkansas, some of which was also reported in "The Nation." Nichols claims that the Arkansas Development Finance Authority (ADFA) was a wholly-controlled financial entity for laundering large sums of cocaine money from Mena, which he says, went through a Florida bank (not named.)

Nichols also made serious allegations of wrong-doing against Rose law firm and Hillary Clinton, charging them with receiving commissions on bond loan applications, contrary to State law. Nichols claims that he stole documents and made copies of them that bear out the truth of his allegations. He also claims that some of the Mena drug money was laundered through a Chicago bank, in which the powerful Democrat politician, Dan Rostenkowski is part owner.

Nichols claims that Roger Clinton, the President's brother did not go to jail for selling cocaine, "they was giving it away" allegedly in return for unspecified favors. Nichols said that "Once he was convicted (Dan Lasater — who was found guilty with Roger Clinton) he and Roger went to a minimum security prison. Holiday Inn we call them. He spent, I think, up to 6 to 8 months and then got out. Unbeknown to anybody, Bill Clinton, granted him (presumably Lasater) a full and complete pardon the day after he got out..."

Nichols accuses Clinton and his Arkansas administration of never going after cocaine smuggling out of Mena: "Not one single major bust was ever made out of Arkansas, out of Mena (Arkansas). Now, imagine that, nearly ten years in its running and never even one truckload of it (cocaine) ever got caught." Nichols went on to make series allegations of wrongdoing against Wes Hubbell, who went to Washington with Clinton, and Hillary Clinton, the Stevens and the Tyson family, politically and financially allied with Clinton while he was the governor of Arkansas. On Tyson, Nichols alleges as follows:

"Don Tyson put in $600,000 or $700,000, all told into all of Bill Clinton's campaigns. Guess what he got out of it? 10 million dollars — and guess from where? The Arkansas Development Financing Authority. And he never paid a dime for it." Nichols also accused a parking meter manufacturer, Parking on Meter (POM) associated with Hubbel, of impropriety, and he said that he tried to get every major news media outlets interested in his story, but that in general, they all refused to touch it. Instead, Nichols says he was subjected to a barrage of verbal and physical abuse that left him virtually discredited.

Nichols said that an associate of his, Gary Johnson an attorney was living in Quapaw Tower condominium. Johnson apparently had a surveillance camera mounted outside his apartment — this, long be fore Geniffer Flowers moved in next door to his condominium. Johnson claims that he saw Clinton entering Geniffer Flowers' apartment on several occasion, with a key.

Johnson said: "I actually saw him go into her condominium. It wasn't that I was standing there looking out of my peephole watching Geniffer Flowers' condominium. It was just that I had gotten the camera. I had the camera before Geniffer Flowers moved in." Nichols said, "guess what he caught on tape? Bill Clinton walking into Geniffer Flowers' apartment on numerous occasions, with a key." Thus far there has been nothing to substantiate Nichols' and Johnson's stories, but as we said, "The Nation" did begin to write about Mena and Wes Hubell, and then, after a few articles, didn't do any follow-up stories — very unlike their journalistic style.

In October 1992, "The Nation" said: "In Hot Springs, where Clinton spoke on Labor Day weekend, I saw the process at work. Here in this louche town of bathouses and former casinos, is where our Bill grew up. You can forget all that agonizing tripe about 'a town called Hope.' The hustling atmosphere evidently impressed him. If we can believe Hillary, who introduced the Guv at the homecoming rally, the first thing they said to each other when he brought her here on an early romantic weekend was: "Just look at all these small businesses...""

The same leftwing magazine published an article in March of 1992, from which the following extracts are taken:

"On the broader question of Clinton's favors to his friends, Larry Nichols — the man fired by Clinton from the Arkansas Development Finance Authority, and the original source of the Flowers story — claims that the connections to the Clintons are practically a requirement for companies seeking loans from ADFA, vastly expanded by Clinton in 1985 to attract capital to the state for the purpose of economic development, offering companies long-term loans financed through the sale of tax-exempt bonds, And, indeed, names appearing in ADFA documents reviewed by my colleagues bear the aroma of Clinton's circle."

"Among the underwriters of the bond issues we have copies of, Stephens Inc. features prominently. The company's chairman, Jackson Stephens and his son Warren have helped Clinton raise more than $100,000 for his campaign. In January the bank Stephens has a controlling interest in, Worthen National, extended Clinton a $2 million line of credit. Another familiar name on the bond issue is the now defunct Lasater and Co. Dan Lasater, who headed the company, is a longtime friend of Clinton and his brother Roger. Both Roger and Lasater were busted for cocaine, the former on a stiffer charge."

"Then there's the Rose law firm, Hillary Clinton's firm whose name adorns both bond issues and loan agreement papers. Hillary Clinton has represented a company owned by Stephens Inc. in litigation. Rose partner Wes Hubbel represented the recipient of the first loan that AFDA made, a company called Park on Meter, or POM, whose name has cropped up in talk about Mena. Hubbel had been secretary of POM in the early 1980s. Hubbel's client in the AFDA deal was Seth Ward, the current president of POM, known as a friend of Clinton. Worthen Bank appears among institutions that have from time to time had liens on POM."

"Clinton and drug policy is another area of vexed confluence. According to Clinton's deputy, John Kroger, Clinton feels 'the real solution to the drug problem is to decrease demand.'...But Clinton also 'supports continued efforts to interdict drugs coming into the U.S.', favoring 'expanding the use of the military, especially for purposes of tracking and stopping small planes coming into the country.' So why hasn't he pursued the drug smuggling trail that leads to Mena, the town and airport in Western Arkansas? Clinton can't claim ignorance of the fact that Arkansas served as a nexus for international drug operations. One of his state prosecutors, Charles Black brought this to his attention in 1988. For five years before that there was a federal investigation joined by Clinton's own State Police. As part of that a federal grand jury was assembled. This grand jury was eventually dissolved, and the local press carried reports that members of the panel had been prevented from seeing crucial evidence, hearing important witnesses and even seeing the twenty nine count draft indictment on money laundering drawn up by an attorney of the Justice Department, Operation Greenback."

"In 1989 Clinton received petitions from Arkansas citizens demanding that he convene a state grand jury and continue the investigation. Winston Bryant, now State Attorney General, made the subject of drugs and Mena an issue of his campaign in 1990. A year later Bryant turned over his state files involving Mena, along with the petitions from 1,000 citizens to Iran/Contra prosecutor Lawrence Walsh, who has since continued to a mass information. (All that Walsh did was continue the coverup.) Later that year, on August 12, 1991, Clinton's advisor on criminal justice wrote to a concerned citizen to say that the Governor understood that the matter of criminal activity in Mena was being studied or otherwise taken up by Bryant, Walsh and Arkansas Representative Bill Alexander."

"Yet with all of this knowledge, Clinton has done nothing. The state Attorney General does not have the power to conduct an investigation, but the state prosecutor does. When Charles Black urged Clinton to allocate funds for such an investigation, Clinton ignored his request. The State Police were taken off the case after the federal government scrapped its investigation. Now the ball is back with Clinton and he continues to do nothing..."

In a later issue, "The Nation" had this to say about Wes Hubbel and Park on Meter. Outlining the history of Clinton's personal creation of the AFDA, the writer went on to say:

"...the ADFA made its first industry loan in 1985 to POM Inc., a parking meter manufacturer based in Russellville, Arkansas. POM, it has been alleged was under secret contract to make components of chemical and biological weapons for use by the Contras, as well as special equipment for 130 transport planes...Such planes were at that time ferrying drugs and weapons in out of Mena...POM's lawyer during those transactions was a partner in Rose law firm, of which Hillary Clinton was, and is, a member. Clinton's state thus appears to have been an important link in the Contra supply line at a time when military aid to the Contras had been banned by Congress."

"We come now to Michael Risconosciouto, a former contract employee of the CIA, who says he worked at Mena on and off between 1988-1989. Risconosciuto was arrested shortly after being named as a witness in the Inslaw case...He was arrested on ten drug related charges and has been convicted on seven...According to Risconosciuto, Mena was part of a network of bases that evolved over time...Mena was crucial because of its central location relative to other bases...Mena was the main drop-off point for narcotics, the other bases serving as distribution points...To Risconoscioto's knowledge, no drugs were ever unloaded at the Mena airport. As with Seal's setup in Louisiana planes flying low altitude would use drag chutes to drop containers of drugs in the surrounding countryside, sometimes into the Ouachita National Forest but more often than not on private land..."

"POM, according to Risconosciuto, was not merely in the business of making parking meters. He says that from the beginning in 1981 the company also made ferry drop tanks...for use on the C-130s." POM management apparently referred the leftwing reporter to the company's lawyer and nothing more was said about POM and its correction with Wes Hubbell and Hillary Clinton's law firm.

The leftwing magazine "The Nation" did another article on Clinton and the accusations made about Gennifer Flowers from which we now present extracts:

"The allegations about Bill Clinton's sex life were first presented in a lawsuit by Larry Nichols, fired by Clinton from his job as marketing director of the Arkansas Development Finance Authority (ADFA). Clinton claims that Nicols was axed for making 700 unauthorized phone calls to Contras in Central America and that the lawsuit is part of a Republican frame-up. The sequence is more complicated, stemming from the State's role, and specifically that of an airport at Mena in western Arkansas in the training and supply of the Contras; also the arms-for-drugs flow between the United States and Central America... A student organization at the University of Arkansas, Fayetville, which has long been investigating the Mena affair, has successfully requested, under F.O.I.A. laws, Nichol's phone toll records, from ADFA. Mark Swaney, a member of this organization, says there were no calls to Central America on the tolls during the relevant period..."

"The Clinton's — Bill and Hillary — are extolled as vibrant and caring, and somehow tremendously together. This version has prevailed in spite of the fact, parenthetically conceded by their admirers, that for a while they were separated and seemingly united only as they approached the presidential campaign. Is lust for power the thing that brought them together? In contrast to the caring Clintons, we are invited to ridicule Flowers as a good time girl..."

"From Sid Blumenthal in the "New Republic (the Socialist's mouthpiece), one of the most effusive pieces of flattery in the history of public relations to the innumerable friendly stories in 'The Washington Post' and 'The New York Times' to the great pooh bahs of perennial punditry, the word has gone forth: Clinton is sound, thoughtful, pragmatic, modern, white, male and safe. And for all the Democratic time servers who have languished for twelve long years he carried — at least until afflicted by mal de Flowers—the fragrance of possible victory..."

There would appear to be a great area of unexplored ground for the newly appointed special prosecutor to rake over, ground that the former special prosecutors Fiske declined to go anywhere near. Perhaps this explains the extreme nervousness of the Democrats in Congress about the removal of Fiske from the investigation. Let us hope that truth will out. Right now, it appears that we are looking at the most successful coverup in the history of American politics.

7

SOCIALIST PENETRATION AND PERMEATION OF RELIGION

"The great civilizations of the world do not produce the great religions as a kind of a by-product; in a very real sense, the great religions are the foundations on which the great civilizations rest." Christopher Dawson, Historian.

"The Christian religion is not a suitable religion for today." Edward Lindeman. Socialist-Christian writer.

While it is true that Fabian Socialism set its sights on penetrating all religions, the real target was always the Christian religion. In its earliest days, the Fabian Society called its one-sheet pamphlets, "tracts," the term used by Christian missionaries, and this was done to deliberately mislead the public as to Fabian Socialism's dislike of organized religion. Perhaps the most evil influence on religious beliefs was the so-called German Rationalization, which came from Bismarck and Marx, who considered religion no more than a social science.

In the United States, the evil Socialist leader, John D. Rockefeller worked to move churches to the left, using lay preacher infiltrators. One of his servants, Paul Blanshard was used for the formation of an organization called "Protestants and Other Americans United for the Separation of Church and State." This doctrine is one of the most successful falsehoods and hoaxes ever perpetrated on the American people. There is no such power in the Constitution, it does not exist.

One of the first Christian churches in America to be "Socialized" was the Grace Church of South Boston, where The Reverend W.D. Bliss was the pastor. A great friend of Sydney Webb, Bliss' missionary zeal on behalf of the Fabian Society was commendable, but his professed Christianity did not extend to teaching the Gospel of Christ. Another corrupter of the Christian religion was Father (later Monsignor) John Augustin Ryan, whose gospel was that taught by the English Socialist, John Hobson. Ryan formed a group called the National Catholic Welfare Council which was used by Fabian Socialists to penetrate and permeate Catholic churches all across America. Ryan went on to become known as "the padre of the New Deal" and was used by Roosevelt get the "blessing of religion for his more controversial New Deal bills."

But the real center of Socialist-religious activity in the United States was the Riverside Church, a Rockefeller "social science Christian" church, funded by the New York City Rockefeller Foundation. From this vantage point, inroads where made into the political life of the nation, particularly through the Dulles Family, who dominated the Federal Council of Churches of Christ in America (FCCA) The FCCA was one of the very first "religious groups" to enthusiastically back Roosevelt's "New Deal."

The 1935, the United States Navy intelligence service named the FCCA as the leader of pacifism: "...This is a large radical pacifist organization...its leadership consists of a small radical group that is always very active in any matter against national defense. "The Dies Committee took sworn testimony from an expert witness who stated as follows: "Apparently, in lieu of promoting Christianity among its several members it (the FCCA) more represents a huge political machine and appears to meddle in radical politics. Its directorate indicates that it interlocks with many of the most radical organizations."

In 1933, the Rev. Albert W. Beaven and 44 co-sponsors, delivered a letter to Roosevelt, in which they strongly urged him to Socialize America. Another "churchman," the Rev Dr. Kirby Page, told Roosevelt to support the Bolsheviks. "The aim of the proletariat in Russia was to establish a better life...It is difficult to find youth anywhere in this world more devoted to the cause of Christ than you'll find in Russia devoted to Stalin...," Kirby said.

Dr. Harry F. Ward, another leading light in the FCCA, actually resigned from the American Civil Liberties Union (ACLU) in 1925 because it barred "totalitarians" from its membership. The year before, Ward — then ACLU's chairman — had spoken out in favor of defending Socialist and Communist causes. This was at a time when Ward was Professor of Christian Ethics at the Union Theological Seminary, New York. Through his excellence in penetration and permeation tactics, Ward was able to subvert three generations of future American church leaders and steer them into the Socialist camp.

The Reverend Niebuhr was another prominent Socialist named by an expert called by Dies Committee hearings. Niebuhr held the post of Professor of Applied Christianity and Dean of the Union Theological Seminary, and was one of the very earliest American Fabian Socialists to push the book, "A New Deal" by Graham Wallas, a leading Fabian Society writer. In 1938, Niebuhr joined the Fabian Socialist American Association of University Professors, which called itself "a progressive educational body." As we know by now, "progressive" is merely another word for "Socialist." Niebuhr was also identified as being the secretary of the Students League for Industrial Democracy (SLID) (which later became the League of Industrial Democracy), the ultra Socialists student's organization that was heavily into radical politics.

Many of the student-members of SLID went on to join the Democrat Party, rather than try to form their own Socialist Party. It was from this beginning that the Democrat Party became infested with Socialists, until today, it is estimated by intelligence specialist contacts of mine, that as much as 86 percent of Democrat Party membership is made up of hard core Socialists. Niebuhr later was to have a profound influence over the Kennedy brothers, Robert citing Niebuhr's book, "Children of Light, Children of Darkness" (a pagan cultist book) as one often books he would take to the moon if he ever had to go there.

Niebuhr's influence ranged far and wide, spreading his "progressive" politics among Socialist members of Americans for Democratic Action (ADA), and LID. During all of his political life, Niehbur preached the "Social Gospel" which later became known as Marxist Liberation Theology. He became a close friend of Arthur Schlesinger Jr, preaching that "capitalism was a sickness" and that violence was in the eye of the beholder. Schlesinger went on to play a very significant role in Socializing America, proving that religious Socialism was a devastating weapon in the right (or wrong) hands. Niehbur openly embraced Marxism (although a totally godless creed and strange belief for a minister said to be as teacher of the Gospel), saying that it was "essentially a correct theory and analysis of the economic realities of modern society."

This so-called "theologian" was also active in controlling the press, having been appointed by Rockefeller to the "Commission on Freedom of the Press." Inevitably, Niehbur was appointed to the Council on Foreign Relations (CFR) on the instructions of David Rockefeller. Thus, in the religious theater of Socialist operations, we see that Fabian Socialism has been very busy in the United States and learned the lesson well that using religion as a means of penetration and permeation of society as a whole, was a very important one. We were led to believe that the Bolsheviks and their Socialist cousins were against all forms of religion. In fact this is not true at all. The Socialist/Bolshevik hatred of religion was directed more toward Christianity than any other religion.

One way in which the Socialists have been able to keep their grip on organized religion is through the Fellowship of Faiths, which was first established as a Socialist organization in 1921 and just recently, completely revived in readiness for the coming One World Government — New World Order. This is an organization meant to control religion — a long-time goal of Socialism — which realized that religion can never be stamped out. Senior Statesman of the Committee of 300, Bertrand Russell put the Socialists attitude to religion in this way: "If we cannot take control of it, then we must get rid of it. " But getting rid of religion was easier said than done, so "control" was the method chosen.

Not all wars thus fought have been able to rid the world of religion. Other

tactics had to devised, such as extensive brainwashing, using the shopworn rela-
tivistic idea that all religions are equal. Proof that the war against Christianity is
increasing in ferocity and intensity can be found in the attack upon the
Constitution of the United States by Socialists like Lloyd Cutler — advisor to
President Carter, President Clinton and his Attorney-General, Janet Reno.
Socialist Cutler seeks to weaken the Constitution so that protection and freedom
to worship and follow one's religion may thereby be abridged.

The shocking mass murder of United States citizens at Waco, Texas is a
recent example of just how far the Socialists are prepared to go to do away with
religious freedom. The events that led up to more Christian United States citizens
being killed than Chinese students in Tienenman Square, are too well known to
be recounted here, but some aspects need clarification and amplification:

The first item to consider is this: Where in the Constitution does it say that
the Federal Government has the right to interfere in the religious affairs of ANY
church, as it interfered and intervened in the affairs of the Branch Davidian
Christian Church? Where in the Constitution does it say that the Federal
Government has the right to decide what is a "cult" and what is not? Let Attorney
General Reno show us where this power is given to federal law enforcement
agencies. The truth of the matter is that it is not found; it is not in the Constitution!

Nowhere in the delegated powers of Congress in Article 1, Section 8, Clause
1-18 is the power to attack a "cult" given. To allow a Federal agency to interject
itself into the Branch Davidian Church and then attack it with force of arms, as
they did in Waco, would take an amendment to the Constitution of the United
States. What happened in Waco was treason and sedition against the Constitution
and the American people. In using military vehicles to attack civilians in a
Christian church we must suppose that the intention was to terrorize citizens and
deprive them of their rights:

Article 1 of the Bill of Rights of the United States Constitution states:
"Congress shall make no law respecting an establishment of religion or prohibit
the free exercise thereof; or abridge the freedom of speech, or of the press, or of
the right of people to peacefully assemble, and to petition the government for a
redress of grievances."

Note the use of the word "shall" which is very much stronger than "will."
Also note the words, "respecting the establishment of religion." Embodied in the
word "establishment" is the implicit understanding that it also means, the act of
establishing, or in plain language, a NEWLY ESTABLISHED ENTITY. In this
case the newly established entity was the Branch Davidian Church. Thus, the
Federal Government was duty bound under the law to PROTECT the Davidians,
NOT MURDER THEM.

The Federal Government went into Waco with the express intention of prohibiting the free exercise of religion by members of the Christian Branch

Davidian Church. It prohibited the Branch David ian members to assemble peacefully. What the Federal Government said, was, "we say that you are a cult and that we don't like your religion, and so we are going to shut your church down." To accomplish this, the Federal Government brought in military vehicles which they then used to assault the church buildings and kill the members of the Branch Davidian Church. On Page E7151 of July 31, 1968, Congressional Record, Justice William O. Douglas said"... It is impossible for government to draw a line between good and bad and be true to the Constitution, better to let all ideas alone." The United States Government chose to ignore this ruling and they tried to go in an simplify religion, to boil it down to good or bad, with the Federal Government the arbiters. The Federal Government tried to make religion a simple affair when it is a very complex one, in which they should not have been meddling under any conditions whatsoever.

The first ten Amendments to the Constitution of the United States are a restriction on the Federal Government. In addition permission to legislate on religion is also denied by Article 1, Section 9 of the constitution. The Federal Government has no absolute powers. The Branch Davidians were entitled to police protection under the powers granted to the State in the 10th Amendment. The Sheriff of Waco failed in his duty when he would not respond to a call for help from a member of the Branch Davidian Church, requesting that his do his duty, that duty being to defend citizens of the State of Texas from marauding Federal agents. Had the sheriff done his duty, he would have taken his men to the site and ordered Federal agents off the property and out of the State of Texas, where they had no jurisdiction. Unfortunately, the sheriff, either our of ignorance of the Constitution or in fear of his own safety, did not interdict the armed and dangerous Federal agents, as he was bound to do by the Constitution.

Under the Constitution of the United States, the responsibility for the protection of "life, liberty and property" belongs to the States and not to the Federal Government. The Emma Goldman case settled that forever. (The perpetrator was tried in a State court and executed by the State for the murder of President McKinley, although the murder of a President was,and still is a Federal crime.) The 14th Amendment, even though unratified did not try to shift responsibility for police protection from the States to the Federal Government. So what we had at Waco was an unauthorized attack on a religious community compounded by the abject failure of the sheriff to protect the citizens of the State of Texas against unlawful, illegal assault by Federal agents.

In consequence, the Branch Davidian citizens of the State of Texas were unlawfully, illegally and with malice aforethought, deprived of life, liberty and property, without due process, and denied a trial by jury, while the sheriff of Waco, responsible for administering State law, stood by and did nothing to stop these attacks. Charges for failing to carry out his duties should be brought against the sheriff of Waco. The immunity clause of Article IV, Part I was grossly violated: "The citizens of each State shall be entitled to all of the privileges and immunities of citizens in the Several States."

The Federal Government under the Constitution of the United States has no power to rule on what is a church and what is a cult. The power of the Federal Government to decided what is a cult and what is a religion is the power to DESTROY ALL RELIGIONS as the Socialists would prefer, and which is their ultimate aim. The 1st Amendment to the Constitution DOES NOT give this power nor is the power delegated to Congress. Instead, what we had was public opinion made by the media, with the repetition for days on end that the Branch Davidian Church was a "cult" as if that was enough legal sanction for the Federal agents to storm the church buildings.

Waco was not the first time that the Federal Government has interfered in religious matters, and most certainly, won't be the last. In pages 11995-2209 of the Congressional Record, Senate, Feb. 16, 1882, we read with horror how the government tried to stop some Mormons from voting. On page 1197 we read part of the debate. "...That right (to vote) belonged to the American civilization and law long before the Constitution was adopted. It is like the right of bearing arms, like many other rights that might be mentioned here, which existed in behalf of the citizens in colonial times in every State; and the provisions which were introduced in the Constitution by way of amendment, as well as in the original instrument, which stand for the protection of these rights, were mere guarantees of an existing right and were not the creators of the right itself."

The Mormons were regarded then as the Branch Davidian church was regarded by the Federal Government. In 1882, the Senate tried to pass a bill that would have appointed a commission of five people to act as judge and jury over the Mormons and stop them from voting. Apart from anything else, this was a violation of the bill of attainder. On page 1200 of pages 1195-1209, Senator Vest made the following statement:

"...For example, no one can presume, we will contend that Congress can make any law in a Territory, respecting the establishment of a religion, or the free exercise of, or abridge freedom of the press, or the right of the people of the Territory peaceably to assemble, and to petition the government for redress of grievances. Nor can Congress deny to the people the right to bear arms, nor the right to a trial by jury, nor compel anyone to be a witness against himself in a criminal proceeding. These powers, and other in relation to the rights of persons, which it is not necessary here to enumerate, are, in express and positive terms denied in the general Government; and the rights of private property have been guarded with equal care."

Upon examination the foregoing statement of fact regarding the protection afforded by the Constitution and its Bill of Rights, we are struck with horror of the Waco situation; The Branch Davidians were not given any protection guaranteed by the Constitution. The powers of police protection were abandoned by the Sheriff of Waco, the Federal Government attacked the members of the Branch Davidian Church, wantonly, savagely and barbarously took their lives, and utterly destroyed their property in defiance of their "rights to private property being guarded with equal care." We can see how far we have regressed since 1882, when the bill to stop the Mormons from voting was defeated.

Why were the Branch Davidians denied every single one of their rights? Why were they treated as an enemy trying to invade our shores would have been treated; with military equipment, helicopters, tanks, bulldozers, and finally, with fire that destroyed them all? Were their rights to a jury trial upheld, if, indeed the Federal Government had any legitimate charge against them before their agents went into church property with guns drawn?

All that has happened, is that the perpetrators of the crimes say, almost blithely, that they take responsibility for the barbarous acts of their servants! What we saw at the brutal massacre at Waco was Socialism/Communism in action. The religion preached by David Koresh may one day have been accepted as an established religion, like Mary Baker Eddy's Christian Science and the Mormons are accepted religions today. These religions might, in their beginnings, have been classed as "a cult," though the word did not have the same connotation then, which it has now. But the Federal Socialist Government was afraid that is what might happen with Koresh, as it had happened with Mary Baker Eddy, so they went in and nipped it in the bud.

Socialism is determined to control religion, and nowhere is this more evident that in their so-called "Fellowship of Faiths." Wars have not been able to rid the world of religion; the Bolsheviks took the lives of 60 million Russian people, the vast majority of whom were Christians. They turned Christian churches into houses of prostitution, stripped them of valuable art, and sold their plunder through the offices of such traitors as Armand Hammer. Christians have been persecuted and killed in terrible massacres, beginning with the Romans and continuing to this day, as we witnessed at Waco.

The Socialists, having realized that they cannot destroy religion by killing its believers and followers, took to trying to control it. They formed the spurious One World Government "Fellowship of Faiths" as a vehicle for taking control of all religions. In tandem with religious control, we are supposed to believe that Communism is dead and that it will soon be archaic. This is not so, Communism will never change. It may do so on the surface, but at the core, there will be little change. What will change is Socialism, as it gains more power and then, when it has taken full control of the world, it will reintroduce Communism as the taskmaster of the peoples of the earth.

Where does the Fellowship of Faiths fit in the scenario? How can it affect political events in a profound manner as is expected of it, and anticipated by its founders? The task of the unification of religion, that is to say, "standardizing" it, fell to Socialist Keddrantah Das Gupta, an executive member of the War Resisters League, and an advocate of armed revolution against our republic. Although dreamed up in 1910, the first formal session of the Fellowship was held in Chicago in 1933. Its true nature was exposed by Sir Rabindrath Tagore, founder of a pro-Communist political movement in India.

Bishop Montgomery Brown, the keynote speaker of the first FF seminar, said, "there will exist a complete World Fellowship of Faiths only when the Gods are banished from the skies and capitalists from earth." Clearly, the Fellowship was a Socialist enterprise from its inception. Sir Rabinddrath, in his written and spoken words, stressed the need for sex education in very young children, We tend to think of sex education for the young as a curse only recently descended upon us, but it actually goes back as far as the priests of Baal and the Egyptian priesthood of Osiris.

It would have been surprising to find Christian ministers and leaders actually accepting the idea of standardized religion and working with the haters of Christianity, were it not for the very same thing happening in the 1980s-1990s. In 1910, the World Friendship of Faiths was being promoted by Sir Francis Younghusband who pointed out that the idea of an East-West union of religions should be brought about. Sir Francis did not say the originator of the idea, Das Gupta, was a rabid Communist, seeking to promote that vile doctrine. Sir Francis gave the history of "standardized" religion as follows:

"The idea occurred to Mr. Das Gupta and he worked for 25 years on it and latterly found a cordial co-operator in an American, Mr. Charles F. Weller...In America a Parliament of Religion assembled in 1893. In Paris in 1904 commenced a series of sessions of the International Congress of the History of Religions. Other sessions were held in Basle, Oxford and Leiden." (All centers for "standardizing" religion and the promoters today of the Marxist doctrine of Liberation Theology.)

"In London in 1924, a Conference of the Living Religions of the Empire (the British Empire) was held. In 1913 in Chicago, continued in 1934 in New York, a Congress World Fellowship of Faiths, convened under the presidency of the Honorable Herbert Hoover and Miss Jane Addams." The presence of Miss Addams at these proceedings was a tip-off that here was rabid Socialism at work under the guise of religion. Miss Addams' history is given in the chapters on Socialist women. The idea was to submerge Christianity in a flood tide of other religions. But Christianity cannot be "standardized," it is unique and stands alone. Its teachings are the basis of capitalism which have since been replaced by Babylonialism, and today, capitalism has been so prostituted and debased as to be unrecognizable as the original system.

Without Christianity, the world will be plunged into a New Dark Age, far worse than anything that has gone before. This should help to explain why the detractors of Christianity are so eager to destroy it, or at least control it, so that it might be watered down, diluted, rendered useless. The Fellowship of Faiths sought to merge Christianity with other religions and so cause the loss of it as unique identity. The idea of a "separation of church and state doctrine" is the work of Socialists inside the United States Government. What it ought to be called, is, THE SUPPRESSION OF CHRISTIANITY WITHIN THE STATE.

Joining the enterprise of "standardizing" religion were Keith Hardie, a Socialist member of the British Labour Party, Felix Adler, founder of the Leftwing Ethical, Culture Society of New York, H.G. Wells, the noted Socialist author, who represented Lord Bertrand Russell. Wells was a member of the secret Masonic society Kibbo Kift Kindred, "Clarte," which had its headquarters in the Grand Orient Nine Sisters Lodge in Paris, the Lodge that played a leading role in the bloody French Revolution.

Moses Hess, an unabashed revolutionary Communists in the world at the time, joined with Wells in support of the Society for Cultural Relations with Soviet Russia. It was inside the confines of the Nine Sisters Lodge that Wells made a statement that was to brand him as a hater of Christianity: "Henceforth the new world government will not brook the competition of rival religious systems. It will have no place for Christianity. There must henceforth be only one faith in the world, the moral expression of the world community."

Annie Besant, a notable member of the Fabian Society, stepped forward to add her name to the list of those who opposed Christianity. Besant was the spiritual successor to Madame Blavatsky, founder of the Theosophy Society and a friend of H.G. Wells. Mr. Charles Wells of the Capitalist-Communist Alliance was a millionaire in his own right at a period in history where the term "millionaire" really meant something.

The task of organizing an American chapter of the Fellowship of Faiths was given to Weller, who quickly received the blessing of Samuel Untermeyer, a leading World Zionist and confidant of President Wilson, who immediately endorsed it after it was presented to him in the Oval Office. As Mr. Samuel Landman of the New York Zionists said, "Mr. Woodrow Wilson, for good and sufficient reasons, always attached the greatest importance to the advice of a very prominent Zionist."

The "good and sufficient reasons" referred to by Mr. Landmann was a packet of love letters written by Wilson to a Mrs. Peck, who in exchange for help promised by Untermeyer to get her son out of a criminal corner, handed the bundle of letters tied with a pink ribbon, either to Untermeyer, or Baruch. Wilson had a great passion for affairs with married ladies, the Peck romance being a particularly long-lasting and torrid one. Foolishly, Wilson conveyed his lovelorn feelings to Mrs. Peck — in writing. It was this indiscretion which is cited as the method used to blackmail Wilson to commit the United States to WWI, which buried the flower of Christian American manhood in the fields of Flanders, and all-but bankrupted this nation. Later, the support of the League of Neighbors, a Socialist "church" front, given to Wilson, almost carried the day for the League of Nations.

Chairman of the Provincial Executive Committee for General Zionist Affairs, Justice Brandeis, was succeeded by Rabbi Stephen Wise, who happened to be a member of the pro-Socialist Emergency Peace Federation front as well as nineteen other fronts. Brandeis was also a member of the London Fabian Society. Many of the old "religious Socialist" organizations are still in existence today, although they have changed their names to move with changing times and circumstances.

Upton Sinclair, rabid Socialist turned author who wrote for the "New Encyclopedia of Social Reform" and was a founder member of the American Fabian League, strongly supported the Fellowship of Faiths. Sinclair consistently gave Christianity a minus during his entire career. What neither Sinclair, Wise, Addams, nor indeed, many of the Fellowship's supporters told the public, was that it was a Freemasonic-inspired movement, through and through. In 1926 the Fellowship of Faiths was a well-established friend of world revolution, dominated by Rosicrucianists on the executive board and committee memberships.

The Threefold Movement started in 1924 by Charles Weller and Das Guptas, held meetings all over the United States and Britain. By 1925 they had held 325 such meetings. Among the leaders of the Threefold Movement were M.S. Malik, a member of the Beni-Israel sect; Dr. A.D. Jilla representing the Parsees; M.A. Dard, representing Mohammedanism; Sir Arthur Conon Doyle (of Sherlock Holmes fame) representing Spiritualism (note: this was the first time it was held out to be a religion), Buddhism, represented by Angarika Dharmapala: Theosophy represented by Annie Besant. The important point to bear in mind in all of this is that all of these religions were, and are, essentially anti-Christian. Another point is that Fellowship of Faiths literature was sold in Communist bookstores all over Britain, Western Europe and the United States.

The First World Congress of the Fellowship of Faiths was opened in Chicago in 1933, hosted by Miss Jane Addams. One of the principal speakers was Bishop Montgomery Brown, National Chairman of the Communist Workers Relief, and a member of fifty other Communist front organizations. In his opening address, Brown said:

"There is one place on earth where they have dared to end exploitation of man — Russia ! In Russia, science has replaced religion which is being stamped out...The USSR is the forerunner of International Communism which will gradually absorb all the capitalist states which are gradually decaying away. If any government, church or institution opposes or stands in the way of this Communist

State, they must be ruthlessly overthrown and destroyed. If world unity is to be attained, it must be arrived at through international Communism, which can only be attained through the slogan: 'Banish Gods from the skies and capitalists from the earth.' Then, and then only, will there exist a complete World Fellowship of Faiths."

Weller and Brown were effusive in their praise of Bishop Brown, Das Gupta stating, "I am sure that others feel as I do, that they have the same beliefs as Bishop Brown, but have not had the courage to speak out and admit it. I want to say that I am thoroughly in agreement with the Bishop's sentiments." Brown wrote a number of works, including one entitled, "Teachings of Marx for Boys and Girls," plus seventeen short books on sex for children which were widely distributed. A survey conducted by the authorities found that all those who were part of the structure and membership of the Fellowship of Faiths were also Freemasons.

The Freemasons established a front to cover their activities at the League of Nations conference in Paris, the organization being called The League of Nations Union. It played a profound role in the deliberations that went on at the Paris Peace Conference which virtually ensured that there would be another world war. As Sir Francis Younghusband said, "We are here to provide a firm spiritual basis for the League of Nations." We can best judge what KIND of a spiritual basis was provided, by simply studying the structure of the United Nations, the League's successor. It is in the confines of the United Nations and its religious executive arm, the World Council of Churches (WCC) that a revival of the Fellowship of Faiths is taking place.

We, in the United States and the West in general, cannot afford to turn a blind eye to this revival. Either we believe that the Christian religion is the basis of the Constitution of the United States, and stand on that, or we shall perish. "Tolerance," "understanding," must not be allowed to blindside us to the truth, and unless we make a stand now, it may well be too late tomorrow. That is how serious the situation has become for the future of the Nation. Either Christianity is the true religion as Jesus Christ has stated, or it is totally without substance. "Tolerance" and "understanding" cannot be allowed to obscure this important principle.

Christianity brought to the world a perfect economic system that has been deliberately prostituted, so that today, it is virtually unrecognizable. The Socialists/Marxists/Communists would have us believe that their system is superior, but when we look at the countries they have controlled — Russia, Britain, Sweden, we see ruination and misery on a grand scale. The Socialists strive mightily to bring their system to bear, which will lead to slavery. Religion is one of the most important areas that they have penetrated, and therefore, the more dangerous. This is not just a religious issue, but also a matter of survival of the

Republic, based upon the laws of God, which include immutable political and economic laws, and not a matter of "democracy" based upon the laws of man. We need to bear this in mind: *Every pure democracy in the history of the world has failed.*

It is important to link these things together, particularly, as I discovered that the Fellowship of Faiths members voted en-bloc for the Socialist ticket in the 1932 elections in which Roosevelt, their Socialist idol, was successful. This was particularly true in both New York and Chicago. The anti-Christian crusade will pick up steam as the big lie spreads around the world that Communism is dead. While it is true that Communism is lying low, SOCIALISM is rampant, particularly in the United States, where our churches have been thoroughly penetrated and permeated by Socialist change agents. To accept the One World Government — New World Order Fellowship of Faiths, we would have to sacrifice Christianity.

A most serious revolution is taking place in the United States. The Weishaupt revolution against the Christian Church has reached new levels of bestiality with the promotion of homosexuality and lesbian ism, "free love" (abortion) and a general lowering of the moral standards of the Nation. One of the principal leaders in this revolution is the World Council of Churches (WCC), the religious arm of the United Nations. WCC activities have resulted in far-reaching changes in the political, religious and economic life of the Nation. The WCC has always known that religion does not stop at the portals of the church.

The Federal Council of Churches (FCC), forerunner of the WCC, had as its plank, penetration and permeate civil government, particularly in the field of education and labor relations. Mark Starr, the British Socialist appointed by Roosevelt to a number of government posts, was used by the FCC to visit factories and distribute the Fabian Society's publication, "What the Church Thinks of Labor," a thoroughly Marxists diatribe against capitalism. The FCC was run on radical Socialist lines according to the methods laid down by Sydney and Beatrice Webb, its founders, and its membership of the Third International shows beyond a shadow of a doubt that the FCC/WCC was, and is, anti-Christian.

The FCC/WCC were run by pagans for pagans as its past history reveals, and as we see it today. One such pagan was Walter Rauschenbach who visited with Sydney and Beatrice Webb and then took their ideas, plus what he had learned from reading Marx, Mazzini and Edward Bellamy, to the Second Baptist Church in New York. Instead of the Gospel of Christ, Rauschenbach preached the gospel of Socialism according to Marx, Engels, Ruskin and the Freemasonic-Socialism of Mazzini.

The FCC/WCC claimed a membership of twenty million, but research proves that its membership was and still is, considerably less. As to the financial support the FCC received and the WCC receives today, research shows that it came from many pro-Communist organizations like the Laura Spellman Fund, the Carnegie Endowment Fund and the Rockefeller Brothers Foundation.

The FCC set the stage for the plague of homosexuality and lesbianism, not to mention "free love" without responsibility (abortion) that has descended upon the Nation. The FCC was, and the WCC is, the staunchest supporters of homosexuality and lesbianism, and were strongly supportive of so-called "constitutional" protection for these groups. Homosexuality is not mentioned as a "right" any where in the Constitution of the United States, and is, therefore a prohibition. "Homosexual rights" are a figment of the overripe minds of Socialist legislators and certain Supreme Court Justices.

In this the WCC was backed by the American Civil Liberties Union (ACLU), who tried to twist and squeeze the Constitution to create non-existent "rights" for those who chose the homosexual way of life. As we shall see in the chapters on law, courts, and the Congress, anyone of standing who protested the acceptance of these non existent "rights," soon found themselves in trouble.

The Fellowship of Faiths was formed for consolidating opinions on religious matters colored with Socialism gathered from around the world One of its strongholds is the Bahai movement. Bahaism was started in Persia in 1844 (today known as Iran), by Mirza Ali Muhammad, also known as "Rab" or "Gate." Unfortunately for "Rab" he was killed by security forces in Tabriz. Bahaism teaches that Zoroaster, Buddha, Confucius and Jesus Christ were leaders who prepared the way for the coming of the Mighty World Educator, Baha u'lla (the Glory of God), whose forerunner, Abdul Baha, died in 1921.

The Bahai movement is very strong in Iran and Australia, and to a lesser extent, England. Since Freemasonry and Theosophy are virtually indistinguishable from each other, and carry elements found in the Bahai faith, it is no wonder that the Bahai religion spread so quickly. Madame Petrova Blavatsky, Co-Mason, Vice President of the Supreme Council and Grand Master of the Supreme Council for Great Britain, creator of Theosophy, greatly favored the Bahai movement which is a convergence of these three streams.

What happened to the Fellowship of Faiths? Shortly before WWI it almost merged with World Zionism and then emergedins the League of Nations. Then, just before WWII, it emerged as the Bahai movement in England, and in England formed itself into the Oxford Group, which was succeeded by Moral Rearmament. Following the close of WWII, it played a key role in the formation of the United Nations (UN) and penetrated the heart of American political life through such outright Socialists organizations as the following:

American Association of University Professors
American Civil Liberties Union (ACLU)
Americans for Democratic Action (ADA)

Committee for Economic Development
Hull House (center for radical feminism)
National Council of Women
The League of Industrial Democracy
Social Democrats USA
Institute for Policy Studies
NATO, political wing
Club of Rome
The Cini Foundation
Cambridge Policy Studies Institute
Committee for a Democratic Majority
Lucius Trust
New Democratic Coalition
War Resisters League
Aspen Institute
Stanford Research
National Organization for Women

The Fellowship of Faiths is an "Olympian" (Committee of 300) project. This ensures that the richest and most powerful people in the world will promote its aims, as we saw in the "Class Reunion" of Fellowship of Faiths held in Chicago in 1993. The American people will have to choose between letting Christian principles go to the wall, or risk a world revolution. This was suggested by Mikhail Gorbachev when he met with Pope John Paul II. Gorbachev suggested a "convergence of religious ideals" which would be the first step toward a revived Fellowship of Faiths in its original name.

But Pope John Paul II reminded him, "Christianity brought into this continent by the Apostles, penetrated into various parts by the actions of Benedict, Cyril, Methuselah, Adalbert, and countless hosts of Saints, is at the very root of European culture." The Pope was not talking about any other religion having bestowed the benefits of civilization upon Europe: He was talking about Christianity. He did not say the growth of a great European culture was due to the Cathars or Albergensians; it was Christianity alone, he said, that brought civilization to Europe.

This is at the root of the hatred felt toward Christianity by the Communist/Marxist/Socialists, who greatly fear that the unifying force of Christianity will be the stumbling block over which their One World Government — New World Order will trip and fall. This is why the Socialist drive to negate and eventually wipe out Christianity, is a matter of urgent necessity. Lord Bertrand Russell's order to Socialism either to take over religion or destroy it, is the basis for Socialism's world-wide drive to penetrate and permeate the Christian religion in particular, and, in the manner of Weishaupt, bore away from the inside, until there is nothing left but a hollowed-out fragile structure to be collapsed by a few strategic blows when the time is right.

The most successful model of this tactic is found in South Africa, where a so-called church leader, the Reverend Heyns bored away from inside the Dutch Reformed Church, while a so-called Anglican "bishop," Desmond Tutu, launched a frontal assault on the Anglican Church. Aided by Freemasons in high posts inside the South African Government, who were willing to commit treason against their people, South Africa was brought down and forced under Communist rule in the person of Joe Slovo, a former colonel in the KGB who uses Nelson Mandela as a front-man puppet. The old saying, "beware of Greeks bearing gifts" can be modified: "Beware of priests and clergymen bearing false, fraudulent Socialist promises." The successful use of religion to bring Socialism into power has been amply demonstrated in Nicaragua, Peru, the Philippines, Rhodesia, South Africa. The United States is next.

8

PLANNED DESTRUCTION OF THE UNITED STATES THROUGH FREE TRADE

No bigger a Trojan Horse sits inside our Republic than "free trade." Elsewhere, we have often referred to it in passing. In this section we would like to fill in some of the details of this monstrous scheme to bring about the destruction of the United States, a long-held cherished dream of the Fabian Socialist in England and their converts in the country. Socialist destruction of our Republic is carried out on many fronts, but none so venomous, seditious, surreptitious and treasonous as so-called "free trade."

Any person who believes in "free trade" needs to be deprogramed and freed from Socialist propaganda-brainwashing. Go back to the beginning of this nation: Clause 1 of Section 8, Article 1, "To collect taxes, duties, imports and excises. To pay debts and provide for the common defense and general welfare of the United States, but all duties, imports and excises shall be uniform throughout the United States." Governor Morris wrote Section 8 and it is interesting to note that he implied that duties are related to paying the bills of the country. There is no mention of graduated income taxes here for that purpose.

The Socialists came along with their treasonous schemes and tried to nullify and repeal this section of the Constitution through the unratified, ultra-vires so-called 16th Amendment to the United States Constitution. They knew that Clause 1 of Section 8, Article I in the Constitution was to prevent the British from inflicting "free trade" on the Colonists. If we read the Annals of Congress and Congressional Globes of the late 1700s and early 1800s, it will quickly be impressed upon us that one of the principal causes of the American Revolution was an attempt by the British East India Company (BEIC) to impose Adam Smith's "free trade" on the colonies.

What is "free trade?" Why, it is just a euphemism for stripping and plundering the American people of their wealth in violation of the United States Constitution. It is the old shell game, brought up to date! "Free trade" was the shell game that the British East India Company (BEIC) used to deprive the American colonists of their wealth, disguising their cut-purse tactics with nice-sounding economic phrases, in themselves, meaningless.

The Founding Fathers did not have the benefit of first hand experience to warn them of the "free trade" wars that would descend on the colonies, but they had the perspicacity and foresight to know that if allowed, "free trade" would wreck the young nation. It was for this reason that President George Washington, having witnessed the terrible devastation wrought in France for the cause of "free trade" and dubbed the "French Revolution," in 1789 declared that it was necessary and proper for the young Republic to protect itself from the machinations of the British government:

"A free people should promote such manufactories as tend to render them independent on others for essential particularly military supplies." — George Washington, First Congress of the United States, 1789.

The Founding Fathers saw from the very beginning that protection of our trade was paramount, and made it virtually the first order of business. No nation which is serious about its sovereignty and protecting the welfare of its people, would allow "free trade." As Joseph Chamberlain said, in his Preface to "The Case Against Free Trade" in 1911:

"Free trade is the negation of organization, of settled and consistent policy. It is a triumph of chance, the disordered and selfish competition of immediate individual interests without regard to the permanent welfare as a whole."

Alexander Hamilton and the Founding Fathers understood that the nation would have to protect its internal market if it wanted to remain sovereign and independent. That was what made America great in the first place: the explosion of industrial progress in the nation, independent of any outside "global trade." Washington and Hamilton knew that to surrender our internal markets to the world would be tantamount to foregoing our national sovereignty.

Socialists know the importance of getting rid of the protective trade barriers of independent nations, as opposed to only now and then breaching them, and they waited their chance to elect Woodrow Wilson for that purpose. As the new President, Wilson's first order of business was to take active measures to smash the tariff barriers erected by Washington and then enlarged and kept in place by Lincoln, Garfield and McKinley.

As we saw earlier, the first order of business of the Fabian Socialist who put President Woodrow Wilson in power was to break down the trade barriers and protective tariffs that had made the United States a great nation in a relatively short time, relative, that is, to the age of older European powers. The NAFT Agreement and GATT take up where Wilson and Roosevelt left off. Both agreements violate the Constitution of the United States and arc the work of The Fabian Society and their American cousins.

The North American Free Trade Agreement is project of the Committee of 300 and a natural extension of the war on American industry and agriculture as set out in the Club of Rome's 1969 Post Industrial Zero Growth position papers overseen by Cyrus Vance and a team of One World Government-New World Order scientists. Breaking down the trade barriers erected by Washington, Lincoln, Garfield and McKinley was long a cherished goal of the Fabian Society. NAFTA is their concoction, their big chance to open the markets of the United States to one-way "free trade' ' and through it, deal a mortal blow to the American middle class.

NAFTA is another triumph for Florence Kelley in that it gets around the Constitution by legislative action. As Judge Cooley said in his work on Constitutional law, page 35: "The constitution itself never yields to a treaty or enactment. It neither changes with time nor does it bend to the force of circumstances." Therefore, neither NAFTA nor any other treaty can change the Constitution. NAFTA is nothing but a crooked, lying, sneaky lowdown scheme to circumvent the Constitution, also an accurate description of GATT.

The first known "free trade" attack on the United States came in 1769 when the Townsend Act was invented by Adam Smith to squeeze revenues out of the American colonies. The NAFTA agreement is designed to squeeze more out of the American worker, or if the workers are unwilling, the workgiver will relocate abroad where wages and life are generally cheaper. In essence, NAFTA has a lot in common with the struggle of the colonists in the period 1769-1776. Tragically, in later years several presidents moved away from trade policies that protected American industry and made the United States the greatest industrialized nation in the world.

Globalism played no part in making America great. Globalism is a catchword of the Madison Avenue media brainwashers to disguise the fact that the so-called global economy touted by Wilson, Roosevelt, Bush and Clinton will eventually reduce America's living standards to that of Third World countries. Here we have a classic case where through Socialism, Americans are fighting again the American Revolution of 1776 to set the nation free of the toils of the fraud that is called NAFTA, with an even bigger fraud called GATT waiting to march onto the battlefield.

In 1992, Bush eagerly picked up the NAFTA ball and began to run with it. Canada was used as a measuring stick to see how well NAFTA would sit with the Canadian people. In this Bush was ably assisted by former prime minister Brian Mulroney. The purpose of NAFTA is to destroy the industrial and agricultural bases of both countries and thereby bring down the middle class. The Post Industrial plans of the Committee of 300 have not progressed fast enough. The situation is rather akin to that which Bertrand Russell described in his desire to kill off millions of "useless eaters." Russell's plan called for a return of the black plague to rid the world of what he called, "excess population."

NAFTA represents a high point in the realignment of transnational policies and the reeducation of those future leaders of American industry and trade who are just now graduating from our institutions of learning. NAFTA may be compared with the Congress of Vienna (1814-1815) which was dominated by Prince Klemmens von Metternich. It will be recalled that Metternich played a leading role in European affairs. He was responsible for the marriage of Arch duchess Marie Louise to Napoleon, which shaped political and economic events in Europe for at least 100 years. Clinton has in essence, "married" the United States to "free trade," which will likewise have a tremendous effect upon this nation for more than 1,000 years.

The Congress of Vienna was marked by lavish parties and glittering events, with an array of dazzling gifts for those who were willing to cooperate with Metternich instead of fighting for the best interests of their country. Similar tactics were used to force NAFTA through the House and Senate, and in the manner of the decision-making debates held behind closed doors in Vienna (the four major powers never allowed the smaller nations to participate) every agreement, every decision of note concerning NAFTA was done in secret, behind closed doors. NAFTA will have a profound deleterious effect upon the United States, the extent and depth of which we have yet to realize.

NAFTA is the turning point in the history of North America, a watershed for the American and Canadian middle class. When combined with EC countries, phase two of the Socialist strategy to take complete of control of trade will have been completed. NAFTA will result in an income of $100 billion for Mexico; it will devastate the American economy through a great decline in its industrial base. A loss of 100,000 American jobs is expected to occur within the first two years of NAFTA being fully implemented, which will send the middle class standard of living plummeting in a manner never before experienced. Pollution will be reexported to the United States through products and food from Mexico.

Foodstuffs from Mexico will contain levels of toxic poisons of all kinds which are forbidden by USDA regulations covering American products. Taking all things into account, the amount of money spent on NAFTA lobbying was close to $150 million. NAFTA lobbying was the most concentrated in the history of the United States, involving a veritable army of specialists and lawyers who overwhelmed the House to vote in favor of the so-called agreement.

The General Agreement on Tariffs and Trade (GATT) is an instrument designed in the United States, based upon Fabian Socialist principles. I don't recall when last something was as little understood by the lawmakers than is this insidious agreement. I contacted scores of legislators, and without exception, not one of them could provide me with an explanation, nor give me facts for which I was searching. GATT was put together at the United Nations Conference on Trade and Employment, held in Cuba, on March 24, 1948. The conference elegates advanced the cause of Adam Smith's "free trade" which they said, would make the world a better place for the ordinary people. While the title, GATT was to come later, the groundwork for this Socialist fraud was laid in Cuba in 1948.

When the agreement reached in Cuba was presented to the House and Senate, it was passed, for the simple reason that it was not understood. Generally, when the House and Senate do not understand a measure before them, the measure gets passed as quickly as possible. This is what happened in the case of the Federal Reserve Act, the United Nations Treaty, the Panama Canal Treaty and NAFTA.

By voting in favor of the NAFTA, the House transferred United States sovereignty to the One World Government in Geneva, Switzerland. This seditious act had a precedent. In 1948, a Republican-dominated House and Senate passed the Trade Agreement Act which arose from the United Nations meeting in Cuba. Hitherto, the Republican Party had held itself out to be the protector of American industry and American jobs, but it turned out to be as false as the Democrat position, and in favor of Adam Smith's Socialist "free trade." A great blow was struck against American industry and trade by the Fabian Socialists in Britain and their American cousins in the United States. The fact that the Trade Agreement Act was 100 percent unconstitutional, and yet it passed, was a cause of sweet satisfaction for the Fabian Society.

By 1962, President John F. Kennedy was calling the sell-out of the American people, "a wholly new approach, a bold new instrument of American trade policy." In his fatally-flawed assessment of where the Fabian Socialists were taking the American people, Kennedy had been fully supported by labor leader George Meaney at the AFL — CIO convention in Florida earlier that year. Congress dutifully passed the legislation, seemingly oblivious of its unconstitutionality.

It was unconstitutional because it gave to the president powers that belonged to Congress, powers that could not be transferred between the three branches of government. The Kennedy administration immediately instituted sweeping tariff cuts, some by as much as 50 percent on a broad range of imported goods. We saw the same unconstitutional actions by Bush and Clinton with NAFTA. Both presidents got unconstitutionally involved in the legislative branch. Bribery may have also been a factor. This is treason.

As the United States entered the twentieth century, the country was on the road to success as no other country had been before it, dating back to antiquity. But the despoilers, the Socialists and their close cousins, the Communists, were lying in wait for America. The United States was built on a solid foundation of protectionism, sound money; there was a rapidly growing industrial base, and thanks to mechanization, agriculture was set to feed our people for centuries to come, no matter what the increase in population might be.

The trade protection measure, the Tariff Act of 1864, which Lincoln signed, increased Customs duties by more than 47 percent. In 1861 Customs receipts brought in 95 percent of the total revenues of the United States. Lincoln, with war on his hands was determined to reinforce the traditional tariff protection and protect it at all costs. His actions on tariff protection, more than anything else, set the United States on the road to two decades of progress in industry, agriculture and commerce, progress that stunned England and made the United States an object of envy — and hatred. There is no doubt that the plot to assassinate Lincoln involved Benjamin Disraeli, England's prime minister and that the decision to murder Lincoln was taken in England because of the president's resolute stand against lowering tariffs on goods from that country.

The United States is in a war to the death. This is not recognized, because there are no big drums of patriotism being banged; no flags flying high, no military parades, and perhaps the key to it all, the jackals of the press are playing "free trade" up as a benefit, not as the mortal enemy of the United States. It is a war on many fronts; just about the entire world is lined up against the United States. It is a war that we are fast losing, thanks to skillfully laid plans of the Committee of 300 given to the Socialists to carry out. Lincoln was one of the first casualties of the trade war.

In 1873, the merchant bankers and City of London financiers combined with their allies on Wall Street to contrive a panic that was due entirely to artificially-created causes. The prolonged depression that followed, badly hurt agriculture, as was the intention of our enemies. Most historian agree that the 1872 anti-United States action was taken to weaken protectionism. The way for yellow journalism to blame protectionism for the depression was opened and has never closed. Thanks to the scurrilous lies that appeared in the press, farmers were led to believe that their problems were caused by trade barriers stopping the flow of "free trade."

Agents of the City of London and Wall Street, aided by the already then kept press, began pounding the pavement of public opinion, and in response to pressure from an ill-informed public, in 1872, a breach in the United States tariff barrier was opened. Custom duties were reduced by 10 percent on a broad range of imported items and by 50 percent, on salt and coal. As any economist knows, and as any properly-taught high school graduate would know, once this happens, it soon follows that manufacturing activity will begin to decline as investors stop investing in real wealth — industrial plants, agricultural implements, machine tools.

But the invaders were partially repelled by the 1900s, and damage was confined to a breach in our redoubt, with the enemy forces unable to beak out into the hinterland. Then came Wilson and the first massive, major assault carried out by anti-tariff protection troops who not only smashed our redoubts, but put the Philistines right in the middle of our camp.

When President Roosevelt came to the White House, the second major assault against our tariff walls was launched. Wilson had paved the way for Roosevelt, and was greatly successful in opening up a breach that led to the highway to the hinterland. Although Wilson did a great deal of damage, which was enlarged by Roosevelt, too much of the tariff wall still remained in place for the liking of Fabian Socialists, Ramsey McDonald, Gunnar Myrdal, Miss Jane Addams, Dean Acheson, Chester Bowles, William C. Bullitt, Stuart Chase, J. Kenneth Galbraith, John Maynard Keynes, Professor Harold Laski, Walter Lippmann, W. Averill Harriman, Senator Jacob Javitts, Florence Kelley and Frances Perkins.

When George Bush was appointed by the CFR to sit in the Oval Office, he tackled his One World — New World Order assignment with energy and enthusiasm, making the NAFTA agreement one of his first priorities. But did Wilson, Roosevelt and Bush have the right to negotiate treaties covering trade matters on their own without, the advise and consent process of the Constitution being observed? Obviously not.

Let us then examine the Constitution and see what it has to say on this vital issue: Article VI, Section 2 "...This Constitution and the laws of the United States which shall be made in pursuance thereof, and all treaties made, or shall be made, under the authority of the United States shall be the supreme law of the land..." The words, "This Constitution and the laws of the United States", says that a treaty is only a law. Law of the Land" relates to the Magna Carta, "and the Judges in every State shall be bound thereby, anything in the Constitution or the laws of any State to the contrary no withstanding."

The word "supreme" in part 2 is NOT "supreme" but ordinary law. To grasp this fully, one has to know the United States Constitution and the historical background that goes with it, which can be found only in the Annals of Congress, the Congressional Globes and the Congressional Records. A full and proper studies of these documents is a prerequisite for understanding what a treaty is. Unfortunately, our legislators never bother to educate themselves through a study of these marvelous journals. Law professors know still less about these mines of information, and therefore, frequently teach constitutional law that is very wide of the mark. It is a case of the blind leading the blind.

"Supreme" was inserted to ensure that French, British and Spanish governments could not backtrack on agreements made over territories ceded to the United States. It was a sufficient way to prevent future governments of these countries on reneging on agreements, but, unfortunately, also caused many Americans to understand that a treaty is "supreme" law. It is impossible for a treaty to be "supreme" when it is only in pursuance thereof. "Can the offspring be greater than the parent? The United States Constitution is always SUPREME at all times and in all circumstances. Laws can never be "supreme" as they are alterable and may have been wrongly passed. The child cannot be greater than the parent.

In spite of what Justice Ruth Ginsberg said about the constitution being flexible, the United States Constitution is not flexible, it is IMMUTABLE. We know that the first rule of any treaty is self preservation. We also know now, that in the United States ALL TREATIES WITHOUT EXCEPTION ARE ORDINARY LAWS AND CAN BE REPEALED AT ANY TIME. A treaty, any treaty, that seriously harms the United States violates the rule of self preservation and can be revoked, even if only by cutting off money to fund it. That is why treaties like the U.N., NAFTA, GATT, ABM, Panama Canal Treaty, are NULL AND VOID, and ought to be revoked by Congress; indeed, would be revoked, if Congress was not dominated by Socialists.

Readers are urged to get a copy of "Law of Nations" by Vattel, the "Bible" used by our Founding Fathers and they will quickly become convinced that a treaty is only a law that can be changed by Congress. In fact a treaty might be described as a "precarious law" because, in essence, it is without substance. Thomas Jefferson said "to hold the treaty-making power boundless, is to make the Constitution blank paper by construction." Congressional Record, House, Feb. 26, 1900.

In addition, the Constitution of the United States expressly forbids the transfer of powers from one branch of government to another. This happened all through the Free Trade Wars and is still going on. The slow, often unnoticed surrender of the legislative to the executive branch of government is what has sapped the strength of the defenders in the Trade Wars. Such actions are unconstitutional and tantamount to sedition and treason against the American people.

The surrender of powers that belong exclusively to the legislative branch of government began with the Payne Aldrich Tariff Act, and the misshapen creature began to grow like the green bay tree. Although the Payne Aldrich Act did not achieve its first goal, it was more than successful in its second; the transfer of legislative powers to the executive. It gave powers to the President, forbidden to him by the constitution in that he could now control Customs duty rates on imports. The House delivered a mortal blow to the very people it was supposed to protect, and allowed "free trade" to rob our workers of their jobs, as manufacturing facilities unable to meet the cut-price, dumping policies of foreign made goods, were forced to close down.

That treason and sedition was committed by those who accepted the Payne Aldrich Tariff Act of 1909 as "law," is today apparent in the NAFTA and GATT agreements. The United States Constitution in Article 1, Section 10 clearly placed matters of trade in the care of the House of Representatives. Section 10 strengthened control by the House over trade matters. The powers of the House were not and are not transferable! It is as simple as that. Any and all "laws," "executive orders," presidential decisions on matters of trade, international agreements, are null and void and must be wiped off the books as soon as government is returned to We, the People. We shall see the huge damage wrought by presidential usurpation of trade powers as we continue.

The Payne Aldrich Tariff Act is typical of the way in which Fabian Socialism acts, always disguising its true intentions behind a facade of lies and more lies. As I have said before, the American people are the most lied to people in the world, and the Payne Aldrich Tariff Act was the high point of lies at the time. Put forward in the House as a tariff protection measure, the real meaning of the act was the exact opposite: it was one giant step forward for the enemies of the American people, the "free traders" and their City of London allies — or is masters a better description of their association?

The Payne Aldrich Tariff Act ostensibly transferred powers to the executive, a transfer that could not and should not have taken place without a constitutional amendment having been passed. Since this did not happen, every trade agreement since 1909 is ultra-vires. If we had a Supreme Court that was not in the hands of the Philistines, we might have been able to turn to it for help, but cannot.

Since the days of Brandeis and "Fixer" Fortas, the Supreme Court has become a Socialist-packed court which has no ears to hear the pleas of We, the People. With passage of the Payne Aldrich Tariff Act, the United States suffered a grave reverse in the Trade Wars, one from which it has never recovered. The Payne Aldrich measure was Socialist "gradualism" in the best traditions of that dishonest political entity.

These sneak attacks on the people of the United States came at a time of our relative innocence. We knew little about Fabian Socialism or of its modus operandi. The book, "The Case Against Socialism: A Handbook for Conservative Speakers" is a guide to the dirty tricks Socialism uses to get its legislation passed and there is no greater dirty tricks Socialist player than President Clinton.

The people of this great United States have been bamboozled by their leaders — beginning with Woodrow Wilson — into believing that such a thing as "free trade" is beneficial for all nations. They will tell us that it was the brainchild of Adam Smith and that David Ricardo, the Socialist's favorite economist, refined the bounds and meaning of free trade. But it all just so much smoke and mirrors. The mythology of "free trade" is so ingrained in the minds of the American people that they believe it really is beneficial! The leadership of the nation, starting with the President on down, has grossly misled the people into this terrible trap.

THE CASUALTIES FROM THIS WAR ARE ALREADY FAR GREATER THAN THE COMBINED TOTALS OF WWI AND WWII. Millions of

Americans lives have already been ruined. Millions live in despair as this relentless war continues to plow under our people. "Free trade" is the biggest single
threat to the infrastructure of the nation — a greater threat than any nuclear attack
could ever be.

Just a few statistics:

Seven hundred and fifty thousand American steelworkers have lost their jobs
since the Committee of 300 unleashed Count Etienne Davignon on this particular
battlefront in 1950.

A million and a quarter of the best paying, stable, industrial jobs related to
and relying upon steel products, were lost in consequence of the death of the steel
industry. This was not because American steel workers were not good workers; in
fact, given the old plants some had to work with, they did very well against unfair
trade practices. But they could not compete with "free trade" imports that under-
sold U.S.-made products because foreign governments heavily subsidized them.
Many of the foreign steel mills were even built with "Marshall Plan" money! By
1994, a total of forty million Americans had lost their jobs due to "free trade"
attacks on their factories, textile mills, production plants.

America grew to be an industrial giant and in the 1880s was leading England
as the world's No.1 industrial nation. This was entirely due to the protection provided local industry by trade barriers. When the Civil War broke out, and up to
close of the nineteenth century, there were 140,000 factories producing heavy
industrial goods with a work force of 1.5 million Americans, probably the best
paid by far in the world at any period in Western history.

By the 1950s, industry and agriculture had created the finest living standard
for America's vast, stable, well-paid middle class, the largest of its kind to be
found anywhere in the world. It had also created a vast market for its goods, an
internal market that its well paid middle class in jobs with guaranteed lifelong job
security supported and helped to enlarge and expand. AMERICA'S PROS PERI-
TY AND JOB SECURITY DID NOT COME FROM GLOBAL TRADE. The
United States did not need world markets to prosper and grow. This was a false
bill of goods sold to the American people, first, by Wilson, and then eagerly, by
Roosevelt, Eisenhower, Kennedy, Johnson, Bush and Clinton.

Thanks to the treason and sedition committed by these presidents and
Congress, imports have steadily risen, until now, in 1994, we can barely keep our
heads above the rising flood waters of cheap-labor imported goods. In the coming year (1995), we shall see casualties skyrocket as the assault by the "free
traders" decimates the livelihood of millions more Americans. There is no end in
sight, yet, our lawmakers continue to retreat, leaving millions upon millions of
wrecked lives behind them. This, more than any other single issue, proves that the
government is not serious about protecting our national sovereignty, WHICH IS
THE FIRST DUTY OF ANY GOVERNMENT.

In this chapter we will only be able to examine a few of the more important treaties, charters and trade "agreements" forced upon the United States by the conniving, cheating, underhand, lying, seditious practices of British and American Socialists. We shall begin with so called "trade agreements." The constitution forbids the transfer of power from one branch of government to another branch. It is called the doctrine of separation of powers and is sacrosanct and immutable, or that is the way it was written by the Founding Fathers. It is illegal, even treasonous to transfer powers, yet we are supposed to believe it was legal for Bush to consult with Mexico and Canada and get the NAFTA agreement up and running. We are supposed to believe that, likewise, Clinton had every right to meddle in NAFTA and now, GATT. Wrong on both counts! Neither Bush nor Clinton had the right to interfere in matters of trade that properly belong to the House.

On this count alone, NAFTA and GATT are illegal, and if we had a Supreme Court that was not making its own predilections instead of upholding the Constitution, it would be so declared. One of the most common tactics used by the "free trade" generals in attacking the United States is to blame "trade barriers" for economic hard times. This is palpably untrue. In looking back over newspaper reports in the "New York Times," the "Washington Post" and others, I found that they never, ever, gave the true picture of what a grave injury "free trade" was doing to this Nation. The incendiary Liberals never let on that the United States was being systematically bled dry from the time that Wilson mounted the first assault on our trade defenses.

The much heralded "Marshall Plan" which is supposed to have saved Europe from ruination was in fact a "free trade" scam. The British people, tired of war criminal Winston Churchill, voted Labor Party leader Clement Attlee, Churchill's deputy Prime Minister and a Fabian Socialist elitist to succeed him. It was Attlee who succeeded Ramsey McDonald, sent "to spy out the land" for Socialism in the United States in the late 1890s. Attlee ranked in the Fabian lists of stars alongside Professor Harold Laski and Hugh Gaitskell, the latter a favorite of the Rockefellers, who chose Gaitskell to go to Austria in 1934 to see what Hitler was up to.

When Chamberlain was ousted because he refused to go along with the Committee's war plans, Attlee was waiting in the wings, and his turn came when he was called upon to replace Churchill. At that time, Britain had not yet repaid its WWI loans to the United States, as it had agreed to do in the Lausanne conference. Yet, in spite of this huge outstanding debt obligation, Britain contracted billions upon billions of dollars of debts that Roosevelt wanted to forget: "Let's forget those silly little dollar signs" said Roosevelt, while urging Lend Lease upon the Nation.

With Labor in power in England, the elite of the Fabian Society immediately put their cherished Socialist schemes into practice nationalizing major industries and providing so-called cradle to grave social services. Of course the British treasury could not meet the huge new financial obligations thrust upon it by the Fabianists, without severely increasing taxes, so Attlee and fellow Socialist John Maynard Keynes, turned to the United States for help. The first artillery barrage on United States taxpayers came in the form of a $3.75 billion loan, which Roosevelt quickly and happily granted.

The $3.75 billion American loan money was used to pay debts incurred by the Socialist government in their mad pursuit of unlimited Socialist spending and Socialist transfer programs. They had yet to come to grips with reality, and when Labor still didn't have enough cash in hand to meet its obligations, the Fabian Brain Trusters got together and dreamed up the Marshall Plan.

Fittingly, the Marshall Plan was unveiled at Harvard University — that hotbed of Socialism in the United States — by Socialist General George Marshall. Cost to the United States taxpayers? A staggering $17 billion over the next five years, which went largely to European countries to fund their State-subsidized industries, so that they could dump their cheaper foreign made goods on the American market, resulting in the loss of millions of good paying, long term industrial jobs.

This had been anticipated by the Fabian Socialist planners, who needed Woodrow Wilson to break open the gates of America's trade barriers, so that foreign-made goods could flood the United States market in the immediate post WWII years, which helped France, Poland, Hungary, and the United Kingdom stabilize their national incomes at the cost of the American worker!

Is it possible that a government such as ours would do such a terrible thing to its own people? Not only is it possible, in reality, our government turned on its people, sending millions of them to stand in breadlines, without jobs and without hope. Our workforce was turned into a line of beggars, desperately trying to understand what had happened to their jobs, and how it had come to pass that instead of working at their old jobs, they were now standing in breadlines or begging for non-existent jobs at some or other employment office.

The Founding Fathers must have turned over in their graves! Had they been around, they would, no doubt have wondered how the descendants of the Colonists, who had fought so hard to throw off taxes imposed by King George III (including a tea tax of one penny per pound), could now to stand back and meekly allow themselves to be taxed out of existence, and have their national income from Customs receipts dry up. They would also probably recoiled in horror from the loss of an estimated $17 billion in Lend Lease debts, which the Socialist-controlled Congress wiped off the books in order to rescue their fellow Socialists in Britain keep the One World Government — New World Order Fabian — Socialist pipe dream going.

Earlier, we emphasized the great damage done to our industrial heartland by the transfer of powers in matters of trade from the House to the executive branch of government. A few case histories will help reinforce our conclusions. But before getting to specifics, it is worthy of note that three United States Presidents, Lincoln, Garfield and McKinley, all staunch defenders of tariff and trade barriers, were murdered for their stand against the "free trade" enemies of this nation. This is well known, but not so well known is the fact that Senator Russell B. Long, one of the most brilliant men ever to grace the Senate benches, was fiercely opposed by the "free traders."

President Gerald R. Ford tried to staunch the severe wounds suffered by industry as imported goods of all kinds began to flood the markets of the nation. For this, he was portrayed by the jackals of the press as a bumbler, a stumbler who could not control his own balance, let alone run the nation. The "free trade" enemies made sure that Ford's stay in the White House was a brief one, especially after Ford signed the Trade Act of 1974, which was the culmination of the efforts of Senator Huey Long to stem the rising flood tide of imported goods.

Long, chairman of the Senate Finance Committee, proposed measures that would strengthen existing tariff protection through Section 201. In terms of Long's "escape clause" (Section 201) companies that were being hurt by imports no longer had to prove their case. But they still had to show that "substantial injury, or the threat thereof" to their business was due to imports. Before Section 201 of the Trade Act of 1974, the cumbersome, time consuming, costly task of proving their case caused many a factory to close down rather than go through a procedure heavily weighted in favor of foreign governments. A shame and a scandal? Yes, but our lawmakers were responsible for this unbelievable state of affairs, not some foreign government or collection of governments.

The heinous fact is that ever since the Wilson presidency, foreign governments have had more standing before U.S. law than our own factory owners and their labor force in matters of trade laws. In anticipation of the move toward "global trade" the United States government even changed the name of the watchdog agency on trade matters from the Tariff Commission, to the United States INTERNATIONAL Trade Commission (ITC) Nobody protested this small step toward selling what remained of our industries down the Global Trade River. Because President Ford signed the Trade Act of 1974, he was vilified as being "anti-free trade" and his stay in office shortened.

In practice, Clause 201 did not provide the promised relief. By the time the full Senate, packed with Socialists masquerading as "liberal Democrats" had finished chewing over the bill, the already unlevel playing field now had a steep uphill gradient against local manufacturers. Notwithstanding Long's specific wording to the contrary, it came out in practice that an industry could only file a case AFTER suffering injury for some time, and even then, there was no guarantee of success, as the ITC might not rule against offending imports. Worse yet, even if the ITC did rule in favor of local industry, the president could still veto the measure.

While all this was going on, hundreds of American companies were forced to close due to unfair competition from foreign goods.

It is difficult to believe that any President of this country would put foreign interests above those of his own people, but this is what happened, time after time, and it is still happening today with the Clinton Socialists in power. The United States Constitution, Section 3 of Article 11 says: "He, (the President) shall take care that the laws be faithfully executed..." None of the Presidents from Wilson to Clinton has taken care to execute the laws protecting our trade, and for that they ought to have been impeached.

After Ford was hit with the charges that he was "anti-free trade," he backed down in his proposed defense of the shoe industry, which had shown a clear hardship case against imported footwear. During the Johnson, Ford, Carter, Reagan, Bush administrations, hundreds of appeals in terms of the Trade Act of 1974 were turned aside, including representations made by the automobile, footwear, garment, computer and television manufacturers, and steel. Clinton is proving to be an even worse enemy of his own people than Wilson and Roosevelt. The Congress and Presidents shot their troops in the back.

A particular case history that is worth recounting concerns the footwear industry, and there are literally scores of similar cases in other industries. At the time that Lincoln came to the White House, shoes and boots were made in small cottage-type, family enterprises scattered around the country. This changed with the advent of the Civil War, but still, thousands of small producers who could not handle Army contracts stayed in business and did very well. There was patently no need to import footwear.

The "free traders" fixed their sights on the footwear industry, which in smaller towns was often the sole employer. Through Congress, the trade barriers against imported footwear began to come under attack. Local manufacturers were accused of causing "inflation" through higher prices. This was completely false. The shoe industry was turning out a good product at a very competitive price. But by the time Lyndon Johnson arrived at the White House, the "free traders" had secured 20 percent of the local market. Then, an alarmed Footwear Industries of America filed a case with the ITC asking for immediate relief, but, as mentioned earlier, Ford gave them no relief.

When Carter arrived on the scene, he too was as petitioned by the Footwear Industries of America. *What is wrong here of course is that the President should have had ANY say in trade matters that rightly belong with the Congress.* But, having already violated the Constitution in a hundred ways, there was no stopping Carter. Instead of coming to the aid of his own people, Carter made an agreement with Taiwan and Korea that was supposed to limit their footwear exports to the

United States, but which in practice, did not ameliorate the situation. The footwear market for imports shot up to 50 percent of the United States market. Carter was deaf, blind and dumb when it came to protecting the livelihood of hundreds of thousands of Americans. Yet this is the same Carter who addressed the nation on television on July 15, 1979:

"The threat is nearly invisible in ordinary ways. It is a crisis of confidence. It is a crisis that strikes at the very heart and soul and spirit of our national will. We can see this crisis in the growing doubt about the meaning of our own lives and in the loss of unity of purpose for our nation." Indeed, and by encouraging "free trade" Carter was responsible for the crisis.

There never was a more hypocritical message to come out of the Oval Office. In the Korean War, General Douglas MacArthur was betrayed by Dean Acheson and Harry Truman. In the Free Trade War, the Footwear Battle was lost because we were betrayed by Jimmy Carter and Robert Strauss.

Next came "conservative" President Ronald Reagan, who did nothing to prevent the flooding of the market by huge amounts of footwear imports from Korea and Taiwan, neither of which countries has never ever imported one single pair of shoes made in the United States! So much for "free trade." As a result of Reagan's studied negligence, shoe imports now hit a new high in 1982, totaling 60 percent of our market. As a matter of grave national importance, it also pushed up the trade deficit by a whopping $2.5 billion and threw more that 120,000 workers in the footwear trade out of a job. Support industries shed 80,000 jobs, a grand total of 200,000 workers tossed on the scrap heap.

As is usual with Socialist propaganda, those who drew attention to the desperate plight of the footwear industry were constantly vilified. "They want to increase inflation — why doesn't the local footwear industry get competitive" the Wall Street Journal, New York Times and Washington Post chorused. This is of course the function of the jackals of the press: Protect the Socialist decision-maker in government and smear as "fascists" or worse, anyone who draws attention to the war.

The truth is that the American footwear industry was very competitive and was turning out good quality products. What the industry could not compete with was the poorer-quality, HEAVILY SUBSIDIZED products coming from Taiwan and Korea, whose governments were putting billions of dollars in subsidies into their footwear industry. This is what is called "free trade." The only thing that is "free" about it is that foreign manufacturers are allowed to dump their subsidized products on the U. S. market free of charge, but our manufacturers are closed out of foreign markets by laws and restrictions — in this case there was not a single hope that American footwear manufacturers could sell in Taiwan and Korea. To this day, no American-made footwear is sold in Taiwan or Korea. This is what is called "free trade."

In spite of five appeals filed within ITC which found that the American footwear industry was suffering irreparable harm from a flood of imports from Korea and Taiwan, Reagan refused to do anything to stem the tide that was now drowning worker and employer alike. The footwear industry found itself out in the cold. It could not turn to Congress, because Congress had transferred its sovereignty to the executive branch, and Reagan in the grip of his Socialist advisors, turned his back on his troops and let the "free trade" enemy troops overwhelm them.

The battle of the footwear industry was just another battle lost by our people in the ongoing Trade War, and it will not be long before we are plowed under by GATT and NAFTA. The Trojan Horse of "free trade" in the Congress will have carried the day for the enemy forces. Our battered troops have no recourse but to retire, leaving millions of wrecked lives behind them. And all of this devastation is wrought in the name of "global trade."

It is well worth calling attention to the similarity of methods used to get the Trade Expansion Act of 1962, and NAFTA onto the books in 1993. Apart from presidential interference in the legislative department, a huge public relations campaign was mounted with the aid of the best and brightest that Madison Avenue could come up with. A press barrage was backed by Howard Peterson of the White House, and the Senate, and the Commerce Department. The pattern was repeated with NAFTA in 1993. NAFTA is on par with the treasonous Monetary Control Act of 1980, signed by Carter.

NAFTA is an illegal "agreement" which cannot pass a constitutional test. Pages 2273-2297, Congressional Record, House, Feb 26,1900 gives the constitutional position regarding "deals" like NAFTA, the Panama Canal, GATT etc: "The Congress of the United States derives its power to legislate from the Constitution, which is the measure of its authority. Any enactment of Congress which is opposed to its provisions, or is not within the grant of powers made by it, is unconstitutional, therefore no law, and obligatory upon no one..."

Judge Cooley, the great constitutional scholar said, "The constitution itself never yields to a treaty or enactment. It neither changes with time nor does it bend to the force of circumstances." The Congress has no constitutional authority to transfer its treaty — making powers to the President, as was done with NAFTA. This is pure sedition. Trade negotiations belong with the House: Article 1, Section 8, Clause 3, "to regulate commerce with foreign nations, and among the several States, and with the Indian tribes." Clearly, neither Bush nor Clinton had a constitutional right to meddle in NAFTA. It is certainly treason and sedition.

On pages 1148-1151, Congressional Record, House, March 10, 1993, "Foreign Policy or Trade, the Choice is Ours," in which the evils of "free trade" are laid bare. It has taken the Socialist 47 years to break down the wise trade barriers erected by Washington, Lincoln, Garfield and McKinley. The cause of the "French" Revolution was "free trade." British Socialists brought depression and panic in France, which opened the doors to the seditionists and traitors, Danton, Marat, The Earl of Shelburne and Jeremy Bentham.

On page 1151 of the above noted Congressional Record, we read: "In 1991 American workers earned an average weekly wage twenty percent below 1972 wage levels. Meanwhile, the textile and apparel industries lost over 600,000 jobs, while steel and automobiles sacrificed another 580,000 positions. Measured in declining income and jobs, the burden of global leadership thus has fallen heavily on low-skilled American workers. Labor intensive manufacturing jobs have moved abroad to low-cost Third World countries, leaving a caste of poorly skilled American workers..."

The Socialist goal to reduce the standard of living of middle class America to that of a Third World Country is somewhere in the region of 87 percent complete, and if matters go as planned, the Clinton administration will soon put the finishing touches to the Trade War at the cost of stabbing the American people in the back. As I have often said, President Clinton was selected to carry out a Fabian Socialist mandate, and "free trade" is only one of treasonous policies he was ordered to carry out.

"All of us have felt how much we need the United Nations if we are really move toward a New World and kinds of relationships in the world in the interests of all countries. The Soviet Union and the United States have more than enough reason to be partners in building it, in shaping new security structures in Europe and the Asian Pacific region. And also in the making of a truly global economy, indeed, the creation of a new civilization." — Mikhail Gorbachev, Stanford University speech, 1990. Substitute "Socialists" for the Soviet Union and it is easy to see that nothing has changed.

The long-range plan of Socialism to break the Constitution of the United States through membership of foreign entities is fairly well recorded, nowhere more so than in the writings of Fabian Socialists and international socialists. We know that the Socialists expects to usher in a world dictatorship through the actions of Communism and Socialism, the one by open and direct methods, and the other by more subtle, hidden means. They expect to triumph through the financial dictatorship of the International Monetary Fund (IMF), which can control governments by forcing free countries through sabotage of their monetary structures, to join international bodies such as the short-lived League of Nations, its successor, the United Nations and a host of peripheral international organizations.

All have a common aim: Destroy the sovereignty of the intended nation — victim by suspension of credit, want of employment, stagnation of industry and agriculture and by super-imposing the laws of an international body over the laws of individual nations. In this book we shall be able to deal with only the United Nations as an example of Socialist surpation of the life's blood of independent nation states.

It is not within the scope of this book to examine how the United Nations charter was set up, other than that it is a Socialist enterprise from the first to the last. Some think of it a Communist enterprise. While it is true that the writers of the United Nations draft were two Soviet citizens, Leo Rosvolsky, Molotov and one American Socialist citizen, Alger Hiss, the charter is a Socialist one, a great victory for the Fabian Society and its American cousins. The United Nations charter fits right in with the Communist Manifesto of 1848.

Had the United Nations treaty/agreement/charter been cast as Communist document, it would not have been accepted by the United States Senate. But the Socialists know their game, and so it was cast as an organization to "keep the peace." Now I have said elsewhere that when we see the word "peace," in any world government document, we must recognize it as Socialist or Communist in origin. That is precisely the nature of the United Nations charter. It is a Communist/Socialist organization. Moreover, the United Nations makes war, it does not keep the peace.

Notwithstanding that the charter was signed by a majority of United States Senators and passed into law, the United States is not a member of this One World Government — New World Order body, and has not for a single minute been a member. There are a number of paramount reasons why this is so: Vattel's "Law of Nations," the "Bible" which provided the sum and substance upon which our Founding Father's international law was based, applies in this case and still stands. This goes back to Roman and Greek law and in itself, is a lifetime study. How many of our so-called Senators and Representatives know anything at all about such matters? Vattel's invaluable book is not part of the curriculum of law schools and is not included in high school and or university text books. The State Department is singularly unversed in this invaluable book, which is why it makes one mess after another in trying to arrange the affairs of this nation without having the faintest knowledge of Vattel's Law of Nations. The United States Constitution stands supreme over all treaties, charters and agreement of whatever stripe and cannot be supplanted by congressional and or executive action.

For the United States to have been a member of the United Nations there would have had to be an Amendment to the United States Constitution passed by all 50 States. Since this did not occur, we are not a member of the U.N., nor have we ever been. Such an amendment would have taken away the power of the House and Senate to declare war and given it to an international body. Because former President Bush attempted to do this at the time of the Gulf War, he should have been impeached for treason against the United States and for failing to abide by his oath of office.

The second point worthy of note is that no more than five Senators actually read the United Nations charter documents let alone properly and constitutionally debated the matter. Such a constitutional debate would have taken at least two years, yet this monstrosity was passed in 1945 in three days! Where such an agreement or bill or whatever is before the Senate and the Senators do not properly debate it, it represents an exercise of arbitrary power. Pages 287-297, Senate, Congressional Record, Dec 10, 1898:

"As a matter of the United States is sovereign, sovereignty and nationality are correlative terms. There can be no nationality without sovereignty and there can be no sovereignty without nationality. As to every matter in the United States as a nation possessed sovereign power, except only where sovereignty has been reserved to the States and or to the people."

Also, from Pomeroy, (on the Constitution) page 27: "There can be no nation without political sovereignty and no political sovereignty without a nation. I shall, not be able therefore to separate these ideas and to present each as a distinct from the other..." Continuing on page 29: "This nation possesses political sovereignty. It may have any organization from the purest democracy to the most absolute monarchy, but considered to its relation with the rest of mankind and its own individual members, it must exist, to the extent of enacting laws for itself as an integral, independent sovereign society among other similar nations of the earth."

Dr. Mulford, one of the finest historians and constitutional scholars said in his book about sovereignty of a nation, on page 112:

"The existence of sovereignty of a nation or political sovereignty, is indicated by certain signs or notes which are universal. These are independence, authority, supremacy, unity and majesty. The sovereignty of a nation or political sovereignty, implies independence. It is subject to no external control, but its action is in correspondence within its own determination. It implies authority. It has the strength inherent in its own determination to assert and maintain it. It implies supremacy. This does not presume the presence of other powers which are inferior..."

As the late Senator Sam Ervin, one of the great Constitutional scholars of this century said many times, "there is no way under the noonday sun that we could have joined the United Nations." Examine the requirements for sovereignty outlined above and it becomes clear that the United Nations is not a nation and that it is entirely lacking in sovereignty. It does not make individual laws for the nation, because it is not a nation. It has no territory of its own, it has no unity and majesty. It is subject to external control.

Moreover the United Nations treaty cannot stand because the United Nations lacks sovereignty. According to "Law of Nations" by Vattel, the "Bible" our Founding Fathers used to frame the Constitution, the United States is forbidden to enter into a treaty with ANY BODY, ANY ENTITY which lacks sovereignty. No one will contest that the United Nations lacks sovereignty so that the United Nations "treaty" passed by the Senate in 1945 is null and void, ultra vires. As a legal instrument it is neither a treaty or a charter and as such it is absolutely worthless, no better than a blank scrap of paper.

The United Nations is a foreign body held together by a collection of ersatz laws, which cannot take precedence over the laws of the United States. To support a position that United Nations laws take precedence over United States laws is an act of sedition and treason. A study of Vattel's Law of Nations and Wheaton's International Law in conjunction with the Constitution will leave no doubt about the accuracy of this. Any Congressman, Senator, or government agent, who supports the United Nations is guilty of sedition.

On pages 2063-2065 Congressional Record, House, Feb. 22nd, 1900 we find this authority: "A treaty is not superior to the Constitution." In diplomatic exchanges between the United States ambassador to France and then Secretary of State Marcy, it is again clearly spelled out: "The Constitution is to prevail over a treaty where the provisions of one conflict with the other..."

When John Foster Dulles, a deep Socialist agent for the British crown was forced to appear before a United States Senate committee of enquiry into the United Nations, like the slippery Socialist he was, he tried to bluff his way through by implying that "international law" like domestic law, could be enforced in the United States. Enforcing "international law" is the very basic bedrock of the United Nations but it cannot be enforced in the United States.

Our contention that the United States is not a member of the United Nations is reinforced by a reading of Congressional Record, Senate, February 14, 1879 and pages 1151-1159, Congressional Record, Senate January 26, 1897. We will not find this vital material in ANY law books. The far left-of-Marx law professors at Harvard, don't want their students to find out about these vital matters.

It makes no difference that the United States Senate "ratified" the U.N. "treaty," charter agreement. Congress cannot pass laws that are unconstitutional, and binding United States law to the subserviency of the United Nation treaty is patently unconstitutional. Any act by Congress (House and Senate) that makes the Constitution subservient to any other body or entity, has no force in law and is of no affect. Clearly, based only on Article 25 of the United Nations treaty, the United States could not have entered into such an agreement.

The Annals of Congress, Congressional Globes and Congressional Records are packed with information on sovereignty and a detailed examination of the material, much of which came from Vattel's "Law of Nations" makes it very clear that the United States was never a member of the United Nations nor can it ever be, unless the vote taken by the Senate in 1945 is subjected to a Constitutional amend ment and then ratified by the 50 States. For further confirmation that the United States is not a member of the United States, we refer readers to pages 12267-12287 of the Congressional Record, House December 18, 1945.

What passed for a constitutional debate on the United Nations Treaty in 1945 can be found in Congressional Record, Senate, pages 8151-8174, July 28, 1945 and in pages 10964-10974 Congressional Record, Senate, November 24, 1945. A study of these records of the United Nations "debates" will convince even the most hardened skeptic of the incredible ignorance of the Constitution displayed by those United States Senators who "ratified" the United Nations Treaty.

Judge Cooley, one of the great constitutional scholars of all times said:

"The Congress of the United States derives its powers to legislate from the Constitution, which is the measure of its authority. And any enactment of the Congress which is opposed to its provisions, or is not within the grant of powers made by it, is unconstitutional, therefore no law, and obligatory upon no one." The 1945 vote taken by the Senate in favor of joining the United Nations is, "therefore no law, and obligatory upon no one."

The 1945 vote on the United Nations agreement was an exercise in arbitrary power and is therefore, null and void, given that it was not constitutionally debated before it was passed by the Senate, in three days: "No treaty/agreement can weaken or intimidate the United States Constitution, which agreements/treaties are no more than law, and like any other law, can be repealed."

So, far from being an immutable document, the United Nations charter/agreement (our legislators lacked the courage to call it a treaty) is null and void and of no consequence and obligatory upon no one. The military are especially enjoined from obeying the laws of a foreign entity, body, or organization, and our military leaders are duty bound to uphold their oath to protect the citizens of the United States. They cannot do this, and obey the laws of the United Nations.

Of all of the international bodies of the One World Government abroad today, none is more insidiously evil than the IMF. We tend to forget that the IMF is the bastard child of the United Nations, both being extensions of the Committee of 300, and the IMF, like the Council on Foreign Relations (CFR) is becoming more openly bold about its true purposes and intentions. The same sinister forces that imposed Bolshevism on Christian Russia, are behind the IMF and its plans to take control of the so-called "global economy."

9

A NATION UNDONE

The vast majority of the American people do not know that the nation has been at war since 1946, nor that we are losing the war. At the close of WWII, The Tavistock Institute for Human Relations at Sussex University and in the Tavistock Center in London, turned its attention to the United States. Its chairperson is Queen Elizabeth II, and her cousin, the Duke of Kent, is also on the board. The former methods deployed against Germany during WWII were now turned against the United States. Tavistock is the acknowledged center of "brainwashing" in the world, and in essence, has been conducting, and is still conducting a massive brainwashing operation against the people of the United States, since 1946.

The main purpose of this endeavor is to assist Socialist programs at all levels of our society, ushering in the New Dark Age of the One World Government-New World Order. Tavistock is active in banking, trade, education, religion and particularly, seeks to break down the Constitution of the United States. In these chapters we will be looking at some of the programs that are intended to make America over until it becomes a slave state. The following are some of the main Socialists organizations and institutions contending against the American people:

BANKING AND ECONOMIC POLICIES:
THE FEDERAL RESERVE BOARD

"Mr. Chairman, we have in this country one of the most corrupt institutions the world has ever known. I refer to the Federal Reserve Board, and the Federal Reserve banks. The Federal Reserve Board, a Government Board, has cheated the Government of the United States and the people of the United States out of enough money to pay the national debt...This evil institution has impoverished and ruined the people of the United States... These 12 private credit monopolies were deceitfully and disloyally foisted upon this country by bankers who came here from Europe and who repaid us for our hospitality by undermining our

American institutions..." Speech made in the House by Congressman Louis T.
McFadden, Chairman of the House Banking Committee, Friday, June 10, 1932.
As has often been said, the Socialist's greatest triumph came with the Federal
Reserve banking monopoly. Socialists-bankers came here from Europe and
England to deceitfully ruin the people of this country through penetration and per-
meation of every facet of our monetary system. These Socialist change agents
could not have accomplished anything without the full cooperation of traitors
within our gates, and they found them in their hundreds, men and women who
were willing to sell the American people out. A notable traitor was President.
Woodrow Wilson, who punched holes through the trade barriers erected by
President. Washington and kept intact by Lincoln, McKinley and Garfield. In
1913, Wilson introduced the Marxist graduated income tax system to replace the
revenues lost from Customs duties and opened the gates to allow the Philistine
bankers from Europe to enter our citadel through passage of the Federal Reserve
Act of 1913.

Few people realize the American banking system was SOCIALIZED with
passage of the Federal Reserve Act of 1913. The commercial banks (we have no
merchant banks in the true British sense) have been "on the dole" i.e., welfare,
since the Socialist banker-thieves were able to get control in that year. What we
have in this country is welfare banking, almost identical to the banking system the
Bolsheviks instituted in Russia. The Federal Reserve banks create debt obligation,
so-called "money" which money does not accrue to the Fed through trading, but
rather through theft from the people. The soft money is stolen directly from the
people. The money that the Federal Reserve banks control, is not honest money;
rather it is fiat money, always inflationary.

Whom can we hold accountable? Whom can we charge with the theft of our
money? No one knows who the stockholders of the largest banking system in the
world are. Is this truly believable? Unfortunately, it is all too true, yet we let this
diabolical situation go on year after year, largely out of ignorance of how the system operates. We, the People, are told to leave money alone, as it is too complicated for us to understand. "Leave it to the experts" say the thieves.

What does the Socialists Federal Reserve do with our stolen money? One of
the things it does is charge us usury, which the system calls the national debt and
which they make into 30-year obligations. These Socialist bankers DO NOTH-
ING to create wealth, they are parasites who live by eating up the substance of the
American people. These parasites have the "right" to make money out of fresh air
and then lend it to the commercial banks at usury and they do it on the credit of
the people.

This is involuntary servitude, for the personal credit of the citizen belongs to
the citizen, and not to the Federal Reserve. By allegedly granting the Federal
Reserve the right to take the individual credit of the citizen for itself, the

Government of the United States allows this parasitical organization to violate the people's 5th Amendment rights, the rights of "life, liberty and property" guaranteed by the Constitution.

Furthermore, the Federal Reserve Board has destroyed the Constitution. Remember, an attack on one part of the Constitution is an attack on the whole Constitution. If one part of the Constitution is torn down, all parts of it are desecrated. Powers delegated to Congress, by We, the People: Section 8, Article 5. "To coin money, regulate the value thereof and of foreign coin and fix the standard of weights and measures." This is article is found in the 17 enumerated powers delegated to Congress by the people. Nowhere did we give Congress the right to transfer this power over to a private banking institution.

Yet, that is exactly what the Congress did in 1913. The bill was introduced for discussion just a few days before the Christmas recess. It consisted of 58 pages of triple-column and 30 pages of fine, closely-printed material. No one could have read it, less still understood it in the few days it was on the floor for discussion. Thus the Federal Reserve Act was ramrodded through the Congress and became an act of arbitrary power — which is what it is called when a bill is not properly debated and passes into law without being fully debated.

Hundreds of excellent books have been written showing the unconstitutionality of the Federal Reserve Act of 1913, so that there is no purpose served by going over it again in this book. Suffice to say that notwithstanding this, the greatest swindle in history, the Federal Reserve banks remain firmly in place as though its history was still a secret. Why is this? Probably it is through fear. Those who have sought to challenge this monstrous Socialist creation in a meaningful way, have been brutally murdered. Members of the House and Senate know that the Federal Reserve is THE heist of the 20th century, yet do nothing to rock the boat for fear of being thrown out of Congress, or even worse.

The Federal Reserve banks were patterned after the Bank of England, a Rothschild Socialist institution which as able to attach itself to the United States following the Civil War, during which period, it leeched off both sides. The monetary system developed for the young American nation by Jefferson and Hamilton was a bimetallism system, 16 ounces of silver to 1 ounce of gold. This was our CONSTITUTIONAL money system, spelled out in Article I, Section 8, Clause 5 and it gave this country unheard of prosperity until the prostitutes of the European central banks were able to subvert it. They did this through the demonetization of silver in 1872, which led to the panic of 1872, all planned by the Socialists.

The Socialists were able to debase our money system to where it was of zero value, then they printed Socialist (Keynesian money) with which they bought up all the prime businesses and real estate. In college courses in economics, the far-left of Marx professors teach that Congress manages our monetary system, but Congress does not, it abdicated the responsibility and gave it into the hands of the

Shylock international bankers to create a welfare, commercial banking system in America. The Rothschilds and their fellow Socialists of the international bank of Shylocks, have put the American people in debt for ever — unless we can find the right leader who will break this chokehold.

The Shylock international bankers, long before the advent of the Federal Reserve Board, looked upon the wealth of this nation with great avarice and were determined to put on pressure until they controlled it. The International Shylock bankers prevented the national bank, during President Andrew Jackson's term, from paying off the Civil War debt, in order to keep the American people tied hand and foot, which we still are. It is well-established that British intelligence fomented and prosecuted the American Civil War, which should have been called International Shylock Banker's War. British intelligence had their agents in place in the Southern States, penetrating and permeating every aspect of life.

When President Jackson shut down the central bank, British intelligence was ready. The Bank Act of 1862 was a Rothschild "scoop" part of the long-range plan to keep the American people in everlasting penury. Although Congress and a patriotic Supreme Court fended off the Rothschild swindlers, the reprieve was short-lived.

Thanks to Trojan Horse Wilson, they got the upper hand in 1913 and plunged this nation into financial slavery, which is the state in which we find ourselves today. As we said in our chapters on education, the Socialists used education to lie to the American public about the Federal Reserve banks, which is one of the reason why it is still tolerated. Its gross excesses and crimes against the American people are not known, although they are spelled out in the hundreds of excellent books on the subject.

But such books are above the ken of those who have less than an a certain standard of education, governed by Socialist control of the school text book industry, which is why so many millions of Americans of all ages find solace in television. Now, if Larry King would hold open, frank discourses opening up information about the evils of the Socialist Federal Reserve, and if the most popular talk show hosts of radio and television would do likewise, we might just get our people excited enough to do something about closing down the Federal Reserve system.

The American public would learn that the first duty of the Congress is to provide and keep a sound monetary system for the United States. The public would learn that we do not have one single honest dollar in circulation. They would learn that the British East India Company and the Bank of England conspired with Adam Smith to pull all gold and silver out of the Colonies, to defeat the Colonists in an economic war that preceded the shooting war.

The American public would learn that for the Federal Reserve Board and the Federal Reserve banks to be constitutional, a constitutional amendment would have to be drafted and ratified by all 50 States.

They will begin to ask questions, "why wasn't this done? Why are we still allowing the private people who own the Federal Reserve to bilk us out of huge sums of money?" They might even put enough pressure on Congress to force it to abolish the Federal Reserve. The American people might learn on the Larry King Show, or from the Phil Donahue Show, that the Federal Reserve banks pay no income tax; that have they have never been audited and pay only $1.95 for every $1000 they receive from the Treasury of We, the People. "What a bargain," we might howl in rage.

An aroused, enraged populace might even shock the Congress into action and force the closure of this Beast of Mammon. The American people would learn that the greatest period of prosperity was the period between the closing of the Shylock central bank by Andrew Jackson and the outbreak of the Civil War. They would learn that the Federal Reserve banks have Socialized commercial banking in this country and that our banks are working on the basis of the system described in the "Merchant of Venice," by Shakespeare.

President Roosevelt told the American people that he was a friend of the poor and the middle class of America, but he was an agent of the Shylock International Banks and Fabian Socialism, from day one. He arranged huge loans to prop up the Socialist government in England, bankrupted by that country's failed Socialist policies, while his own people stood in bread lines, and in 1929, the same foreign interests manipulated the stock market crash that took billions of dollars off stock prices, which the predators were then able to buy up at 10 cents on the dollar. The Federal Reserve banks engineered the crash through the New York Federal Reserve bank. On pages 10949-1050 of the Congressional Record, House, June 16, 1930, we find the following:

"More recently the Federal Reserve Board has made American industry the victim of a single series of manipulations in the interest of European credit which caused the stockmarket to crash and present industrial depression. Those manipulations began in Feb. 1929 with the visit to this country of the governor of the bank of England and his consultations with the Federal Reserve Board head, the subject of these conferences being anxiety as to the financial situation in Great Britain (reeling from Socialist programs that had bankrupted the country) and the fall of the pound sterling.

"The British and French had invested $3 billion in the American stock market, and the purpose was to stop the drain of gold to the United States by breaking American security values. Their first effort in March, 1929, caused by public proclamations of the Federal Reserve (from its New York branch) calculated to scare investors caused a minor panic in March. The second effort, beginning in August, 1929, was made by sales and short sales of British and French investors by American bankers and the panic of October 1929..." The Federal Reserve banks were responsible for the 1929 crash and subsequent depression.

Today, in 1994, the Federal Reserve Board, under the chairmanship of Socialist Alan Greenspan, is choking the feeble life out of the American economy, because Greenspan's masters in London have told him to keep inflation down to 1.5 percent, even it means the loss of 50 million jobs. Today, our membership of the World Bank, the Bank of International Settlements and our willingness to compromise our sovereignty by falling in line with the dictates of the International Monetary Fund (IMF) bodes ill for the future and would indicate that the Committee of 300 is gearing up for another world war.

Nowhere in the Constitution is there found a power that authorizes the United States Government to fund so-called international banks like the World Bank and the IMF. To find this power one has to look in Article 1, Section 8, Clauses 1-18, but it would be futile to search for it because it is not there. We have no constitutional power authorizing the funding of foreign banks, hence such action is unlawful.

Spurred on by the Socialist in England, President George Bush pushed hard to pass the One World Government — New World Order trade bills of NAFTA and GATT which would rob the United States of its sovereignty and depredate industrial and agricultural jobs, throwing millions of Americans out of work. "Global trade" is an old aim of Fabian Socialism which it has striven to achieve since 1910, in its effort to break up the favorable trade position of the United States and reduce the standard of living of the American blue collar and white collar middle class, to that of Third World countries.

However, Bush ran out of time and so the baton in the relay race was passed to President Clinton, who succeeded in having the NAFTA "treaty" passed with the aid of 132 "progressive (Socialist) members of the Republican Party. In 1993, the Fabian Socialist's dream of "global trade" took a giant step forward with the passage of NAFTA and the signing of the General Agreement on Tariffs and Trade (GATT) measure that ended America's unique position of being able to provide a good standard of living and jobs for its unique middle class.

It would take an Amendment to the Constitution of the United States to make the NAFTA and GATT treaties lawful. First, there in is no provision or power in the Constitution that allowed Presidents Bush and Clinton acted in a 100 percent unconstitutional manner by getting involved in the details of these treaties, which are solely in the domain of the legislative branch. There is a constitutional prohibition against the three branches of government delegating their powers to each other, Pages 108-116, Congressional Globe, Dec. 10, 1867:

"We agree in the proposition that no department of the Government in the United States, neither the President, nor Congress nor the courts, possess any power not given by the Constitution."

There is no provision for giving away U.S. sovereignty in the Constitution, but that is what our Trojan horse enemies did when they negotiated directly with these One World Government — New World Order purveyors of the NAFTA and GATT treaties, in pursuance of the International Socialist agenda.

FOREIGN AID

The "sacred cow" of the Fabian Socialists was getting other people's money (OPM) to fund their Socialist excesses. We know about the $7 billion dollar loan engineered by John Maynard Keynes to bail out the failed Socializing of the British people via the Labor Party. We also know about the Socialist scheme to fund other foreign countries via the so-called foreign aid appropriations bill, an event that costs the American people close to $20 billion annually, where we play Santa Claus to some of the most undeserving nations in the world, whose failed Socialist policies we continue to prop up. The House and Senate fail lamentably to even make a pretense of screening bills for their constitutionality before they allow them to come to the floor. If they did their job properly, foreign aid bills would never reach the floor of the House and Senate. *This is a crime against the American people, best described as sedition.*

Foreign aid serves two purposes; it destabilizes America and helps the Committee of 300 take control of the natural resources of countries funded by coercion of the American taxpayers. Of course there are countries that have no natural resources, such as Israel and Egypt, but in these cases, foreign aid become a geopolitical consideration, but still remains, involuntary servitude or slavery. Foreign aid began in earnest with President Roosevelt when he gave away an estimated $11 billion to Bolshevik Russia and $7 billion to the British Labor Party Government.

Is their any grant in power in the Constitution of the United States that would make provision for this astonishing annual giveaway?

The answer is, "NO" and it would require an amendment to the Constitution to make foreign aid legal, but it is doubtful whether such an amendment could be properly drafted, as foreign aid violates the clause forbidding slavery (involuntary servitude). To put it bluntly, foreign aid is treason and sedition. The members of the House and Senate know it, the President knows it, but this does not stop the annual theft of billions of dollars from the American workers. Foreign aid is theft. Foreign aid is involuntary servitude. Foreign aid is Socialism in action.

THE MIDDLE CLASS

Of all the people most hated by the Marxist/Fabian Socialist/Communists and their American cousins, none outranks the unique American middle class, which has long been the bane of the existence of Socialism. The middle class is what made America the mighty nation it became. Trade wars were and are aimed at the middle class, personified by the so-called "global economy." The criminally degenerate efforts of Presidents Wilson and Roosevelt, and later, Carter, Bush and Clinton, to smash down the trade barriers that developed and protected the middle class, are told elsewhere in this book. What we want to do in this chapter is to look at where the middle class stands in mid-1994.

The middle class is the greatest social triumph of the 20th century for our Confederated Republic, which was properly and well run, up to 1913. Born out of sound monetary policies, trade barriers and protectionism, the middle class was the rampart against all of the hopes of Karl Marx to bring revolution to America were dashed to pieces. The expanding middle class which began in earnest between the time that Andrew Jackson outlawed the central bank, and the Civil War, continued during both world wars. But since 1946, something has gone wrong. Elsewhere we have explained the war waged against the American middle class since 1946 by the Tavistock Institute, a war we are losing hands down.

The equality of blue-collar workers in good-paying industrial jobs with an assured future was the first target of the Club of Rome's Post Industrial-Zero Growth blueprint for the destruction of our industrial base. Blue collar workers enjoyed parity income with white collar workers and together, they formed a formidable middle class, not the "working class" of Socialist European countries. This was THE political fact recognized by the Socialists as a big obstacle to their plans to ruin America. Thus, industry, which supported the middle class, had to be eviscerated, and it was, and still is, being cut up, section by section, with NAFTA and GATT doing the slicing.

One thing I have always emphasized is that the Socialists never give up. Once they set their goals, they will pursue them with a tenacity of purpose that is almost frightening. I have traced the decline of the economic and political power of the middle class to the beginning of the 1970s, following the implementation of the Club of Rome's Post Industrial-Zero Growth plan. By 1973, the foundation-floor upon which the middle class rested, began to show signs of serious sinking as job prospects and earnings prospects began collapsing. So much so, that by 1993, for the first time ever, job losses among white collar workers equaled job losses of blue collar workers. Since the 1970s, and particularly in 1980, the Census Bureau reported middle class incomes plummeting.

What Socialism achieved through the destruction of trade barriers, increased taxation and an ongoing onslaught against the work-place, is the emergence of a new class in America, the working poor. Literally millions and millions of former blue collar and white collar workers have fallen through the yawning cracks in their former solid middle class foundation, jobs based on industrial employment, protection of trade. The middle class found itself making up the more than 60 million Americans, roughly 23 percent of the population, who can be described with accuracy, as the working poor, those whose incomes are less than enough to cover the cost of the basic necessities of life.(Yet, we can afford to give $20 billion in "foreign aid" to strangers).

One of the most destructive shots fired against the middle class in the trade war was the so-called oil shortage generated by the deliberately planned 1973 Arab-Israeli conflict combined with war on nuclear power stations. The Socialists have closed down nuclear energy — the cheapest and safest form of energy and the least polluting, and made our industrial heart beat on oil — better yet, imported oil. Had the nuclear power program for this country not been utterly savaged by the Socialist-controlled "environmentalist" shock troops, the country would have by now experienced a zero need to import oil, so detrimental to our economy in general and, in particular, to our balance of payments situation. In addition, by shutting down nuclear power stations, the Socialists slashed an estimated one million jobs annually from the payrolls.

The rising cost of oil fanned by the Arab-Israeli war and loss of nuclear energy, forced productivity lower, which in turn considerably lowered wages, impacting on the economy, as lower wages discouraged spending. Starting from 1960, we find that the median family income rose by almost 3 percent annually right up to the 1973 Arab — Israeli War. No doubt this is what Kissinger meant when he said the war had a far wider impact on the American economy than at first thought.

From 1974, real wages of blue and white collar workers fell by a whopping 20 percent. By 1993, the number of workers forced to take part time jobs who were formerly fully employed in blue collar jobs, almost doubled from the year before. Likewise, white collar workers in stable industry-related jobs, found themselves becoming "permanent temporaries" in ever increasing numbers. The number of temporary former blue collar workers is now around 9 percent, with white collar workers in the same category around 10 percent of the total workforce. The foundation upon which the middle class was built was not only cracking and sinking, it was beginning to totally break up.

Although government statistics only admit to an average unemployment rate of between 6.4 percent and 7 percent, the real rate is closer to 20 percent. With the downsizing of defense contracts an estimated loss of 35 million jobs is the reality of the situation when we take into consideration the impact of NAFTA and GATT on the job market. North Carolina's textile industry is expected to shed two million jobs in the second year of a fully operational GATT.

Irving Bluestone of the Institute of Policy Studies says his survey of steady, industry-related jobs, the sole source of wages that support a middle class family, found that 900,000 good-paying industrial jobs were lost each year starting in 1978 to 1982, that is, almost 5 million high-quality blue collar jobs in five years. There are no other statistics of a similar nature covering the period 1982 to 1994, but, if we take the same number, 900,000 — and we know the number is higher — then it is reasonable to suppose that in 12 years the number of such jobs lost, and which will never return, amounted to 10 million well-paying long-term industrial jobs. Now we begin to get the real figures about unemployment, and not only that, we get the real picture of the QUALITY jobs lost forever, thanks to the onslaught of the Club of Rome and the Tavistock Institute against the American workplace.

President Clinton will pay a price for his trade war on the American people, that price will include a single term. Clinton has plumped for a global economy, which inevitably means employment insecurity in America. Bringing down the last trade barrier by GATT has sent our economy whirling into the maelstrom of decreased spending as a cause of increased joblessness. Clinton is learning the hard way that you can't have your cake and eat it. Global economy + deficit reduction = HUGE JOB LOSSES. There is no chance that the country can take another four more years of Clinton's Socialist administration, with a rising tide of temporary, low paid jobs swamping former well-paid, long-term industrial jobs.

The middle class is vanishing, but their voice can still be heard, and their message must be, "to hell with a global economy and to hell with deficit reduction. WE WANT GOOD PAYING, STABLE, LONG TERM EMPLOYMENT!" Even though the United States is just lately been forced into a global economy, the devastation is clearly visible with hundreds of solid, stable corporations forced to lay off their trained work force in droves.

What we have today in 1994 — and this has developed since the Arab Israeli War — is a Wall Street/Las Vegas economy. McDonald stock is high, but flipping hamburgers is no substitute for a well-paid long term industrial job. So while McDonald stocks do well on Wall Street, can the United States make do with an economy in which well-paid jobs are becoming an endangered species? An article in the Los Angeles Times said that in 1989, one in four American jobs were partime, a frightening rise over the 1972 figures, but the ratio in 1993 was one in three, or one third of all jobs in American were temporary jobs. The bottom line is that no industrial nation can survive the rate of attrition in well-paying industrial jobs and not go whirling out of control into an abyss of destruction.

The United States is losing the battle against the forces of Socialism spearheaded by the Tavistock Institute. In the next two years we are going to be faced by a huge increase in competition forced upon us by "global economy" where nations with millions of semi-literate people will be taught to turn out goods at slave-labor pay rates. What will the work force in the United States do then? May we remind you that this is the logical result of policies implemented by Woodrow Wilson, policies that were to destroy the internal market of the United States. Our work force of skilled industrial blue collar workers will very soon be haunted by the specter of no jobs at all, and we are going to find these workers grabbing at any kind of a job to halt the slide of their standard of living, or, indeed, just to keep bread on the table.

Clinton ran his campaign on promise to the middle class. How many of the jobless remember his speech, "The rich get the goldmine and the workers get the shaft"? That was before he was ordered to meet with Jay Rockefeller and Pamela Harriman who told him very bluntly, "you are delivering the wrong message. The DEFICIT is what the message is." Thereafter, Clinton suddenly began to preach the Socialist gospel of cutting the deficit, without mentioning that it could only be done at the cost of millions of jobs.

Then Clinton did the other thing Socialists are good at; he made a promise that government would reshape everything. But the worry has grown; Clinton hasn't been able to convince workers that a lower deficit is better than full employment. A recent poll showed that 45 percent opposed to 26 percent of Americans thought unemployment a more serious problem than the deficit. Clinton also told us that we are enjoying a recovery, but this does not ad up, as contrary to the normal pattern, when recovery means less people are working at involuntary part-time lower-paid jobs, this time the percentage has GROWN. *In 1993 there were more than 6.5 million people working in temporary lower-paid jobs.*

Of the much vaunted claim that the Clinton administration created 2 million jobs last year, we should note that 60 percent of these jobs were in restaurants, health care, bars, hotels (bellmen, porters, doormen). The drive to "globalize" (read destroy) the American domestic market begun by Woodrow Wilson, has gone into high gear with Clinton. The dramatic results from this destructive program can be measured by the following:

- In Automobiles, imports rose from 4.1 percent to 68 percent from 1960 to 1986.
- Clothing imports rose from 1.8 percent in 1960 to 50 percent by 1986.
- Machine tool imports rose from 3.2 percent in 1960 to 50 percent in 1986.
- Machine tools are THE most important indicator of the true economy of an industrial nation.
- Electronic imports rose from 5.6 percent of the market in 1960 to 68 percent of the market in 1986.

The Fabian Socialists with their false "global economy" promises completely undermined the United States as the greatest industrial nation the world has ever seen. The tragedy contained in these figures translates to MILLIONS UPON MILLIONS of good paying, long term, stable jobs, which are now lost FOREVER, sacrificed on the alter of Fabian Socialism's dream of a One World Government — New World Order dictatorship. The American worker was lied to by Presidents Wilson, Roosevelt, Kennedy, Johnson, Bush and Clinton, who have jointly and severally committed high treason against the United States. As a result of this treasonous policy carried out by a succession of Presidents, domestic investment, public and private fell by half from 1973 to 1986, sloughing off millions of good-paying long term jobs.

As of this time, mid 1994, apart from the pathetic slogans offered by the political candidates of both parties, the middle class crisis has not been, and is not being addressed. This is not to say that the politicians are unaware of it. On the contrary, they hear from their constituents every day, as they grow more and more angry over problems they do not understand, an anger that leaves them with little patience with the Washington government's inability to bring these problems that are affecting them so drastically, under control. The politicians will do nothing to look for solutions to the crises, because the solutions that are readily available run contra to the Club of Rome's dictatorial, Post Industrial Zero Growth blue print. Any effort to bring the middle class disaster to national attention, will be choked off before it can get started.

There is no other crisis that compares with the middle class crisis. America is dying. Those who could turn things around are unwilling or afraid to do so, and the situation will continue to deteriorate until the patient becomes terminally ill, a point soon to be reached, probably in less than 3 years. Yet, no attention is being paid to this, the most massive change taking place, which truly compares with the massive changes wrought by the Civil War. The last election reflected the situation in voter turnout; people have got tired of voting and seeing no results. The crisis condition of the United States remains, so why take the time and trouble to vote? There is no confidence in America's future — that is what being without a meaningful job or any job at all does to the human spirit.

Since the 1930s, the power hungry continue to grab more and power. The Communist Party U.S.A., also known as the "Democratic Party" got their Socialist President Roosevelt to pack the Supreme Court with justices who regarded the Constitution merely as an instrument to be twisted and squeezed to suit Socialist programs. The 10th Amendment became their football, to be kicked all over the place. I analyzed major Supreme Court decisions since the "packing house" was established, and found that this court never, in a single instance, prevented the power-hungry from grabbing what they wanted.

States rights were trampled underfoot by the Roosevelt stampede and it continues to this very day. Beginning with the Roosevelt administration, government has expanded and contracted the Constitution like an accordion player playing the right tune. What the Supreme Court did, and what it is still doing, is redistributing the rights and powers vested in We, the People, in favor of the Federal Government. That is why we are faced with the imminent death of the middle class, and the destruction of the Constitution of the United States.

What is needed is an urgent program that would turn the country around and save the middle class. Such a program would call for the utter defeat of the Democrat Party, which party has lied to and misled the American people since the Wilson administration: an education program that would excise Socialism in its entirety, abolish the false unconstitutional "separation of Church and State," a

.

house cleaning of the Supreme Court (which could be closed down during the procedure), the Federal Reserve closed down and the national debt abolished.

When Warren G. Harding was elected to the White House, the United States was in chaos as it is now. Credit was overextended, the Federal Reserve was madly manipulating the currency and causing inflation with the attendant massive crop of business failures. Commodity prices had been artificially lowered by foreign pressures, and unemployment was widespread. The Federal Reserve-created National Debt had ballooned. We were still at war with Germany, a ruse to suck more "reparations" out of that country. Wilson's taxes were at an all time high.

On assuming office, Harding made a list of what ailed the United States and then forced the Congress to stay in session for two years to solve the problems. Harding attacked the Shylock International Bankers and their Wall Street allies. He said what Jesus Christ before him had said, "I will drive you out of the temple." Harding told the Shylock bankers that there would be no more foreign entanglements, no war foreign wars, no national debt, "the last of which all-but destroyed the Republic."

Harding relieved the credit crunch and enacted new tariff taxes that protected local industries. Government employees were cut to the bare minimum, a budget was established. Immigration was restricted to protect our borders against the hordes of anarchists flowing in from Eastern Europe and to protect our labor market. Harding instituted new tax regulations that cut income taxes by hundreds of millions of dollars each year, and he signed a treaty of peace with Germany and told the League of Nations to fold up its tent and depart our shores.

But Harding did not live long enough to enjoy his signal victories over the Philistines, whom he had driven out of our camp in total disarray.

On June 20, 1923, while on a political trip to Alaska, he fell ill and died. His death was caused by kidney failure, the clearest indication that a powerful poison had somehow been administered to him. We need a man like Warren Harding, whose courage knew no bounds. We must search and find the "new Warren Harding" who will restore the programs that would have saved America from the monstrous grip of Socialist evil doers.

The nonsensical "deficit reduction is king" notion must be brought into proper perspective. If the deficit was zero tomorrow, the crisis of the middle class would not be eased. Even Clinton's $50 billion public investment program has been forgotten. Wall Street' s eviscerating of our industries must be stopped, which means exposing the gnomes of the bond market. The trade barriers erected by Washington and maintained by Lincoln, Garfield and McKinley must be reinstated. A drive must be made to educate the public about what unlimited, untaxed imported goods, also known as "free trade," does to our economy. This would bring a dramatic return to full employment: It would also bring the Nation into direct confrontation with the foreign powers who rule this country.

The "brave new world" of Clinton is without substance. There are no foreign markets for American goods, and this is how it has always been. The only thing that has changed with a "global economy" is that our defenses were breached and imported goods came flooding through gaping holes in the dykes. This is at the root cause of the middle class crisis. Whereas, it was always that American manufacturers were able to supply a rising local demand because of steady blue and white collar jobs, our position became untenable when Wilson said that we must not be afraid of "competition!" In 1913, the United States had a closed market with full employment, a rising economy and long range prosperity, Customs revenues paid the government bills up to 1913, when the Socialists got Wilson to tear down the dykes protecting our standard of living.

In a closed market, our manufacturers could afford to pay good wages: by so doing they created purchasing power and an effective demand for their products, which meant full employment, long term permanent job security. All that Socialist (Democrat) Presidents from Wilson to Clinton have offered the American worker is a slim chance to sell some goods in China, Japan or England, in return for a low-paid job of sorts, so that by degrees, especially with the full force of NAFTA and GATT brought to bear on them, they will find themselves accepting a constant lowering of their standard of living and be thankful for the opportunity to work at any job, no matter what it might be. This is called, "free trade." This is the future of the American middle class.

The net effect of "free trade in a global economy" will be the disappearance of the American middle class, (clerical, blue collar and white collar) the class that made America great. The top 500 companies shed more than 5 million middle class workers over the past 13 years. Some future leader may react in alarm when the full extent of the ravaging of the middle class becomes dearer. At that time, the only alternative for the leader of this nation, will be to stem the tide of "free trade," which means a return to tough, trade barriers. That will be a humiliating defeat for the Socialists who run the Democrat Party, but one which they will have to accept if America is not to become like Russia; the possessed and the dispossessed.

To sum up the tragedy that has come down on America: A global society means a middle classless society in America. "Free trade" has already eroded the standard of living of the middle class to where it is no longer comparable with what it was in 1969. The American middle class was not made by "free trade" or a "global economy." The middle class was made out of trade barriers and a secure protected market for locally manufactured goods. Trade barriers did not give rise to inflation. Starting with Woodrow Wilson, a succession of Presidents has lied to the American people and generally, succeeded in getting this blatant lie accepted as truth.

Socialism is a ghastly failure. Putting aside its pious platitudes of enriching the lives of the ordinary people, Socialism's sole purpose was always to enslave people and gradually bring about the New Dark Age of a One World Government — New World Order. Even when in full control of the British Government, and notwithstanding the billions of "foreign aid" dollars America poured into the British treasury to shore up Socialist programs, Socialism proved to be a colossal flop.

Sweden was one the countries that elected to go the Fabian Way. We have already met the Socialist idealists, Gunnar Myrdal, and his wife, both of whom played a major role in wrecking education in America. For more than 50 years, Stockholm was the pride of Socialists everywhere. Myrdal was a minister in the Swedish cabinet for many years, and played a leading part in introducing Socialism to Sweden, its leaders well contented they had proved that Socialism works.

From the 1930s onwards, Sweden was synonymous with Socialism. All politicians of whatever party were committed Socialists, their differences being only in degree, not in principles. French, British, Indian and Italian Socialists flocked to Stockholm to study the "miracle" at work. The foundation of Sweden's Socialist state was its welfare program. But where does Sweden's proud Socialism stand today, in 1994? Well, it is not exactly standing, it is more like the Leaning Tower of Pisa, leaning more and more toward capitalism with each passing month.

Sweden's politicians are learning that voters do not vote altruistically, and that the age of ideal Socialism is dead and only remains to be buried. The Swedish Socialists who blatantly interfered in South African politics and marched in protest against the United States involvement in Vietnam, are discovering that their Socialist vocabulary is outdated in a country where everything has gone to hell. Swedish Socialists sat down at the table to sup with International Socialism, only to find that their dinner guest had departed with the silverware. Sweden fell victim to the lies and false promises of Socialism. Today, the country is in an economic shambles and it will take fifty years for Sweden to work itself out of the mess, that is, presuming it will be permitted to do so. Britain was destroyed by Socialism a long time ago. Now, it is America's turn. Can the United States survive a near fatal overdose of Socialist poison, administered by the Socialist Communist Democrat Party of the United States? Only time will tell, and time is what the American blue collar, white collar, clerical worker middle class no longer has.

Implicit in all of the programs of the Wilson, Roosevelt, Kennedy, Johnson, Carter, Bush and Clinton presidencies, although not spelled out, is that the socializing of the United States is the great goal toward which Socialism is working. This will be accomplished through new forms of ownership, control of production — meaning the choice to destroy industrial plants is theirs — is essential if the Socialists are to advance their plan to move the United States, and then the rest of the world, ever more swiftly and surely into a One World Government New World Order of the New Dark Age of total slavery.

The absolutely false picture that Socialists have painted of themselves as a benign, friendly organization whose only interests in bettering the lot of the common people is not correct...Socialism has another brutal, vicious face, one which history reveals will not hesitate to kill if that is what it takes to Socialize the United States.

Nothing can describe the vicious side of Socialism better than the statement made by Arthur Schlesinger: "I don't know why President Eisenhower doesn't liquidate Joe McCarthy the way Roosevelt did Huey Long." Huey Long's "crime" was that he truly loved America and all of its people, the very first American politician to fully understand what Roosevelt was doing to the United States. Huey Long spoke out for the middle class, which he correctly perceived as the target of the Socialist, and he spoke out against Socialism on every possible occasion.

Great hatred of Long was expressed by the Socialist/Marxist/Communist machine in the United States, whom they called, "the personification of the fascist menace — the man most likely to become the Hitler or Mussolini of America." So hungry were the little people of America for a spokesman for their downtrodden situation, that it is believed Long received up to 100,000 letters a day. Roosevelt went into a rage at the mention of the name of Huey Long and feared that Long would succeed him as the next President of the United States.

A blizzard of Socialist propaganda flew against Huey Long. There never was such an unprecedented campaign of all-out hatred directed against a single individual; it was frightening, it was awesome. Roosevelt went into near epileptic fits every time Huey Long revealed further truths about the Socialists programs Roosevelt was about to impose. Huey Long lashed out at Roosevelt's British Fabian Socialist "deals," urging the people to: "Defy this kind of autocracy, defy tyranny." Roosevelt tried to have Long impeached for tax evasion, but Long came out of it without a blemish to his character.

The Roosevelt camp were left with only one option: "Murder Huey Long." *The cause of deep concern was Long's move to assert Sates rights.* He refused so-called "federal money" and told a wildly enthusiastic audience in Louisiana that he was going to sue the Federal Government and get an injunction to remove all federal agencies and their offices from the borders of the State of Louisiana. Roosevelt took great fright; this was an action of which the Federal Government lived in daily fear, one that could sweep the States and cut back the functions of the Federal Government until it was operating inside the confines of the first 10 Amendments of the Constitution of the United States, its wings clipped, its agencies confined to the District of Columbia.

"Defy this kind of autocracy, defy this kind of tyranny" Long cried when he discovered that the Federal Government was attempting to block the sale of Louisiana State Bonds, bonds which would provided the revenue the State needed to replace the "Federal funds" he ordered the State not to accept. In 1935, with Roosevelt as nervous as a cat up a tree, Long went to Baton Rouge to visit his friend, Governor Allen. As he left the Governors office, a man shot him. The assailant, a close friend of Roosevelt, was Dr. Carl Weiss, who was gunned down by Long's guards, too late to save him, and Weiss lay dead.

Huey Long was transported to hospital, where he lingered between life and death. In his near-death state, Long had a vision of Americans from all walks of life who needed his leadership. He cried out to God, "Oh Lord, they need me. Please don't let me die. I have so much to do, God, I have so much to do." But Long died, felled by a Socialist assassin. Lincoln, Garfield, McKinley, all tried to protect America against the ravages of the Socialists, all paid with their lives. So did Congressman L.T. McFadden, Senator William Borah, Senator Thomas D. Schall and President Kennedy, after renouncing Socialism.

Socialism is far more dangerous than Communism, because of its inherent, evil slow approach to forcing drastic, unwanted changes upon the people of the United States. There is only one way to overcome *this violently dangerous menace,* and that is for the whole people to be educated to where they recognize what they are up against and toss Socialism out, neck and crop. This can and MUST be done. "Unity is strength." There are more of our patriotic people than there are Socialists. All we need is leadership and an educated people to stand fast in the face of the vicious tyranny which every president Since Woodrow Wilson has helped fasten around our necks. The Socialists can't shoot us all! Let us rise up and smite the Philistines in a show of great unity. We have Constitutional power to do just that.

EPILOGUE

Americans and indeed the world sat around waiting for the hammer of Communism to strike, little realizing that a greater danger to the Republican nation state such as ours, was Socialism. Who in the Cold War era feared Socialism? The number of writers, commentators and forecasters who said this, could be counted on one hand. Nobody thought that Socialism was anything to worry about.

The Communists played a major trick on is, keeping our collective eyes fixed on Moscow while the most terrible damage was being wrought at home. I have always maintained throughout the twenty five years I have been writing, that the greatest danger to the future well being of our nation lay in Washington, not Moscow. The "evil empire" mentioned by former President Reagan is not Moscow but Washington and the Socialist camarilla controlling it.

Events unfolding as we come to the close of the 20th century bear out the accuracy of that contention. In 1994 we have a Socialist at the helm of the nation's affairs, ably assisted by a Democrat Party that adopted Communism/Socialism in 1980, and with more than 87 percent of the Democrats in the House and Senate showing their Socialist colors, attempts by the people to change the course of the nation via the ballot box are not going anywhere.

The "surplus to requirements" population of the world — and this includes the United States — is already being decimated by laboratory made mutant viruses that are killing hundreds of thousands of people. This process will be speeded up in terms of the Club of Rome's Global 2000 genocidal blueprint — after the mobs have served their purpose. The experiments begun in Sierre Leone with Lassa fever and media visna mutant viruses is being brought to perfection in the laboratories of Harvard University in August of 1994. A new, even more deadly virus than AIDS is about to be released.

Already released and working with deadly efficiency are the new flu viruses. These mutant flu viruses are believed a 100 percent more effective than the "Spanish flu" viruses tested on French Moroccan troops in the fading days of WWI. Like the Lassa fever viruses, the "Spanish flu" virus got out of control, and in 1919, swept the world and killed more people than the total military casualties of both sides in WWI. There was no stopping it. Casualties in the United States were horrendous. One out of every seven people in big cities in America were swept away by "Spanish flu." People fell ill in the morning from fever and a debilitating tiredness. Within one or two days, they died — by the millions.

Who knows when the new flu mutant viruses will strike? In 1995 or perhaps the summer of 1996? Nobody knows. Also waiting in the wings is Ebola fever, its proper title, "Ebola Zaire" named after the African country of Zaire, where it first surfaced. Ebola fever cannot be stopped; it is a merciless killer, which acts fast and leaves its victims horribly contorted and bleeding from every opening in the body. Recently, Ebola Zaire has surfaced in the United States, but the news media and the Centers for Disease Control are saying little about it. Research experiments have been going on with Ebola viruses at the U. S. Army Medical Research Institute involving this and other highly dangerous viruses.

What is the purpose behind unleashing these dreadful killer viruses? Population control is given as the reason, and if we read the statements made by Lord Bertrand Russell, Robert S. McNamara and H.G. Wells, the new killer viruses are merely what these men said was coming. In the eyes of the Committee of 300 and the Socialist camarilla, there are just too many unwanted people on the earth.

But that is not the whole story. The real reason behind the planned global mass genocide is to create a climate of instability. Destabilize nations, set people's hearts fluttering with fear. War is part of that plan, and in 1994, war is everywhere. There is no peace on earth. Miniscale wars rage in what was the Soviet Union; in former Yugoslavia the war goes on between the factions artificially created in the first place by British Socialists. South Africa will never again be the land of peace it once was; India and Pakistan are not far behind. This is the result of years and years of careful Socialist planning.

There are 100 more nations today than there were in 1945. Most of these are built on a shaky alliance of tribal-ethnic divisions with religious differences, differences in culture. They will not survive, having been created and placed on the shelf to await the destabilization process. The United States is being thrust into similar divisions thanks to clever long range Socialist planning. America in 1994 is ripe to be riven apart by racial, ethnic and religious differences. America long ago ceased to be "one nation under God." No nation can survive cultural differences, especially where language and religion play a crucial role.

The Socialist are forging ahead through President Clinton to exploit this fact of life, which we try to hide every 4th of July. The next decade will be one in which these divisions boil up and over. America will be divided by income, lifestyle, political outlook, race and geography. A huge wall, which the Socialists have been building since they put President Woodrow Wilson in office, is almost finished. This wall will divide America into the have and have nots — with the middle class in the latter category. America WILL become like any other Third World country. Beautiful cities will be ruined by lack of social services and police protection as local and state governments, deliberately starved of revenues, are unable to meet the rising costs of services and protection.

Crime will spread to the suburbs. Formerly safe suburbs will be come crime infested suburbs. It is all part of the Socialist plan to break up major cities and scatter population groups — even into your safe neighborhoods, which in ten or more years are likely to be as crime ridden and gang-infested as the inner cities of major American cities are now.

Illegitimacy rates won't be controlled by abortion, because abortion is directed toward stemming the middle class birth rate. Madame Kollontay's Socialist abortion and free love was always intended as a brake on the middle class becoming too powerful. The illegitimate birth rate will grow and grow among the working poor. There is now a population explosion of illegitimate babies who are growing up fatherless with mothers unable or unwilling to care for them. This is Fabian Socialism in action, the evil dark side of Fabian Socialism that was always kept out of sight.

The new underclass now coming up in America will consist of millions of unemployed and unemployable, which means a huge floating, unstable population that can only turn to crime for survival. Suburbs are going to be flooded with the underclass and its street gangs. The police will not be able to stop them—and for a while they will be allowed free rein to do the destabilizing work for Socialism.

The beautiful suburb in which you now live is likely to be the ghetto of the year 2010, populated by thousands of gangs whose members live by the sword. "Going to Mayberry" will become more common as these vicious young thugs expand their areas of operations.

The vast majority of Americans are totally unprepared for what lies just ahead. They are lulled into complacency by Socialist promises that can never be fulfilled. While the United States faces its "Dunkirk," our people look more and more to government to solve problems that were created by Socialism in the first place, problems neither President Clinton nor his successors have any hope of solving, simply because it is deemed necessary to DESTABILIZE America.

Bitter hard times lie ahead, all the Democrat Party promises are just so much sounding cymbals. Lacking education, training, jobs — with industrial employers either wiped out or relocated in foreign countries — unemployed mobs will roam the streets in search of a living they were promised by the Socialists. When they have done their work, and America is destabilized, the "excess population" will be wiped out by mutant virus diseases, faster than we can ever imagine.

This is what the SOCIALIST predicted they would do, but few paid any attention to the promises of Bertrand Russell and H.G. Wells. Americans are more concerned about baseball and football, to the extent that historian of the future will marvel at how mass political psychology was not recognized by the people, and resisted. "They must have been fast asleep not to see it" will be the harsh judgment of future historians.

Can anything be done to stop the ravaging of this nation? I believe what is needed is to arouse the super-wealthy in the conservative ranks — and there are many of them — and get them to support a foundation that would teach a crash course on the Constitution of the United States, based solely on the reading of the Annals of Congress, the Congressional Globes and the Congressional Record. These documents contain the finest information about the Constitution together with a great deal of information about Socialism and its plans for a One World Government — New World Order, the new Dark Age of slavery.

Armed with this information, millions of citizens could challenge their representatives who vote for unconstitutional measures. For instance, if 100 million informed citizens challenged as unconstitutional Crime bill, and gave notice that they would not obey the provisions of the measure because it is 100 percent unconstitutional, it would never have passed the House and Senate. This is the only route left for patriotism to express itself. It can, and it must be done.

The hour IS late. To those who respond to the Socialists plans to bring the United States down to the level of any Third World country, "this is the United States, it can't happen here," I would say, "IT IS ALREADY HAPPENING." Who would have thought a few scant years ago that an unknown, obscure governor of a relatively unimportant state would become the President of the United States — even though 56 percent of the voters voted AGAINST him? This is SOCIALISM IN ACTION, forcing unpopular, unwanted changes upon the United States.

THE LEGACY OF SOCIALISM; A CASE HISTORY

At 9.40 a.m. Friday, September 30, 1994, Richard Blanchard, a 60 year old architect was shot in the neck after stopping for a red light at the edge of San Francisco's Tenderloin district. As Blanchard sat in his car in broad daylight, waiting for the light to change, two 16 year old thugs approached him, pointed a gun at him and demanded money. At that moment the light changed and Blanchard tried to drive away. He was shot in the neck and today lies totally paralyzed and on life supports in hospital.

As the law now stands, the 16-year old thug may not be named nor can his photo be published. According to a report in the San Francisco Examiner, Blanchard's friend, Alan Wofsy stated: "It means someone in San Francisco is not safe stopping at a red light during a regular working day. It takes away the whole innocence of life. The idea that you have to be vigilant in carrying out your normal daily tasks because your life may be taken away, means there are no more boundaries to civilized behavior. Another part of this tragedy is that this is a man whose hands were everything to him. Over nothing a man is reduced from being a wonderful architect to being a paraplegic."

The police response to this nightmare was, "roll up your windows and lock your car doors. If someone sticks a gun in your face give him whatever he wants. It's not worth losing your life over a watch or your wallet." This is the legacy of Socialism: "Yield to criminal thugs because the police cannot protect you, and having been disarmed by Socialist legislation that is 100 percent unconstitutional, you can no longer protect yourself."

After arch-Socialists Art Agnos and Diana Feinstein (both former mayors of San Francisco) left office, San Francisco was what they had made it, a Socialists nightmare. Had Mr. Blanchard been allowed his constitutional right to carry a gun in his car, the thugs, knowing this, would likely have thought twice about approaching him, or any citizen bearing arms.

But thanks to the unconstitutional actions of Socialists like Feinstein, the citizens of California and many of the other States have been disarmed and are now advised to "stand and deliver" in the face of criminals carrying guns. What would the Colonists, who refused to pay a tax of one penny a pound on tea, think of modern America and such an official admission of total, abject failure by the State to protect its citizens?

Blanchard's tragic story is repeated a thousand times a month across the United States. What is needed is a return to the Constitution, with a sweeping away of all gun laws and soft Socialist laws that protect criminal thugs like the one who shot Blanchard. Every citizen has the right to keep and bear arms. If this were widely advertised and generally known that citizens were exercising that right, the crime rate would plummet. No thug would dare to approach a motorist with a gun in plain view.

The tidal wave of Socialism is sweeping all before it. That tidal wave has to be confronted very soon and turned back, otherwise the United States is headed for extinction in the manner of ancient Greece and Rome. Police departments tell us they are understaffed and don't have the financial resources to confront the crime wave. Yet, in the same breath Clinton forces through an unconstitutional so-called "Crime" bill that is largely a Socialist transfer program with very little help for our police.

In Washington D.C., the nation's crime capital with more restrictive laws on gun ownership that in any other city, the mayor recently appealed to the President to send in the National Guard to deal with black on black gang violence. Clinton said no, but he did authorize money from the budget to assign park police and the secret service to street patrols. The results were dramatic; a 50 percent drop in gang-related shootings.

Then, the money ran out and the secret service and park police were withdrawn from the streets of Washington D.C. Shootings and violence returned. "We just don't have the money to continue that program," a White House spokesman told ABC television. WHY NOT? How can we afford to give away $20 billion in FOREIGN AID, which is 100 percent unconstitutional and yet cannot afford to fund essential crime prevention programs in Washington, the one place where the Federal Government does have jurisdiction in matters of police protection?

That is the legacy of Socialism, the road to slavery.

SOURCES AND NOTES

"Foreign Affairs." CFR Journal, April 1974. Gardner, R.

"An Interview with Edward Bellamy" Frances E. Willard, 1889.

"Boston Bellamy Club." Edward Bellamy, 1888.

"Fabianism in the Political Life of Britain 1919-1931." John Strachey.
Also "Left News," March 1938.

"Rand Institute School of Studies Bulletin 1952-1953." Upton Sinclair.

"The Economic Thought of John Ryan." Dr. Patrick Gearty.

"Socialist-Communist Collaboration." Zigmunt Zaremba, 1964.

"Corruption in a Profit Economy." Mark Starr.

"United States Advisory Commission." Mark Starr.

"Americans for Democratic Action." (ADA)

"The Case Against Socialism: A Handbook for Conservative Speakers."
Rt. Hon A.J. Balfour, 1909.

"The Fabian News" Bulletin 1930, mentions Rexford Tugwell as an associate of
Roosevelt and Governor Al Smith of New York, and again in "Who's Who,"
1934. Tugwell was also closely associated with Stuart Chase author of "A New
Deal." Tugwell served in the Economics Department of Columbia University.

"The Fabian Society." William Clarke, 1894.

"New Frontiers." Henry Wallace.

"A New Deal." Stuart Chase, 1932.

"Philip Dru, Administrator." Edward Mandell House, 1912.

"Great Society." Graham Wallace

"Beveridge Plan." William Beveridge. Became the "blueprint" for Social Security in the United States.

"Socialism, Utopian and Scientific." Federick Engels, 1892.

"Bernard Shaw." Ervine St. John, 1956.

"The Supreme Court and the Public." Felix Frankfurter, 1930.

"The Essential Lippmann-A Philosophy for Liberal Democracy." Clinton Rossiter and James Lare.

"John Dewey and David Dubinsky." Pictorial Biography, 1952.

"Hugo Black, The Alabama Years." Hamilton and Van Der Veer, 1972.

"A History of Zionism." Walter Lacquer.

"The Affluent Society." John Galbraith, 1958.

"Pillars of Society." A.G. Gardiner, 1914.

"Bulletin of the Rand School of Social Sciences." 1921-1935.

"The Other America: Poverty in the U.S." Michael Harrington, 1962

"History of Socialism." Morris Hilquit, 1910.

"Holmes-Laski Letters." The correspondence of Mr. Justice Holmes and Harold Laski. De Wolfe, 1953.

"Intimate Papers of Colonel House" C. Seymour, 1962.

"The Economic Consequences of Peace." John Maynard Keynes, 1925.

"General Theory of Economics." John Maynard Keynes, 1930.

"The Crisis and the Constitution, 1931 and After." Harold J. Laski, 1932.

"From the Diaries of Felix Frankfurter." Joseph P. Lash, 1975.

"Harold Laski: A Biographical Memoir." Kingsley Martin, 1953.

"Memories of a Socialist Snob." Elizabeth Brandeiss, 1948.

'The National Livelihood Plan." Prestonia Martin, 1932.

"Felix Frankfurter Reminiscences." Philip Harlan, 1960.

"Commentaries on the Constitution of the United States." Joseph Story, 1883.

Everson vs. Board of Education. This was the first Socialist triumph in reversing religious clause school cases. There was no legal precedent to support Everson's argument before the court. There is nothing in the Constitution to support the so-called "wall of separation" described by Jefferson and it is not part of the Constitution. The First Amendment was NOT intended to wall off the state from religion, which is what the Everson case suddenly found constitutional. How could a mere figure of speech uttered by Jefferson — and then only in relation to the State of Virginia — suddenly become law? By what constitutional mandate was this done, and by what precedent? The answer is NONE in both cases.

The "wall of separation" was an excuse for Frankfurter to exercise his bias against the Christian religion and in particular, against the Catholic Church. Again we say, THERE IS NO CONSTITUTIONAL PROVISION FOR THIS MYTHICAL "WALL OF SEPARATION BETWEEN CHURCH AND STATE." In this, Frankfurter was greatly influenced by anti-Catholic Harold J. Laski and Justice Oliver Wendell Holmes, both hardened Socialists. Laski held that "education that is not secular and compulsory is not education at all...The Catholic Church should be confined to Limbo..and above all, St. Augustine...The incapacity of the Catholic Church to tell the truth...makes it impossible to make peace with the Roman Catholic Church. It is one of the permanent enemies of all that is decent in the human spirit." Moreover, Black was a passionate reader of Scottish Rite of Freemasonry publications, which vehemently condemned the Catholic Church. Yet, we are expected to believe that Justice Black did not exercise extreme personal prejudice in ruling in favor of Everson!

"Selected Correspondence 1846-1895." Karl Marx and Frederich Engels.

"Edward Bellamy." Arthur Morgan, 1944.

"Fabian Quarterly." 1948. The Fabian Society.

"An American Dilemma." Gunnar Myrdal, 1944.

"Fabian Research." The Fabian Society.

"Reflections on the End of an Era" Dr. Reinhold Niebuhr, 1934.

"The History of the Fabian Society." Edward R. Pease, 1916.

"The Roosevelt I Knew." Frances Perkins, 1946.

"The Fabian Society, Past and Present." G.D.H. Cole, 1952.

" The Dynamics of Soviet Society."

"The United States in the World Arena." Walt W. Rostow, 1960.

"Labour in Britain and the World" Dennis Healey January, 1964.

"The Age of Roosevelt." Arthur Schlesinger, 1957.

"The Fourth of July, 1992." Edward Bellamy, July 1982.

"Mr. House of Texas." A.D.H. Smith, 1940.

"New Patterns for Primary Schools." Fabian Society, September 1964.

"The Coming American Revolution." George Cole, 1934.

"H.G. Wells and the World State." Warren W. Wagner, 1920.

"Education in a Class Society." Edward Vaizey November, 1962.

"Socialism in England." Sydney Webb, 1893.

"The Decay of Capitalist Civilization. " Beatrice and Sydney Webb, 1923.

"Ernest Bevin." William Francis, 1952.

"Social Security." The Fabian Society, 1943. (Adaptations from the Beveridge plan.)

"The New Freedom." Woodrow Wilson, 1913.

"Recovery Through Revolution." (Said to be the thoughts of Lovett, Moss and Laski) 1933.

"What an Education Committee Can Do in Elementary Schools." Fabian Society, 1943.

"The American Fabians" ADA periodicals, 1895-1898.

"Roosevelt to Frankfurter." December, 1917. Letters of Theodore Roosevelt, Library of Congress.

"Wealth Against Commonwealth." Henry Demarest Lloyd, 1953.

"The Need for Militancy: The Socialism of Our Times," 1929. Contains statement made by Roger Baldwin advocating revolution in the United States.

"Freedom in the Welfare State" address by Senator Lehman in which he falsely claims "Founding Fathers instituted welfare state." Published in 1950.

"Rexford Tugwell" quoted in the Rand School Bulletins, 1934-1935.

"American Civil Liberties Union (ACLU)." Formed in January 1920, it was called Civil Liberties Bureau. Many of its ideas taken from book, "The Man Without a Country" by Philip Nolan. The statement made by Robert Moss Lovett: "I hate the United States! I would be willing to see the whole world blow up, if it would destroy the United States" approximates sentiments expressed by Nolan in his book. June, 1919 issue of "Freedom," talks about formation of ACLU, names names, including founder the Rev. John Nevin Sayre. Other ACLU sources "Freedom Through Dissent" June 30, 1962. Also, Rogers Baldwin, ACLU founder member "The Need for Militancy" and Laidler's "The Socialism of our Times."

"Walter Reuther." President of United Automobile Workers Union. Worked closely with League of Industrial democracy. Taken from "Forty Years of Education." LID, 1945. See also Congressional Record House, October 16, 1962 pages 22124-22125. Also Louisville Courier Journal." "Sweden: The Middle Way,"

Mar quise Child. "The Southern Farmer," Aubrey Williams (1964 report House UnAmerican Activities Committee.)

"Woodrow Wilson." Material taken from "The New Freedom" Arthur Link,1956. Albert Shaw, editor of the "Tribune" Minneapolis. Shaw also wrote "Review of Reviews." "The Year 2000: A Critical Biography of Edward Bellamy" by Sylvia Bowman, 1958. "International Government" published by Brentanos New York, 1916. Senate Investigating Committee Senate of the State of New York 1920. This committee investigated the Rand School for seditious activities. Wilson was ordered by MI6 to destroy Military Intelligence Bureau files on subversive elements in the Fabian Socialist orbit, which order Wilson carried out. Reported in "Our Secret War" by Thomas Johnson. "An American Chronicle" Ray Stannard Baker,1945. "Record of the Sixty Sixth Congress" pages 1522-23, 1919. Hearing of the Subcommittee on Judiciary, 87th Congress January 9-February 8 1961. "The Road to Safety." Arthur Willert, 1952. "Fabian News" October, 1969. "Note for a Biography." July 16 1930. Also, the "New Republic." "Social Unrest" by Rev. Lyman Powell, 1919. (Powell was Wilson's old friend.) "Mr. Wilson's War." John Dos Passos, 1962. "The New Statesman" article by Leonard Woolf, 1915.

"Florence Kelley," (real name Weschnewetsky.) Kelley's story is told in "Impatient Crusader, Florence Kelley's Life Story" by Josephine Goldmark, 1953. "Survey" magazine Paul Kellog Editor. "The Nation," Freda Kirchway. "The Roosevelt I Knew," Kelley, 1946. Kelley was a "social reformer's reformer" and director of the League of Industrial Democracy (LID) 1921-1922, national secretary of the National Consumers League and innumerable Fabian Socialists front organizations.

Senator Jacob Javitts. Closely allied with the Fabian Society in London, received congratulatory cable from Lady Dorothy Archibald. "Freedom in the Welfare State" symposium applauded Javitts and his work on behalf of Socialism Javitts voted for ADA-Socialist proposals earning a near-perfect scorecard of 94 percent. Participated in "Democracy Round Table: Needed A Moral Awakening in America" in 1952. Others who sat with Javitts included Mark Starr, Walter Reuther and Sydney Hook.

"Constitutional Powers of a President." Found in Section II of the Constitution of the United States.

Congressional Record Feb. 27,1927. "General Deficiency Appropriation Bill."

"Congressional Record, House, June 26 1884 Page 336 Appendix thereto." Here we find why education is the means by which the Socialist onslaught may be blunted.

"The Mind and Faith." A. Powell Davies, edited by Justice William O. Douglas. Davies, the Unitarian Church supporter of Justice Hugo Black also wrote "American Destiny (A Faith for America") in 1942, and "The Faith of an Unrepentant Liberal" in 1946. The impact that Davies made on Justices Douglas and Black is seen in the Socialist issues looked upon with favor by these two Justices in Supreme Court decisions in which they participated.

"Brave New World" Julian Huxley. In this work Huxley calls for a hugely expanded totalitarian Socialist state that would rule with an iron fist.

"Communism and the Family." Madame Kollontay. In which she expresses outrage and indignation over parental control of children and the role of women in marriage and family life.

"Brave New Family" Laura Rogers. Surprisingly like the title of Huxley's "Brave New World." Rogers lays out the strategy long demanded by Socialists to gain control of children and take them away from parental control along the lines suggested by Madame Zinioviev, wife of Gregori Zinoviev, hardened Soviet Commissar.

"Congressional Record, Senate S 16610-S16614." Shows how Socialism tries to undermine the Constitution.

"Congressional Record, Senate February 16, 1882 pages 1195-1209." How Mormons were interfered with by Senate Committee and how it violated Bill of Attainder.

"Liberties of the Mind." Charles Morgan. In reference to so-called "psychopolitics."

"Communist Manifesto of 1848." Karl Marx.

"Congressional Record, Senate, May 31 1924, pages 9962-9977." Describes how American Communists disguise their programs as Socialism and explains that they differ only by degree.

INDEX

A

Aaron, Nan..................................107

Abzug, Bella 95, 105, 106

Acheson, Dean......................133, 177

Ad Hoc Committee on Public Education on Sexual Harassment...106

Addams, Jane.....89, 94, 97, 100, 156, 158, 171

Adler, Felix 157

Alden, R. W. 36

Aldrich, Nelson 70

Alliance for Justice 106

American Association of University Professors..........................150, 161

American Civil Liberties Union.......43 65, 76, 80, 106, 125, 150, 154, 161, 215

American Economic Association.....36

American Fabian........4, 25-27, 33-35, 38, 52, 70, 101, 110, 150, 158

American Federation of Teachers 3

American Socialist Party..........52, 140

Americans for Democratic Action...4, 15, 16, 18, 51, 133, 151, 161, 211

Amery, L. S. 21

Angarika Dharmapala...................158

Arkansas Development Finance Authority 143-145

Aspen Institute 162

Association for Improving the Condition of the Poo 96

Association of University Women ..96

Atlee, Clemment...........................20

Austin, Warren 71

B

Bahai Movement..........................161

Baker, Ray S. 4, 55, 71, 90

Baldwin, Roger....26, 44, 45, 125, 215

Bank Act of 1862..........................190

Barden, Graham 74, 76

Barker, Granville 91

Baruch, Bernard 37, 42, 54, 68, 113, 132

"Basis of the Fabian Society" 1, 24

Bayh, Birch 24

Beaven, Albert W. 150

Bellamy, Edward.........18, 33, 48, 109, 122, 160, 211, 214, 216

Bemis, E.W....................................36

Benton, William B. 104, 105

Besant, Annie 2, 21, 92, 93, 100, 157, 158

Beveridge Plan 95, 212, 215

Beveridge Report............................14

Beveridge, William............91, 98, 212

Bevin, Earnest...............................13

Biddle, Francis................................51

Black, Hugo 66, 70, 74, 76, 77, 80, 115, 212, 217

"Blackstone's Commentaries With Notes" 111

Blanchard, Paul..............................43

Blavatsky, Petrova 93, 161

Bliss, W. D....................................49

Bluestone, Irving...........................195

Bolshevik Revolution............5, 23, 27, 28, 30, 117, 118, 125, 132

Borah, William.....................73, 203

Boston Bellamy Club.........18, 25, 210

Boston Nationalist Club 18

Bowles, Chester 22, 171

Branch Davidian Church at Waco ......
64, 65, 66, 152

"Brandeis Briefs"..............9, 13, 83, 94
110, 122, 123

Brandeis, Louis 9, 13, 42, 43,
68, 73, 107, 121, 122, 123, 137

Brave New Family in Missouri 87

"Brave New World" ..86, 87, 200, 216

British East India Company...........165,
166, 190

British Petroleum............................121

Brockwood Labor College 3

Brothers Fund 104

Brown vs. School Board,
Topeka, Kansas 83

Bryan, William Jennings.................117

Burger, Warren 107, 116

Burrows, Herbert.............................93

Bush, George....27, 46, 53, 59, 63, 83,
121, 171, 192

C

Cambridge Policy Studies Institute.....
162

Cambridge University.....................121

Carnegie Endowment Fund..........161

Carnegie Foundation 82, 85

Carter, Jimmy 78

Case Against Free Trade................166

Center for Law and Special Policy..106

Chamberlain, Joseph...........8, 89, 166

Chase, Stuart 4, 11, 120, 124, 132,
171, 211, 212

Chiang Kai Shek 121

Christian Book Club...........................2

Christian Temperance Union 96

Cini Foundation.............................162

Civil Liberties Bureau 44, 215

Civil War 43, 57, 67, 94, 116, 121,
122, 174, 178, 189, 190, 191, 194, 198

Clinton, Bill..22, 42, 83, 143, 144, 147

Club of Rome................162, 167, 194,
196, 198, 205

Co-parenting Program 87

Coffin, William Sloane 22

Cole, Margaret 3, 93

Committee for a Democratic
Majority...162

Committee for Economic
Development 162

Commons, John R............................36

"Communism and the Family" 87,
92, 96, 106, 217

Communist International..................7

Communist Manifesto of 1848........8,
11, 12, 23, 24, 32, 71, 84, 86, 137,
182, 217

Communist Workers Relief 158

Congress of Vienna 168

Constitution of the United States....5
9, 30, 32, 33, 34, 39, 62, 76-79, 82,
103, 104, 106, 119, 122, 123, 152-154,
159, 161, 167, 172, 181, 187, 192,
198, 202, 208, 212, 216

Council of Foreign Relations 15

Cox, Archibald 21

Cripps, Stafford 3, 12, 14, 33, 91

Crossman, Richard 3, 14, 81

Currie, Lauchlin 121, 132

Cutler, Lloyd 152

D

Dard, M.A. 158

Debbs, Eugene V. 48

Democrat Convention of 1940 97

Democrat Party 2, 4, 17, 31, 34, 38, 91, 99, 116, 124, 129, 137, 140, 142, 151, 198, 200, 201, 205, 207

Devereux, Arthur 18

Dewey, John 70

Dicks, H.V. 70, 72, 75, 81, 212

Dies Committee 127, 150

Disraeli, Benjamin 170

Dole, Robert 112

Douglas, Paul 48, 51

Douglas, William O. 111, 115, 153, 217

Doyle, Arthur C. 93, 158

Dukes, Paul 153, 217

Dulles, John Foster 68, 184

Dutch Reformed Church 163

E

Eastern Spring Conference of Professional Schools 26

Edwards, Albert 15

Eisenhower, Dwight 66, 120

Elliot, Charles W. 56

Engles, Friedrick 92, 212, 213

Ervin, Sam 183

Ethical Society of Culture 1

Everson vs. Board of Education 76, 213

Executive Orders 42, 59, 62, 109, 112, 119, 173

F

"Fabian News" 9, 22, 25, 90, 100, 122, 211, 216

Fabian Research Center 3

Fabian Socialism 1, 2, 4-7, 12-14, 16, 18, 19, 20, 24, 25, 26, 30, 32, 34, 35, 45, 50, 56, 61, 69, 90, 92, 93-95, 98-101, 115, 128, 130, 132, 140, 141, 149, 151, 173, 191, 192, 195, 207

Fabian Society 2-10, 12, 14, 15-18 20, 24, 25, 27, 32, 35-38, 40, 44, 48, 49, 50, 52, 55, 61, 65, 68, 69, 70, 78, 89, 90, 92, 98, 99, 101, 104, 121, 138, 157, 169, 182

Fabian Society Summer Schools 94

Failed Socialist Policies 15, 193

Federal Council of Churches ...150, 160

Federal Reserve Act of 1913 ...188, 189

Federal Reserve Board ...21, 187, 189, 190, 191, 192

Fellowship of Faiths 93, 151, 155-162

Fellowship of New Life 18, 25

Fels, Joseph 56

Feminism ..9, 90-93, 95, 106, 108, 162

Filene, Edward 125

"fireside chats" 56, 119, 127

Flowers, Gennifer 144, 147

Ford, Gerald 177

Foreign Aid............193, 194, 201, 210

Fortas, Abe 67, 70, 82, 115

Foster, William Z. 52

"Four Pillars of the House of
Socialism"...11

"Fourteen Points" 118

Fowler, Henry 21

Frankfurter, Felix....19, 42, 44, 50, 61,
66, 68, 70, 80, 97, 102, 106, 112, 113,
115, 123, 125, 127, 132, 133, 137,
212

"free love" 35, 60, 84, 92, 106
107, 160, 207

Freedom Planning Group 132

G

G.I. Bill 74

Gaitskell, Hugh 61, 175

Galbraith, John 212

GATT 5, 53, 166-169, 172, 175, 180,
192-196

General Agreement on Tariffs and
Trade 168, 192

"General Deficiency Bill" 58

General Federation of
Women's Clubs 95

George, Henry 1

German Rationalization................149

Girl's Friendly Society America 96

Glendower, Elizabeth......................94

Goldberg, Arthur.................21, 68, 70

Goldman, Emma 28, 153

Goldmark, Josephine 123, 216

Gollancz, Victor 2

Graduated income tax.......28, 33, 37,
38, 39, 42, 164, 188

"Great Society" 4, 8, 11, 137, 138

Greenspan, Alan 192

Gulf War 27, 53, 59, 121, 182

Gunther, John 21

Gupta, Das 156

Guptas, Das.....................................158

H

Hale, William B. 57

Hamilton, Alexander.....................166

Hammer, Armand 155

Hampstead Historical Club 7

Hardie, Keith...................................157

Harriman, Averill.........13, 21, 99, 171

Harriman, Pamela ..45, 50, 91, 142, 197

Harrington, Michael 140

Hart, Philip 51

Harvard Socialist Club 18, 35, 136

Hayle, William B. 38

Health care reform..........................50

Henderson, Arthur 9, 41

Heritage Foundation....................126

Hess, Moses....................................157

Hicock, Lorena 105

Hill, Anita 105-107

Hill, Lister 74

Hillman, Sydney 42

Hillquit, Morris 48, 52, 111

Hines, Walter 41

Hiss, Alger 68, 126, 182

Hobson, John Atkins 122

Holmes Oliver Wendell 127, 213

Hopkins, Harry 97, 98, 101, 120, 121, 130

House, Edward Mandel 4, 41, 42, 61, 99, 100, 116, 120, 130, 212

Howe, Fred C. 54, 126

Hubell, Wes 144

Huebsch, B. W. 42

Hull, Cordell 126

Hull House 94, 99-101, 162

Humphrey, Hubert.......................22

Huxley, Aldous.........................86-87

I

Institute for Pacific Relations....15, 134

Institute for Policy Studies............162

Inter-Collegiate Socialist Society ...47, 52, 69, 70, 138

International Association for Labor Legislation..96

International Bankers Association....54

International Confederation of Free Trade Unions.................................94

International Ladies Garment Wokers Union.................................3

International Monetary Fund........16, 130, 181, 192

International Students Congress 20

International Trade Commission ..177

J

Jackson, Andrew 8, 22, 140, 190, 191, 194

James, E. 36

Javitts, Jacob..............51, 67, 171, 216

Jilla, A. D. 158

Johnson, Jim 143

Johnson, Lyndon....................132, 178

Jones, James K. 72

Justice Department 115, 145

K

Kahn, R. F. 129

Keddrantah Das Gupta 156

Kelley, Florence 31, 42, 43, 48, 61, 62, 70, 71, 73, 78, 83, 92, 94, 96, 109, 113, 120, 122, 123, 124, 167, 171, 216

Kenan, George F. 21

Kennedy, John F...................2, 17, 19, 140, 169

Keynes, John Maynard.........5, 12, 56, 72, 97, 98, 121, 127, 130, 131, 139, 176, 192, 212

King, Martin Luther 21

Kissinger, Henry 10, 138

KKK "Clarte" 93, 100, 157

Kollontay, Alexandra....61, 91, 92, 106

Korean War 134, 179

Kuznetsov, Vasily 135

L

Lamont, Thomas...........................137

Landman, Samuel 157

Lansbury, George 55, 116

Lasater, Dan 143

Laski, Harold 2, 5, 7, 13, 17, 20, 24, 32, 37, 45, 56, 60, 61, 66, 71, 91, 101, 104, 123, 127, 128, 137, 171, 175, 212

Lattimore, Owen 15, 104, 121

Laura Spellman Fund 104, 161

"Law of Nations" ..172, 182, 183, 184

Lawrence, Susan 93, 98, 99

League of Industrial Democracy....18, 47, 48, 53, 70, 151, 162, 215, 216

League of Nations 55, 118, 136, 158, 159, 161, 181, 199

League of Womens' Voters.............96

Left Book Club............................2, 12

Lend-Lease 127

Lewin, Kurt 81

Liberation Theology..............151, 156

"Liberties of the Mind" 32, 217

Likert, Rensis.................................85

Lincoln School of Teachers College..70

Lindsay, A. D. 21

Line Item Veto...........5, 61, 62, 66, 67

Lippmann,Walter 4, 35, 42, 53, 55, 61, 69, 90, 101, 118, 124, 127, 130, 132, 136, 137, 141, 171

Lockhart, Bruce........................28, 117

Lodge, Henry Cabot 17

London School of Economics.....3, 11, 14, 17, 19, 71, 104, 123

Long, Huey..............................202, 203

Lovett, Robert M. ..43, 57, 94, 101, 215

Lubin, Isadore 50

Lucius Trust 162

Lusk Committee...........................49

Lusk Laws...............................110-111

M

MacGowan, Kenneth 18

Malik, M. S. 158

Malzberger, Benjamin....................82

Margaret Bent Lawyers Achievement.................................106

Marshall, John 107

Marshall Plan.................174, 175, 176

Martin, Prestonia 50, 89, 97, 213

Marvin, Cloyd H. 74

Marx, Karl...................2, 7, 11, 32, 35, 47, 49, 57, 118, 139, 194, 213, 217

"Maternity and Infancy Act"..........96

McCarthy, Joseph 16, 28, 104

McCorvey, Norma 106

McDonald, Ramsay........2, 12, 69, 102

McFadden, Louis T..........71, 102, 103, 132, 188

McKinley, William 28, 40, 117, 153, 166, 167, 177, 180, 188, 199, 203

McNamara, Robert S.....135, 139, 206

Meade, Margaret................21, 81, 85

Meaney, George 169

Mediation Commission On Industrial Unrest 20

Mediation Committee....................45

Mendelssohn, Moses 1

Mennen Williams, G.......................21

Mezes, Sydney 37, 136

Milholland, Inez.............................93

Mill, John Stuart..............................1

Miller, David...............................118

Milner, Alfred 28, 56, 118

Mirza Ali Muhammad 161

Moley, Raymond V. 132

Mondale, Walter 22

Moral Rearmament 161

Morgan, Charles 32, 217

Morganthau, Henry.........................98

Mosely, Oswald..........................9, 101

Muggeridge, Malcolm 21, 22

Myrdal, Gunnar....73, 79, 82, 84, 171, 201, 214

N

NAFTA.................5, 53, 138, 167, 169, 171, 172, 175, 180, 192, 193, 194, 195, 200

National Abortion Rights Action League...106

National Abortion Rights League ..92

National Bureau of Economic Research 104

National Catholic Welfare Council..... 111, 149

National Congress of Mothers and Parent-Teachers Association 95

National Consumers League....94, 96, 97, 110, 216

National Cooperative Commonwealth Society 24

National Council of Jewish Women... 96

National Council of Labour Colleges..3

National Council of Women 162

National Education Association 71, 75, 81, 85

National Federation of Business and Professional............................95

National health plan 32

National League of Women Voters ... 92, 95

National Organization for Women.... 106, 162

National Planning Association 104

National Recovery Act...............26, 54

National Training Laboratories 85

National Women's Law Center.....106

New College Law School...............106

"New Deal" 4, 11, 20, 29, 51, 97, 98, 99, 101, 102, 103, 111, 120, 124, 125, 128, 131, 138, 150, 211, 212

New Democratic Coalition............162

"New Encyclopedia of Social Reform"...............................158

"New Freedom" 37, 38, 214, 216

"New Frontier" 4, 17, 32, 137, 138

"New Republic" 1, 18, 19, 45, 56, 101, 136, 138, 147, 216

New School for Social Research 3

"New Statesman" 17, 22, 90, 102 216

New World Order.....9, 23, 30, 53, 64, 68, 78, 88, 91, 123, 136, 151, 160, 162, 167, 171, 182, 187, 192, 193, 197, 201, 202, 208

New York Foreign Policy Association .. 132

New York Nationalist Club 110

Nichols, Larry 143, 145, 147

Nitze, Nina 56

North American Free Trade Agreement.....................................167

"Nueva Vita" 6

O

"Operation Greenback"..............145

Organization for the Advancement of Women.........................106

"Origin of the Family".....35, 92, 106, 109

"Our Soviet Ally"..............................2

Outcome Based Education..............85

Overman Committee on Bolshevism.. 45, 92, 106

Ovington, Mary White....................83

Owen, William H. 78

Oxford Group...............................161

Oxford University.........36, 88, 90, 142

P

Page, Kirby.......................................150

Palmer, Mitchell.....................124, 128

Panama Canal Treaty 27, 169, 172

Pankhurst, Emily..............................93

Parents as Teachers 87

Paris Peace Conference......4, 55, 118, 123, 136, 159

Patterson, Franklin W......................71

Payne Aldrich Tariff Act........172, 173

Payne-Townshend, Charlotte..........90

Pearson, Drew................................120

Pease, Edward R...............36, 52, 214

Perkins, Frances.............48, 49, 94, 96 98, 99, 113, 119, 121, 129, 132, 171

Perot-Gore Debate 39

Peterson, Howard...........................180

"Philip Dru, Administrator".....42, 43, 99, 212

Pinchot, Amos..................................19

Planned Parenthood 106

Plessy vs. Ferguson 75

Political Action Group.....................83

"Political and Economic Planning" .102

Political parties....................48, 53, 59

Post Industrial Zero Growth...167, 198

Pound, Roscoe 45, 121

Priestly, J. B. 21, 102

"Psychopolitics".........29, 32, 108, 216

Q

Quintas Fabian.................................7

R

Rand, Ayn..13

Rand School.....49, 110, 111, 214, 216

Rand School of Social Science 126, 132, 212

Rauschenbach, Walter..................160

Reed, John 69, 136

Reese, John Rawlings......................10

"reforms" 9, 11, 19, 25, 29, 30, 49, 84, 86, 87, 90, 96, 104, 113, 122

Reno, Janet 152

Republican Party 31, 140, 169, 192

Reuther, Walter...............51, 215, 216

Richardson, Bill 68

Riverside Church...........................150

Rockefeller Brothers Foundation...161

Rockefeller, David 13, 70, 151

Rockefeller, Jay 142, 197

Rockefeller, John D........................149

Rogers, Laura...........................87, 217

Roosevelt, Eleanor.............20, 31, 48, 50, 94, 96, 97, 99, 105, 132

Roosevelt, Franklin D. 31, 42, 58, 96, 119, 124

Rostenkowski, Dan 143

Rostow, Walt Whitman......26, 68, 82, 132, 134, 135

Rosvolsky, Leo 182

Royal Commission of London University 90

Royal Institute for International Affairs...15, 40

Rumsey, Mary....................................99

Rusk, Dean.............134, 135, 138, 139

Russell, Bertrand 8, 10, 21, 55, 130, 151, 157, 162, 168, 206, 207

Ryan, John Augustin 111, 149

S

Sayre, Francis B. 45

Schlesinger, Arthur J. Jr. 29, 121, 122, 132, 151

Schlesinger, Arthur M. Sr. 45, 48

Schneiderman, Rose 125

School busing....................................53

"Scientific Socialism" 32

Seligman, E. R. 36

Separation of Church and State....43, 49, 58, 62, 63, 74, 75, 149, 157, 198

Seymour, Charles 116

Shaw, Albert......................36, 37, 216

Shaw, George Bernard.....5, 7, 14, 35, 90, 108, 130

Shawcross, Hartley.............................3

Sieff, Moses I. 102, 103, 132

Silverman, Sydney............................21

Simpson, Adlai 133

Sinclair, Upton 36, 45, 52, 94, 158, 211

Slaughterhouse decisions................79

Smith, Adam......39, 40, 165, 173, 190

Smith, Al 94, 111, 128, 211

Smoot, Dan 31

Social Democrats USA 162

Social Security................14, 50, 91, 98

"Socialism Of Our Times" 19, 215

Socialist Garland Fund 3

Socialist goals 17, 32, 58

"Socialist Hands Across The Sea" ...15

Socialist International 7

Society for Physical Research..........93

Solarz, Stephen.................................68

Sorenson, Theodore 51

Spellman, Laura.....................104, 161

Stanford Research 162

Starr, Mark.........2, 126, 160, 211, 216

Stassen, Harold 120

Steed, Wickham................................21

Stettinus, Edward...........................120

Stevens, Adlai 21

Stevens, Harlan................................48

Stone, Harlan..........................98, 113

Strachey, John 1, 2, 14, 211

T

Tagore, Rabindrath 156

Tariff Act of 1864 170

Tavistock Institute for Human
Relations.......10, 81, 85, 137 138, 186

Taylor, Maxwell.............................135

Tennessee Valley Authority Project....
126

Theosophy................................2, 161

Theosophy Society...........93, 157, 158

Thomas, Clarence ..103, 104, 107, 108

Thomas, Norman.........19, 31, 43, 136

Threefold Movement.....................158

Toynbee, Arnold 21, 56

Trade Act of 1974..................177, 178

Trade Agreement Act....................169

Trade Expansion Act of 1962........180

Trade Tariffs 39, 102

Truman, Harry......................3, 75, 179

Tugwell, Rexford Guy.....................26

Turtle Bay.......................................57

Twentieth Century Fund 125

"Two Worlds" 31

U

Union Theological Seminary.........150

United Nations 21, 52, 59, 94, 128,
134, 159, 160, 161, 181-185

United Nations Conference on Trade
and Employment...........................169

United Nations Economic
Commission for Europe..................82

United States Advisory Commission...
3, 210

"The Unseen Hand" 31

Untermeyer, Samuel........73, 111, 157

V

Vickers Hall, Peter 126

Vietnam War 55, 135, 138, 141

Volcker, Paul 21

von Metternich, Klemmens 168

W

Wald, Lilian......................................99

Wallace, Henry 4, 17, 32, 132, 211

Wallas, Graham........3, 4, 5, 8, 11, 20,
24, 55, 68, 96, 98, 99, 123, 150

War Resisters League 156, 162

Warburg family 57

Ward, Harry F. 150

Warren, Earl 73, 77, 79, 82, 86,
107, 116

Waye, Nora 143

Webb, Beatrice.............2, 6, 9, 12, 22,
49, 90, 91, 92, 97, 130, 160

Webb, Sydney.........3, 5, 8, 18, 25, 36,
50, 55, 81, 89, 93, 98-101, 111, 118,
125, 130, 149, 214

Wedgewood Benn, Anthony..........21

Weicker, Lowell...............................22

Weishaupt, Adam..............................2

Weiss, Carl....................................203

Weller, Charles...............................158

Wells, Charles.................................157

Wells, H.G. 6, 10, 13, 19, 93, 100, 157, 206, 207, 214

Wentworth, Thomas 33

West, Rebecca.................................21

White, Harry Dexter.................14, 68

Whitney Straight, Dorothy....101-104

Wilkinson, Ellen.............................93

Willard, Cyrus.................................18

Wilson, Harold.............................120

Wilson, Woodrow.........11, 19, 32, 36, 37, 41, 48, 58, 79, 101, 110, 116, 136, 157, 166, 173, 176, 188, 196, 197, 200, 203, 206, 215, 216

Winant, John G.................................14

Winchell, Walter.............................120

Wiseman, William ...32, 113, 116, 117

Women's International League 96, 100, 101

Women's Legal Defense Fund 106

Women's Trade Council..................97

Women's Trade Union League 96

World Bank.............................62, 192

World Conference on Education....78

World Council of Churches...159, 160

"World Curriculum" 86, 87

"World Revolution" 23, 28, 58, 61, 64, 90, 91, 94, 158, 162

World Youth Congress Movement..... 126

Worthen National 145

Y

Younghusband, Francis.........156, 159

Z

Zinoviev, Lelina 96